Manifesto for Global Democracy

Manifesto for Global Democracy

Two Essays on Imperialism
and the
Struggle for Freedom

Arjun Makhijani

The Apex Press

New York

Cover Design and Front Cover Art: Mary Ellen McCourt
Back Cover Art: Cathie Sullivan
Interior Design: Mary Ellen McCourt

Library of Congress Cataloging-in-Publication Data

Makhijani, Arjun

Manifesto for global democracy : two essays on imperialism and the struggle for freedom / Arjun Makhijani.
p. cm.
The first work "On freedom and equality", is a new essay. The second work "From global capitalism to economic justice", published in 1992 by Apex Press, is an exact reprint. The two are being issued together under a new, but related book title.
Includes bibliographical references.
Contents: On freedom and equality : the struggle for global democracy -- From global capitalism to economic justice : an inquiry into the elimination of systemic poverty, violence and environmental destruction in the world economy.

ISBN 1-891843-24-9 (hardcover : alk. paper) -- ISBN 1-891843-21-4 (pbk. : alk. paper)
1. Capitalism. 2. Democracy. 3. Imperialism. 4. Distributive justice. 5. Environmental policy. 6. Economic history--20th century. I. Title

HB501.M252 2003
320'.01'1--dc22
2003058250

Published by the Apex Press,
an imprint of the Council on International and Public Affairs,
located at 777 United Nations Plaza, Suite 3C, New York, NY 10017.
Its publications office may be reached at (800) 316-2739 or (914) 271-6500,
P.O. Box 337, Croton-on-Hudson, NY 10520.
Web site: www.cipa-apex.org.

Printed in the United States of America by
Capital City Press
Montpelier, Vermont

CONTENTS

Borders*
By Yevgeny Yevtushenko

In every border post
                there's something insecure.
Each one of them
                is longing for leaves and for flowers
 They say
        the greatest punishment for a tree
is to become a border post.
The birds that pause to rest
                on border posts
 can't figure out
        what kind of tree they've landed on.
I suppose
        that at first, it was people who invented borders,
and then borders
        started to invent people.
It was borders who invented police,
                armies, and border guards.

. . . .

While borders still stand
                we are all in prehistory.
Real history will start
        when all borders are gone.

Reprinted by permission of Yevgeny Yevtushenko

*Excerpted from the poem, "Fuku," in Yevgeny Yevtushenko, *The Collected Poems 1952-1990*, edited by Albert C. Todd with the author and James Ragan (New York: Henry Holt, 1991), pp. 586-587.

Preface to

Manifesto for Global Democracy:

Two Essays on Imperialism and
the Struggle for Freedom

This book combines my 1992 book, *From Global Capitalism to Economic Justice*, also published by Apex Press, with a new essay *On Freedom and Equality*, which explores the roots of exclusionary apartheid ideas of freedom and contrasts them with the universal ideas championed by Mahatma Gandhi and Rev. Martin Luther King, Jr. This new essay was originally meant as a preface to a second edition of *From Global Capitalism to Economic Justice,* but it grew to be a major piece in its own right, though obviously related to the book. Hence, the two are being issued together under a new, but related, book title.

Arjun Makhijani
Institute for Energy and Environmental Research
Takoma Park, Maryland
301-270-5500

On Freedom and Equality:
The Struggle for Global Democracy

Arjun Makhijani

The Apex Press
New York
2004

*This essay on freedom and equality is dedicated to
my friend and colleague in the struggle for
peace, justice, and nuclear disarmament,
Louise Franklin-Ramirez*

ACKNOWLEDGMENTS

Ben Schiff, Professor of Politics at Oberlin College, gave me truly valuable comments that led me to drastically revise much of my initial approach to this new essay. I also was inspired by *The Heart of Whiteness*, the book that he and June Goodwin wrote in 1992, about Afrikaners of all political persuasions, at a time when the walls of apartheid in South Africa were beginning to crumble. I think the work is essential reading if the struggle against global apartheid is to be waged in a Gandhian spirit.

I want to thank Maria Jimenez, Director of the Immigration Law Enforcement Monitoring Project (ILEMP) of the American Friends Service Committee, who shared her seminal, inspiring paper on the right of global mobility with me. Her critique of a draft of the section on borders was crucial to the development of some of the ideas in it. Finally, her work on the U.S.-Mexican border is exemplary of the kind of practical work that needs to be done in order to get to the beginning of history to which Yevtushenko's beckons us all.

Yevgeny Yevtushenko graciously gave me permission to reprint an excerpt about borders from his amazing poem, Fuku. The "Iron Curtain" is gone. But another one, present even then, dividing the fearful wealth of the few from the misery of the many, porous to the fruits of cheap labor, but not to the workers, has now risen into full view. It is maintained, like the other one was, by lead bullets and a vast governmental apparatus. It is the divide of global apartheid, described in *From Global Capitalism to Economic Justice*.

I am grateful to Mike Davis, who allowed me to reproduce some of the photographs of famine in Victorian India from his archival collection, which show some of the history of how global apartheid was created. Three of them are reproduced in the following pages. The Web site of the Institute for Energy and Environmental Research also has pictures of Louise Franklin-Ramirez, who, for more than two decades, has been the leading organizer of the commemoration of the atomic bombings of Hiroshima and Nagasaki in Washington, D.C. Ben Wisner recounted to me some of the activities around the statue of Gandhi in Tavistock Square in London. His photograph of that statue is also at www.ieer.org. Some historical data on food and population are also being posted on the website of IEER in a special issue of *Science for Democratic Action*, IEER's newsletter.

I benefited greatly from comments by Ward Morehouse, who has been generous with his time and has been the publisher of so much that I have written. John Steinbach, Allison Macfarlane, Jenice View, Michele Boyd, Lisa Ledwidge, Annie Makhijani, Nicole Deller, and Mary Lou Nelson also gave me useful suggestions. I am also very thankful also to Lois Chalmers, the librarian of the IEER, for her document research and fact checking though, of course, I alone am responsible for the contents of this essay.

The focus on the ruling structure of the West in this essay, as in the following essay, and specifically on the United States within that structure, is not because it is better or worse than others in the past, but because it is the one that today shapes and controls the world that we, the people of the world, including especially the people of the United States, must change. Further, I also happen to admire many of the ideas of Tom Paine, whose work, *Common Sense,* inspired the U.S. Declaration of Independence. He was part of his time, as are we all, and one must see his life work in that context. But he was also well ahead of it.

I am grateful for the generosity of the C.S. Fund that enabled me to write this essay as a part of my work at IEER, and for the extraordinary flexibility that has been accorded to me in the use of the grant. The unrestricted general support of IEER's individual donors was also of significant help in allowing me to continue my research and writing. It has been far more difficult for me to write this than it was to write the original book. I hope that it is a helpful complement and update. Finally, I'm grateful to the readers of *From Global Capitalism to Economic Justice,* because of whom it will be reprinted for the third time, this time as part of this larger book.

Arjun Makhijani
February 2003

ON FREEDOM AND EQUALITY:
THE STRUGGLE FOR GLOBAL DEMOCRACY

MR. PRESIDENT, the times call for candor. The Philippines are ours for-
ever, 'territory belonging to the United States,' as the Constitution calls
them. And just beyond the Philippines are China's illimitable markets....We will not renounce our part in the mission of our race, trustee,
under God, of the civilization of the world. And we will move forward to
our work with gratitude for a task worthy of our strength and thanksgiv-
ing to Almighty God that He has marked us as His chosen people, hence-
forth to lead in the regeneration of the world.
...

The Declaration [of Independence] applies only to people capable of self-
government. How dare any man prostitute this expression of the very
elect of self-governing peoples to a race of Malay children of barbarism,
schooled in Spanish methods and ideas? And you who say the
Declaration applies to all men, how dare you deny its application to the
American Indian? And if you deny it to the Indian at home, how dare you
grant it to the Malay abroad?
...

And so the Declaration contemplates all forms of government which
secure the fundamental rights of life, liberty, and the pursuit of happiness. Self-government, when that will best secure these ends, as in the
case of people capable of self-government; other appropriate forms
when people are not capable of self-government.

—Senator Albert J. Beveridge, in the U.S. Senate, January 9, 1900[1]

We're giving the forces of evil, the forces of the antichrist, room in our
government. That's the ANC [African National Congress].

—Dominee (Reverend) Pieter Nel, an Afrikaner minister 1992[2]

A true revolution of values will lay hands on the world order and say of
war, 'This way of settling differences is not just.' This business of burning human beings with napalm ...cannot be reconciled with wisdom, justice, and love....

---

[1] Albert J. Beveridge, "In Support of An American Empire," *Congressional Record, 56* Cong., I Sess.
[1900], pp. 704-712. Available at http://www.mtholyoke.edu/acad/intrel/ajb72.htm.

[2] As quoted in June Goodwin and Ben Schiff, *Heart of Whiteness: Afrikaners Face Black Rule in the
New South Africa* (New York: Scribner, 1995), p.22.

America, the richest and most powerful nation in the world can well lead the way to this revolution of values. There is nothing, except a tragic death wish, to prevent us from reordering our priorities, so that the pursuit of peace will take precedence over the pursuit of war.

—Martin Luther King, Jr. in Beyond Vietnam, April 4, 1967[3]

The dozen years since the accompanying essay was completed, at the sunset of the U.S.-Soviet clash, have seen the hopes of millions of people for a new dawn of freedom and equality across the world dashed because of a process of globalization that has put the interests of corporations and capital ahead of those of the people. Inequalities within and between countries are immense. A few hundred people now have more wealth than the poorest two billion.

It is a telling part of the rules of the World Trade Organization, created in 1995, that a country may protect its military industries under the rubric of national security[4] but may not protect its water supplies under the rubric of the essentials of life. In response to darkening prospects, new forms of solidarity are emerging worldwide, locally and transnationally. People are rising up to protect their water resources, as they did in Bolivia against Bechtel Corporation, whose sales are twice Bolivia's Gross Domestic Product. Bechtel filed a lawsuit against Bolivia after Bolivia cancelled the contract. But Bolivia has found interesting company. On July 1, 2002, the Board of Supervisors of the City of San Francisco, where Bechtel has its headquarters, passed a resolution in solidarity with the people of Bolivia, and asked Bechtel to drop its lawsuit.[5] Slowly and hesitantly, a struggle for global democracy and survival, and in opposition to militarist, corporate-dominated globalization is emerging.[6]

---

[3] Martin Luther King, Jr. "Beyond Vietnam: A Time to Break Silence," speech delivered at the Riverside Church, New York City, April 4, 1967. Available at http://www.hartford-hwp.com/archives/45a/058.html. Viewed on October 23, 2002.

[4] The government procurement exception, Article XXIII of Annex 4(b), the government procurement rules to the founding WTO Agreement reads in part: "Nothing in this Agreement shall be construed to prevent any Party from taking any action or not disclosing any information which it considers necessary for the protection of its essential security interests relating to the procurement of arms, ammunition or war materials…" Available at http://www.jus.uio.no/lm/wta.1994/iia4b.html#3620. This clause is similar to one in the 1947 GATT agreement. The term "protection" is used here in the sense of foreign trade and/or investment protection. GATT, the General Agreement on Tariffs and Trade, in place since 1947, had essentially the same rules exempting military industries from its free trade provisions. Text available at http://www.jurisint.org/pub/06/en/doc/05.htm.

[5] See "Bolivia vs. Bechtel" on the website of Public Citizen at http://www.citizen.org/cmep/Water/new/articles.cfm?ID=7978.

[6] For a collection of essays on this subject, see Dean Ritz, ed., *Defying Corporations, Defining Democracy: A Book of History and Strategy* (New York: Apex Press, 2001).

Global inequalities, and the repression they require for their maintenance, have been increasingly compared to South African apartheid operating on a global scale – that is, to global apartheid.[7] As Richard Falk has pointed out in his analysis of globalization, the facts are so compelling that the analogy has suggested itself even to establishment thinkers:

> Thomas Schelling, long notable as a war thinker who influenced the outlook of the United States strategic community during the formative period of the cold war, poses for himself the question about what model of authority at a state level might 'an incipient world state resemble.'[8]

Schelling's answer, which he himself found "stunning and depressing," was that a world state under present conditions would look like South Africa under apartheid.[9] But the political units of the world system are states, which have dominant nationalities, whose place in the world scheme is analogous to that of the Whites in South African apartheid. In this system, borders are the instruments of segregation. The struggle for democracy in a global society, then, is, in essential ways, the global equivalent of a struggle for civil rights and for desegregation.

The period since the Berlin Wall fell has seen the intensification of corporate-dominated economic globalization, including the creation of a new supranational body, the World Trade Organization, to complement the World Bank and the International Monetary Fund (IMF). These developments have entrenched the domination of multinational capital over people.[10] There have been increasing restrictions on the mobility of the vast majority of people in the world. Anti-immigrant sentiment has risen and draconian laws against immigrants, documented or not, have been passed, even as the Western powers demand that Third World countries open up to Western capital and commodities. The walls within the European Union have come down *as part of the same process* by which walls against the majority of the people of the Third World have become higher and more bloody.

---

[7] Gernot Kohler, whose essay bearing the title "Global Apartheid" I noted in the first printing of *From Global Capitalism to Economic Justice,* seems to have created the term in the early 1970s. Others have also had this insight before my analysis in that book was published. Adam Hochschild pointed out the similarity in an article in *Mother Jones.* ("In the Final Days." *Mother Jones*, November 1980). To be sure the analogy is not exact.

[8] Richard Falk, *Predatory Globalization* (Malden, MA: Polity Press, 1999), pp. 13-14.

[9] *Ibid.*, p.14.

[10] For a series of essays on the connections between promotion of corporate interests and the Cold War, see David Horowitz, ed., *Corporations and the Cold War* (New York: Monthly Review Press, 1969).

Over a decade ago, when I wrote the accompanying essay on global capitalism, the limitations on freedom and the conditions that were attached to it in the capitalist countries, most of all in the United States, remained well under the political radar screen of the vast majority of people. Since September 11, 2001, people in the United States have not only been stunned by the murderous attacks on that date; vast numbers have also been aghast at the speed and severity of the curbs on rights and freedoms at home.

As the "War on Terror" has evolved, it has become more and more analogous to the worst phases of the Cold War, and in terms of suppression of constitutional rights, perhaps more extreme. Once more the United States is supporting dictators and torturers abroad in the name of freedom. Once more, the U.S. government appears to have taken upon itself to decide which governments are fit to be in office and which shall be overthrown, which are evil, which are good.

The terrorist attacks of September 11, 2001, mark the definitive end of the post-Cold-War period, a time invested with many hopes of ridding the world of weapons of mass destruction and of cooperation in matters of economics and environment. There were many early gains in the late 1980s, until the mid-1990s. Then a slow erosion began that has assumed breathtaking proportions since September 11, 2001. A year following that date, the United States seemed a strangely different place. The *New York Times*, in reviewing a year of federal government policies of secrecy, the proposed program of spying using methods strongly resembling the communist East German *Stasi*, and the curbs on basic constitutional rights that had been imposed over the year, had put the Bush administration's actions in the same camp as those of "the enemies of freedom abroad":

> As the Bush administration continues down its path, the American people need to make clear that they...will not allow their rights to be rolled back.... Fear is no guide to the Constitution. We must fight the enemies of freedom abroad without yielding to those at home.[11]

Suddenly, the core of the argument is about the nature of freedom not only among the peoples and in the places that have long suffered its denial, but also in the United States, which has, in the eyes of many, regarded itself as the natural home of liberty. Specifically, it has come up in the context of

---

[11] "The War on Civil Liberties," *New York Times* editorial, September 10, 2002. This specific program is now prohibited by law, but other draconian governmental intrusions on privacy are being considered, developed, and put into place. See for instance, the Department of Defense news briefing of November 20, 2002 at http://www.politechbot.com/p-04186.html, viewed on November 30, 2002.

the question "why do they hate us?" that many Americans have asked insistently since September 11, 2001. For instance, President Bush, in his address to a joint session of Congress, nine days after the attacks, said:

> Americans are asking, why do they [the terrorists] hate us? They hate what we see right here in this chamber — a democratically elected government. Their leaders are self-appointed. They hate our freedoms — our freedom of religion, our freedom of speech, our freedom to vote and assemble and disagree with each other.
>
> They want to overthrow existing governments in many Muslim countries, such as Egypt, Saudi Arabia, and Jordan. They want to drive Israel out of the Middle East. They want to drive Christians and Jews out of vast regions of Asia and Africa.
>
> These terrorists kill not merely to end lives, but to disrupt and end a way of life. With every atrocity, they hope that America grows fearful, retreating from the world and forsaking our friends. They stand against us, because we stand in their way.[12]

This answer — "because they hate our freedoms" — has been accepted widely in the United States, though far from universally. It leaves out some crucial facts that are central to understanding the nature, scope, and cost of those freedoms, and hence does not inform us whether the problems arise from the hate of the freedoms or the manner in which they are acquired and maintained.

President Bush did not note how severely limited and conditional these freedoms have turned out to be in practice as the jailings of citizens and non-citizens, without lawyers or even formal charges, have shown. His speech does not throw light on the cost of freedoms in the United States to people outside the United States. President Bush did not note that Saudi Arabia is not free. Egypt is not free. Jordan is not free. All three are U.S. allies (as of this writing). Nor did he note that the United States has stationed troops in Saudi Arabia, to all appearances against the wishes of most of the people of that country. He did not mention oil, the central reason for the intense U.S. and Western interest in the Persian Gulf region for the better part of a century and for the presence of U.S. troops in Saudi Arabia in particular.

The spontaneous analogy to Pearl Harbor made by many in the United States in the wake of the terrorist attacks of September 11, 2001, is reveal-

---

[12] George W. Bush. "Address to a Joint Session of Congress and the American People" (Washington: White House, Office of the Press Secretary, September 20, 2001). Available at http://www.whitehouse.gov/news/releases/2001/09/20010920-8.html.

ing in an unintended way. The intended comparison is that the two were surprise attacks; pure "evil" opposed to the goodness and democracy of the United States. Yet, oil was a crucial element in both.

There was considerable political and economic conflict between the imperialist ambitions of Japan and those of the United States in the Pacific and hence ample indication that a Japanese attack sometime, someplace was likely. War was in the air in 1941 and a Japanese attack was expected, just as there were ample indications of the September 11 attacks beforehand, if not of the exact manner, date, time, and place. In 1940, the United States had moved its Pacific fleet to the base in Pearl Harbor. Using its economic and military muscle, including a freeze on financial assets in July 1941, the United States created a virtual oil embargo against the Japanese militarists who sought control of Indonesian oil in their quest to conquer and subjugate Asia.[13] The oil belonged neither to the U.S., nor to Japan, nor to the Dutch imperialists who then ruled Indonesia, but whose own country was then occupied by the Nazis. The Indonesians themselves, to whom the oil belonged, did not enter any of the big power calculations. The Japanese imperialists attacked the U.S. fleet at Pearl Harbor in an attempt to remove the main military obstacle on their route to Indonesian oil.

September 11 was also largely about oil. Osama bin Laden and al Qaeda derived much of their Saudi political support from popular opposition to the extended U.S. military presence in Saudi Arabia and U.S. support of an unpopular and, by all independent accounts, corrupt Saudi regime. The U.S. military presence as well as its support of the Saudi regime are both centered on the control of the vast pool of oil under Saudi sands – the largest proven petroleum reserves in the world.[14]

It is indicative of the popular hostility to the U.S. military presence that the Saudi government has been reluctant to allow the U.S. government to investigate the Saudi connections to crimes of September 11, even though a majority of the hijackers were Saudi citizens. This echoes the earlier Saudi reluctance in the case of the bomb attack on the Khobar Towers, where U.S. military personnel were killed. But Saudi Arabia has not only oil; it is also the land where the two most holy shrines of Islam are located.

---

[13] Daniel Yergin, *The Prize: The Epic Quest for Oil, Money, and Power* (New York: Simon & Schuster, 1991), p. 318. A dated but still useful reference on the politics of oil is Robert Engler, *The Brotherhood of Oil: Energy Policy and the Public Interest* (Chicago: University of Chicago Press, 1977).

[14] Saudi Arabia has proven recoverable oil reserves of about 264 billion barrels (of 42 gallons each), amounting to about one-fourth of the world's total. See the U.S. Energy Information Administration Web site at http://www.eia.doe.gov/cabs/saudi.html. Viewed on 5 November 2002.

The United States had already been building alliances with repressive governments in Central Asia, well before September 11, 2001, in the pursuit of oil and natural gas. [15] This interest also involved Afghanistan, which was seen as a desirable route for one or more pipelines to get Central Asian gas, and possibly oil, to the open seas without going through the Persian Gulf or Russia. Talks between a U.S. oil company and the Taliban were abandoned in 1998 after the terrorist attacks on two U.S. embassies in Kenya and Tanzania. The War on Terror has served as an occasion to consolidate these U.S.-Central Asian alliances with a large military presence. [16] In brief, President Bush's speech does not inform us about the scope of the word "our" in his phrase "our freedoms." Who is in? Who is out? What are the criteria? Is there an empire-building element in this war?

The words "we" and "our" often refer to those who are considered to be "civilized." Consider for instance, Attorney General John Ashcroft's speech of February 19, 2002, to the National Religious Broadcasters Convention regarding the War on Terror. He said:

> But the call to defend civilization from terrorism resonates from a deeper source than our legal or political institutions. Civilized people — Muslims, Christians and Jews — all understand that the source of freedom and human dignity is the Creator. Civilized people of all religious faiths are called to the defense of His creation.
>
> …
>
> We are a nation called to defend freedom — a freedom that is not the grant of any government or document but is our endowment from God.[17]

---

[15] Michael T. Klare, *Resource Wars: The New Landscape of Global Conflict* (New York: Metropolitan Books, 2001). The extent of the overlap between U.S. oil politics, Saudi Arabia's government and elites, the Taliban, Osama bin Laden and his family, Pakistani intermediaries, the terrorist attack of September 11, as well as the U.S. government's response to it is still unclear. The considerable prior interest in a route for Central Asian gas and oil through Afghanistan and Pakistan is not in doubt; it continues to play a role in the politics of that area in the post-Taliban phase. One account arguing for a close link is by Jean-Charles Brisard and Guillaume Dasquié, *Forbidden Truth: U.S.-Taliban Secret Oil Diplomacy and the Failed Hunt for bin Laden*, translated from the French by Lucy Rounds with Peter Fifield and Nicholas Greenslade (New York: Thunder's Mouth Press/Nation Books, 2002).

[16] For some points regarding about the problematic nature of the War on Terror in Afghanistan, see Arjun Makhijani, "A Complex, Ill-Defined War on Terrorism," *Medicine and Global Survival*, February 2002. Available at http://www.ippnw.org/MGS/V7N2Aftermath.html#Makhijani. Islamic fundamentalism has, of course, been promoted by the United States also. Among the groups most prone to violence in the name of Islam today are those that were associated with the U.S.-sponsored opposition to the Soviet occupation of Afghanistan between December 1978 and 1989.

[17] Attorney General John Ashcroft, prepared remarks to the National Religious Broadcasters Convention, February 19, 2002. Available at the Department of Justice Web site http://www.usdoj.gov/ag/speeches/2002/021902religiousbroadcasters.htm.

Where the Attorney General's view might leave Hindus, Buddhists, Sikhs, Jains, Zoroastrians, Confucians, deists like Tom Paine, many tribal people, not to mention agnostics or atheists, is unclear, to say the least. But the underlying idea in Mr. Ashcroft's speech that the United States is a power for global good and for global democracy, is a deeply rooted messianic belief across much of the U.S. political spectrum. It is in this context that the United States government is set upon exercising a degree of power in the world that makes it prosecutor, judge, jury, and executioner even as it violates and undermines its own commitments regarding security and human rights under international law. [18]

This is a moment of grave peril. Large-scale violence is being sponsored by both governments and non-governmental groups, as the ideology of intolerance and hatred against religious groups, nationalities, immigrants, and the dispossessed is taking hold across the world. It is a time when we need, as never before, to seek inspiration in the struggle for global democracy in the lives and examples of Mahatma Gandhi, Rev. Martin Luther King, Jr., and the anti-apartheid struggle in South Africa led by Nelson Mandela. Their struggles were in broad conformity with Jefferson's assertion that he knew "but one code of morality for men whether acting singly or collectively." The goal of achieving such a morality and accountability in public life has been considered important enough in U.S. political culture that this remark is part of the inscription at the base of his statue at the Jefferson Memorial in Washington, D.C. The violence of terrorism, whether governmental or non-governmental, is at its root a violation of that principle. In retrospect my failure to integrate the lessons of the great non-violent freedom struggles of our time explicitly into the accompanying, earlier essay seems to me to be the largest single gap in the thinking and the framework I set forth in it. I will make an attempt to remedy the problem in this essay on the nature of the struggle for global democracy in the present context.

Two Concepts of Freedom

Two concepts of freedom have long contended for the soul of society. In the first, human freedom is reserved for a select few. The Afrikaner votaries of apartheid exemplified by Dominee Nel, the European-Americans who, under the rubric of Manifest Destiny, claimed a God-given right to occupy the continental United States and conquer, confine, expel,

---

[18] See Nicole Deller, Arjun Makhijani, and John Burroughs, eds., *Rule of Power or Rule of Law?: An Assessment of U.S. Policies and Actions Regarding Security-Related Treaties* (New York: Apex Press, 2003) for an analysis that covers U.S. obligations and compliance relating to a variety of treaties.

or kill those in the way (Native Americans and Mexicans), and Senator Beveridge's views that extended those ideas across the oceans are illustrations of the ideological school that freedom is divisible and exclusionary.

The supposed lack of any one of a number of things is enough to justify conquest, expropriation, exploitation, and even genocide — fitness, civilization, modernity, Christianity, supposed deficiency in intelligence due the size of brains or craniums (an argument also applied to women in the last half of the nineteenth century), the possession of too much of something (such as melanin), or too little (such as technology). In other words, this concept of freedom is based on inequality for which a variety of earthly and divine sanctions have been invented. It creates choice, prosperity, and mobility for some, at the cost of limiting or reducing it for others, generally with some rationalizing and moralistic cover. We might call this the apartheid school of freedom. Another feature of this school is that the select few often claim that the prerogative of exclusionary freedom is actually for the benefit of the subjugated — bringing democracy, technology, modernity (often tellingly symbolized not by science or rationality, but by MacDonald's and Coca-Cola) achieved at great cost to the select few ("the White Man's burden," "foreign aid," and so on).

The core argument is as old as slavery, across cultures and civilizations. Aristotle supported and rationalized slavery:

> For there is one rule exercised over subjects who are by nature free, another over subjects who are by nature slaves. The rule of a household is a monarchy, for every house is under one head: whereas constitutional rule is a government of freemen and equals. The master is not called a master because he has science, but because he is of a certain character, and the same remark applies to the slave and the freeman.[19]

Saint Augustine endorsed the prerogatives of the slave master to own, dominate, and punish slaves as part of Christian doctrine. In his monumental work, *Concerning the City of God Against the Pagans*, one of the founding philosophical-theological works of institutional Christianity, he argued that a person who was a slave was being punished for his prior sins as part of a divine plan. He must therefore submit to the slave-master, the *paterfamilias*, who, as part of the same plan, had the *duty* to mete out punishment to the slave during worldly existence. God would take care of everyone equally, according to their merits (including obedience). After

---

[19] Aristotle, *Politics*. Translated by Benjamin Jowett; with introduction, analysis, and index by H.W.C Davis. Reprint of Oxford University Press edition of 1905 (Mineola, N.Y.: Dover, 2000), p. 37.

death.[20] This doctrine is remarkably similar to the one that has been (and is) used across cultures and through the ages to subjugate women to the fathers of their households. Another analogy is to be found in the subjugation of *Dalits* in India, the so-called "Untouchables" in the Hindu hierarchy, consigned to the lowest rung of the economic and social existence by the upper castes.

The second concept of freedom does not consign the hope of equality to the life hereafter. The opening of the modern period, in the last half of the eighteenth century, saw the ringing calls "all men are created equal" and "liberté, égalité, fraternité," for which the U.S. and French revolutions are justly renowned. In many ways, Tom Paine united the best aspirations of both. He was the author of *Common Sense*, the pamphlet that inspired the Declaration of Independence. He also participated in the French Revolutionary Parliament and thought that the 1793 constitution "of the French Republic the best organized system the human mind has yet produced," and objected to it on but one ground – that "the right of suffrage [regardless of property or taxpaying status] is not maintained."[21]

In the revolutionary France of 1791, workers and peasants on the streets not only took up the cause of their own freedom, but also denounced slavery and supported the slave revolt then occurring in San Domingo, a Caribbean colony central to the economy of France and to the slave trade. An agent of the slave-owners in France described the scene thus: "One spirit alone reigns here, it is horror of slavery and enthusiasm for liberty."[22] C.L.R. James, in his classic history of the Haitian revolution, summed up the spirit of universality that prevailed:

> Henceforth the Paris masses were for abolition, and their black
> brothers in San Domingo, for the first time had passionate allies
> in France.[23]

The central differentiating characteristic between these two concepts of freedom relates to equality. Institutionalized inequality is the hallmark of the exclusionary concept of freedom. The active and universal recognition

---

[20] St. Augustine, *Concerning the City of God Against the Pagans*. Translated by Henry Bettenson in 1972; reprinted with a new introduction by John O'Meara (London: Penguin, 1984), pp. 874-876.

[21] Philip Foner, ed., *The Life and Major Writings of Thomas Paine* (New York: Citadel Press, 1993), p. 607. The quote is from Paine's introduction to "Agrarian Justice." But even Tom Paine excluded women from his idea of universal suffrage.

[22] As quoted in C.L.R. James, *The Black Jacobins: Toussaint L'Ouverture and the San Domingo Revolution*. 2nd ed. revised (New York: Vintage, 1963), p. 120.

of humanity, whether of the oppressed or of the oppressor, that is the main message of Gandhi and King, is in stark contrast to this idea. For instance, during India's independence struggle, Gandhi said that the British were welcome to stay in India so long as they stopped robbing it. King exhorted Blacks to approach the struggle for freedom with love. Nelson Mandela approached the South African anti-apartheid revolution in the same spirit. Like Beethoven's magnificent music written when he could not hear, Mandela created this deeply human, universalist formulation of freedom during his own imprisonment:

> It was during those long and lonely years that my hunger for the freedom of my own people became a hunger for the freedom of all people, white and black. I knew as well as I knew anything that the oppressor must be liberated just as surely as the oppressed. A man who takes away another man's freedom is a prisoner of hatred, he is locked behind the bars of prejudice and narrow-mindedness. I am not truly free if I am taking away someone else's freedom, just as surely as I am not free when my freedom is taken from me. The oppressed and the oppressor alike are robbed of their humanity.[24]

In all three struggles, the humanity of the oppressors was amply affirmed. There have also been enduring gains for the oppressed in political terms, such as the right to vote. During the anti-apartheid struggle in South Africa, millions of people joined hands across the world; students, governments of towns and cities in the United States and Europe, and so many others lent support to the anti-apartheid struggle. Independent India provided the African National Congress with a haven in Asia. Sweden did so in Europe. Many Africans, in turn, supported the struggle of African Americans for civil rights. Gandhi's non-violent struggle for equality had its start in South Africa.

But, if we survey the results of the struggles for independence in India, against apartheid in South Africa, and for civil rights in the United States, some crucial questions remain unresolved and there has even been retrogression. The legacy of gross inequality and discrimination and economic deprivation at the hands of economic forces, integrated from local to global, remains stubbornly entrenched even though the melanin content of the

---

[23] James 1963, *op. cit.*, p. 120.

[24] Nelson Mandela, *Long Walk to Freedom: The Autobiography of Nelson Mandela* (Boston: Little, Brown, 1994), p. 544.

ruling elites has increased somewhat. Tribal people in India have recently been declared "encroachers" in forestland, some of which is being taken over by World Bank-financed monoculture forestry. *Dalits* remain, in large measure, at the bottom of the social ladder. A murderous variety of Hindu chauvinism has ascended in electoral politics in large parts of India, especially in Gandhi's home state of Gujarat. In South Africa the demands of international finance and protection of property, which was originally obtained by expropriation and grotesque use of force, has reached such dimensions that Blacks have been forcibly evicted from their homes as squatters in operations reminiscent of the apartheid regime. In the United States, *de facto* school segregation prevails, despite intensive desegregation efforts. Even the right to vote won again by African Americans in 1965 (as it was in 1870) is being gradually eroded. Disproportionately large numbers of them, especially young men, have been deprived of the right to vote in several states by the simple expedient of deeming many non-violent crimes, including drug possession, as felonies and then denying felons the right to vote even after they have served their sentences.[25]

This continuing violence, repression, and marginalization that is inflicted daily on billions of people is a central result of the process of corporate-dominated globalization. Third World elites are, to a large extent, willing junior partners in the new scheme of commercial empire, which has many

---

[25] Marc Mauer, "State Disfranchises Those Who Have Paid Their Debt," *Miami Herald*, July 28, 2002. Available at http://www.miami.com/mld/miami/3742792.htm.

[26] I encountered a small illustration of this willing, junior partnership on a recent visit to Calcutta (now called Kolkata). The main ballroom in one of the fancier hotels there is named after Robert Clive, the conqueror of Bengal in 1757. The ravages, robbery, and corruption inflicted by Clive and his troops and the officers, agents and employees of the East India Company laid Bengal (including today's Bangladesh and West Bengal, where Calcutta is located) to waste, leading to a famine that killed about 10 million people during 1770-1771. The elites in India seem to have forgotten, for few of them seem to remember or at least care enough to demand a change. A Britisher not only remembered, but wrote a book about the tax that was central to the violence: the salt tax. See Roy Moxham, *The Great Hedge of India* (New York: Carroll & Graf, 2001). As is well-known, Gandhi initiated a massive civil disobedience movement around the salt tax, galvanizing millions to action in resistance to British rule.

[27] India's grain surpluses are nearly 60 million metric tons and growing at an average of 10 million metric tons per year. Over 10 million children under three years are severely malnourished (at 18 percent of the total). (Amy Waldman, "Poor in India Starve as Surplus Wheat Rots," *New York Times*, December 2, 2002). Less than 15 percent of the *growth* in the surplus would provide 1,000 calories per day to every severely malnourished child. See also Sudha Ramachandran, "India, the Politics of Starvation," *Asia Times*, November 12, 2002, available at http://www.globalpolicy.org/socecon/develop/2002/1112starvation.htm, viewed on December 3, 2002 and Radhakrishna Rao, "The Mirage of India's Food Surplus," September 7, 2001, on the web at http://www.india-syndicate.com/sci/rrenv/7sept001.htm, viewed on December 3, 2002. Both the latter articles point out that India is subsidizing exports of grains even as many of its people are starving.

parallels to the ones created by European and British government-chartered companies, like the East India Company in times past.[26] One indication of a return to grim times is that children are starving in India, while India is exporting food and has enormous grain surpluses, some of which are rotting in poor storage facilities.[27] In some ways the situation is worse, for the Indian government is following the IMF formulas of cutting "subsidies" for food and starving the poor even though it has historically high and rising foreign exchange reserves and therefore has no need of IMF loans.[28]

Exclusionary freedom, generalized apartheid

The core of any form of apartheid, whether local or global, is the assertion of power by the privileged, under the guise of superiority, for the overall purpose of securing unequal economic benefits, often with the accompanying rationalization that it is, after all, for the benefit of those who are being dominated. Such privilege cannot long be maintained without the threat and use of violence, intimidation, and fear that creates exclusion by race, caste, nationality, or gender. Since the United States now leads the perpetuation of global apartheid, it is important to consider the specificity of the U.S. historical background to it. (Not that any other power, using any other religion or ideology would do better. There is ample evidence, past and present, that it would not). [29]

It was during Andrew Jackson's time that the fervor for land-grabbing in the name of God, Christianity, and civilization, soon to be known as "Manifest Destiny," reached fever pitch, giving modern form to U.S. nationalism.[30] Indeed, the use of the term "nation" to describe the United States became popular among northerners during the heyday of Manifest Destiny, among other things as a code-word for a Whites only westward

---

[28] India's foreign exchange reserves in mid-2002 were over $55 billion. They have been growing at about $5 billion per year over the last decade. See Y.V. Reddy, "India's Foreign Exchange Reserves: Policy, Status, and Issues," special lecture by the Deputy Governor of the Reserve Bank of India, May 10, 2002. Available at http://www.bis.org/review/r020510f.pdf, viewed on December 3, 2002. Some reserves are necessary for financial stability, but large and growing reserves are viewed as an important component for attracting foreign investment.

[29] Germany, for instance, had a view parallel to the British-U.S. ideas of promoting democracy or civilization among the conquered, when it became a global power at the end of the nineteenth century. The Berlin elite of the time described their goal for world power as "world political freedom." The Nazis were their direct economic heirs, since the main economic goal of that latter regime was the re-establishment of German imperialist power, which Germany lost with World War I.

[30] John William Ward, *Andrew Jackson: Symbol for an Age* (Oxford: Oxford University Press, 1955); Anthony F.C. Wallace, *The Long, Bitter Trail: Andrew Jackson and the Indians* (New York: Hill and Wang, 1993).

expansion at the expense of Native Americans.[31] In the same period "federalism" came to be a code-word for southerners' assertion of their slave-owning property prerogatives at the expense of African-Americans. Jacksonian democracy extended suffrage to White men regardless of property, but did so on trails covered with tears, broken treaties, and blood.

It was a time when European settlers were terrorized by the idea of violence by Native Americans, just as southern slave-owners, mindful of the Haitian revolution, were terrorized by the idea of a slave revolt. And both these kinds of violence did occur, sometimes with terrible ferocity against innocents. Nat Turner's small army of rebellious slaves, longing to be free, not only killed male slave-owners, but also women and children, on the night that they decided would be the start of their war of independence. Native Americans not only fought soldiers in valiant wars of resistance to European conquest. From time to time they also visited terrible acts of violence upon settlers and their families.

It is not a rationalization of such violence, but rather an assertion of historical truth, to note that it was rooted in and was a reaction to the violence and injustice of slavery and genocide initiated and sustained by an invading and oppressive system that denied the humanity of slaves and Native Americans. Here are three examples of privation and terror experienced by slaves from the life of perhaps the best known of Nat Turner's African-American contemporaries, Frederick Douglass:

1. About parents:

> I never saw my mother, to know her as such, more than four or five times in my life; and each of these times was very short in duration, and at night.... Very little communication ever took place between us. Death soon ended what little we could have while she lived, and with it her hardships and suffering. She died when I was about seven years old, on one of my master's farms, near Lee's Mill [in Maryland]. I was not allowed to be present during her illness, at her death, or burial....
>
> Called thus suddenly away, she left me without the slightest intimation of who my father was. The whisper that my master

---

[31] Anders Stephanson. *Manifest Destiny: American Expansion and the Empire of Right* (New York: Hill and Wang, 1995), Chapter II. Of the pre-Civil War period, he notes: "Opposing slavery did not mean that one was in favor of a free, multiracial citizenry living in republican harmony, though to their credit some radical abolitionists did so argue. Instead, one tended to be against *mixtures* as well as unfree labor. Loud calls for a 'free' state often signaled an attempt to keep blacks out, coupled, at best, with some colonization scheme to rid oneself of blacks already present." p. 29 (emphasis in original).

was my father, may or may not be true; and, true or false, it is of but little consequence to my purpose whilst the fact remains, in all its glaring odiousness, that slaveholders have ordained, and by law established, that the children of slave women shall in all cases follow the condition of their mothers; and this is done too obviously to administer to their own lusts, and make a gratification of their wicked desires profitable as well as pleasurable; for by this cunning arrangement, the slaveholder, in cases not a few, sustains to his slaves the double relation of master and father.

2. About an aunt:

Before he commenced whipping Aunt Hester, he took her into the kitchen, and stripped her from neck to waist, leaving her neck, shoulders, and back, entirely naked. He then told her to cross her hands, calling her at the same time a d——d b—-h. After crossing her hands, he tied them with a strong rope, and led her to a stool under a large hook in the joist, put in for the purpose. He made her get upon the stool, and tied her hands to the hook. She now stood fair for his infernal purpose. Her arms were stretched up at their full length, so that she stood upon the ends of her toes. He then said to her, "Now, you d——d b—-h, I'll learn you how to disobey my orders!" and after rolling up his sleeves, he commenced to lay on the heavy cowskin, and soon the warm, red blood (amid heart-rending shrieks from her, and horrid oaths from him) came dripping to the floor. I was so terrified and horror-stricken at the sight, that I hid myself in a closet, and dared not venture out till long after the bloody transaction was over....

3. About work:

I lived with Mr. Covey one year. During the first six months, of that year, scarce a week passed without his whipping me. I was seldom free from a sore back. My awkwardness was almost always his excuse for whipping me...
...

Mr. Covey's ....life was devoted to planning and perpetrating the grossest deceptions. Everything he possessed in the shape of learning or religion, he made conform to his disposition to deceive. He seemed to think himself equal to deceiving the Almighty. He would make a short prayer in the morning, and a long prayer at night; and, strange as it may seem, few men would at times appear more devotional than he....

> If at any one time of my life more than another, I was made to
> drink the bitterest dregs of slavery, that time was during the first
> six months of my stay with Mr. Covey. We were worked in all
> weathers. It was never too hot or too cold; it could never rain,
> blow, hail, or snow, too hard for us to work in the field. Work,
> work, work, was scarcely more the order of the day than of the
> night. The longest days were too short for him, and the shortest
> nights too long for him. I was somewhat unmanageable when I
> first went there, but a few months of this discipline tamed me.
> Mr. Covey succeeded in breaking me. I was broken in body,
> soul, and spirit....[32]

Slavery and near-slavery continued into the twentieth century, in
Stalin's Soviet Union, in Hitler's Germany, and in global capitalism, where
it is still rife. It enters the world economy in a variety of ways, from silk to
sex. For example, a million children are forced into the international sex
trade each year; many of them are "bought and sold like chattel" in what is
a multi-billion dollar global business.[33]

Yet, if we are to reflect on Gandhi and King, we must also note that the
violence of the oppressed has been used as a trigger by powers of European
origin as a rationale for conquest and the appropriation of land and other
resources. There is ample evidence that those powers that wanted conquest
sometimes also incited violence, for instance, by sending settlers as
advance parties into areas they were not supposed to occupy. Such incite-
ments, real and imagined, have occurred throughout U.S. history (and not
only U.S. history). Examples include militant settler forays into Mexican
territory as a prelude to the U.S.-Mexican War of 1846-48 and the provocations leading up to the Gulf of Tonkin resolution of the U.S. Congress of
1964.[34] Whether incitement has been a pattern enough to be part of U.S.
foreign policy culture in its military aspect is beyond the scope of this
essay, but, I believe, well worth detailed examination, given the evolution
of world events since the fall of the Berlin Wall in 1989.

---

[32] Frederick Douglass, *Narrative of the Life of Frederick Douglass, An American Slave*, Made available by Project Gutenberg, in 1992, at ftp://ibiblio.org/pub/docs/books/gutenberg/etext92/
duglas11.txt. Viewed on December 24, 2002, originally published in Boston in 1845.

[33] Carol Bellamy, Executive Director of the United Nations Children's Fund (UNICEF), in a
December 12, 2001, Reuters story, "Millions of children in commercial sex trade-UNICEF," by
Marjorie Olster, at http://in.news.yahoo.com/011212/64/1as8l.html and the corresponding November
28, 2001, UNICEF press release, "UNICEF Warns: Demand for Child Sex is Linked to Spread of
HIV/AIDS," at http://www.unicef.org/newsline/01pr93printer.htm.

[34] For details regarding the 1964 provocations, see Daniel Ellsberg, *Secrets: A Memoir of Vietnam and
the Pentagon Papers* (New York: Viking, 2002), Chapters 3 and 4. For a summary of settler politics
and U.S. military affairs regarding the U.S.-Mexican War see James M. McPherson, *Battle Cry of*

The War on Terror is in keeping with this history. For instance, the Cold War had an aspect of resistance to the oppression and violence of Stalinism so far as the internal structure of the West was concerned. But so far as core Western aims in the Third World were concerned, and therefore for the majority of the world's people, it was not about freedom at all. One need look no farther than Winston Churchill, whose famous speech at Fulton, Missouri in 1946 marks the rhetorical beginning of the end of the wartime alliance with the Soviet Union and the start of the Cold War. He was an unabashed imperialist. In 1942, in the thick of his leadership of Britain against the Nazis, the same year he was making his call for "blood, sweat, and tears" to preserve British freedom, Churchill also famously promised that "I have not become the King's first minister in order to preside over the liquidation of the British Empire." He did preside over an Indian famine, in Bengal in 1942-43, that killed about three million people[35] and jailed Gandhi, Nehru, and other Indian leaders, who pointed out the contradiction between the British determination to keep India in chains while asking for full Indian cooperation in the fight for freedom against the Nazis.[36]

One U.S. objective was the conversion of the colonial to a commercial empire that it would dominate. In keeping with this goal, the maintenance of inequality and control over the world and its resources was an explicit objective of the U.S. policy during the Cold War. I have cited some evidence for that in the next essay, but a quote from a 1948 policy paper on Asia by George Kennan, the liberal intellectual architect of Cold War containment policy, is particularly revealing regarding the *intent* to maintain inequality:

Freedom: The Civil War Era (New York: Ballantine Books, 1989), Chapter 2. Southerners had their own version of Manifest Destiny that emerged from the conflicts over whether the newly acquired territories resulting from that war could have slave-labor-based plantation agriculture. In the 1850s, there were various misadventures originating in the South to capture Cuba and Nicaragua for the extension of such plantation agriculture there. There was even a school of thought that advocated that the extension of U.S.-owned slave-labor-based plantations through Central America, all the way to the southern tip of South America, and back up into the Caribbean. McPherson 1989, *op. cit.*, Chapter 3.

[35] No famine was officially declared despite the large number of deaths, though some official relief efforts were initiated in August 1943. The British Governor of Bengal, Sir T. Rutherford, wrote: "The Famine Code has not been applied as we simply have not the food to give the prescribed ration." Amartya Sen, *Poverty and Famines: An Essay on Entitlement and Deprivation* (Oxford: Clarendon Press, 1981), Chapter 6 and Appendix D. Sen explains that 1943 was the peak year for deaths, but excess deaths continued for years after that. The Rutherford quote is on p. 79 of the 1982 paperback edition.

[36] On being denied freedom, Gandhi, Nehru, and others initiated the historic Quit India movement in 1942, which led to their arrest and imprisonment. A useful review of Churchill and the end of the British Empire is provided by William Roger Louis, "Churchill and the Liquidation of the British Empire," March 29, 1998. Available at http://www.westminster-mo.edu/cm/scholar/291998.pdf, viewed on December 28, 2002.

Furthermore, we have about 50% of the world's wealth but only 6.3% of its population. This disparity is particularly great as between ourselves and the peoples of Asia. In this situation, we cannot fail to be the object of envy and resentment. Our real task in the coming period to devise a pattern of relationships which will permit us to maintain this position of disparity without positive detriment to our national security. To do so, we will have to dispense with all sentimentality and daydreaming; and our attention will have to be concentrated everywhere on our immediate national objectives. We need not deceive ourselves that we can afford today the luxury of altruism and world-benefaction.[37]

Despite Kennan's secret advice at the time, the public rhetoric of the United States was about promoting development and democracy so people could flourish and vote and worship as they pleased.

There is still talk about promoting democracy today, though more stark statements about re-establishing imperialism have also re-emerged after nearly a century of disrepute. But the establishment goal of domination has also been clearly articulated this time. For example, the draft post-Cold War military strategy, formulated in 1992 by the Pentagon when it was headed by then-Defense Secretary Dick Cheney, was to prevent the emergence of any rival. The implicit "regional defense strategy" is that the United States would "prevent any hostile power from dominating a region whose resources would, under consolidated control, be sufficient to generate global power. These regions include Western Europe, East Asia, the territory of the former Soviet Union, and Southwest Asia."[38]

A task force whose members now occupy senior positions in the current Bush administration published a report in September 2000 that now appears to be a formal part of the U.S. government's policy for permanent hegemony.[39] The report's goal was to promote Cheney's 1992 concept of

---

[37] U.S. State Department Policy Planning Study #23, 1948. This quote is taken from excerpts published in Thomas H. Etzold and John Lewis Gaddis, eds., *Containment: Documents in American Policy and Strategy 1945-1950* (New York: Columbia University Press, 1978), pp. 226-227. Kennan also drafted a famous essay in *Foreign Affairs* in July 1947 advocating "containment" of the Soviet Union — which was made into a nuclear-tipped policy in NSC-68 (drafted mainly by Paul Nitze).

[38] "Excerpts from the Pentagon's Plan: 'Prevent the Re-Emergence of a New Rival'," *New York Times*, March 8, 1992. The strategy was drafted in the Pentagon in 1992 when Cheney was Secretary of Defense in the administration of then-President George H.W. Bush. Cheney is, as of the time of this writing, in 2002, Vice-President in the administration of George W. Bush, and a leading voice in U.S. foreign and military policy. See the discussion below on the September 2000 report of the Project for a New American Century and its aftermath.

[39] Jay Bookman, "The President's Real Goal in Iraq," op-ed *Atlanta Journal-Constitution*, September 29, 2002. Available at http://www.accessatlanta.com/ajc/opinion/bookman/2002/092902.html.

military dominance. It concluded as follows:

> At present the United States faces no global rival. America's grand strategy should aim to preserve and extend this advantageous position as far into the future as possible.
>
> …
>
> This report proceeds from the belief that America should seek to preserve and extend its position of global leadership by maintaining the preeminence of U.S. military forces.[40]

These sentiments mirror in the military sphere Kennan's ideas in the economic one expressed more than half a century ago, when the idea of the "American century" first gained considerable currency.

The imperial enterprise at the beginning of the twenty-first century seems curiously like that in the last part of the nineteenth century and the first part of the twentieth. During the first part of that time, the imperialist contest for Central Asia and the Arabian regions of the Ottoman Empire revolved around the British desire to control its "lifeline" to India, "the jewel in the crown." With the conversion of the British and other navies from coal to oil during World War I, and the rise of the Indian independence movement, the Persian Gulf region (starting with Iran, then Iraq, and then the rest) became the center of the imperialist quest, the new supply end of the "lifeline," with Winston Churchill playing a central role in much of the proceedings.[41] The growing role of oil (and hence of oil transport routes) was passionately expressed by Senator Bérenger of France in 1918. Oil was

> the blood of victory. Germany had boasted too much of its superiority in iron and coal, but it had not taken sufficient account of our superiority of oil. As oil had been the blood of war, so it would be the blood of peace. At this hour, at the beginning of peace, our civilian populations, our industries, our commerce, our farmers are all calling for more oil, always more oil, for more gasoline, always more gasoline. More oil, ever more oil![42]

Bookman lists the positions in the administration of the prominent members of the organization, Project for the New American Century, which published the report.

[40] Thomas Donnelly, et al., *Rebuilding America's Defenses: Strategy, Forces, and Resources for a New Century* (Washington, D.C.: Project for the New American Century, September 2000), p. i and iv. Available at http://www.newamericancentury.org/RebuildingAmericasDefenses.pdf.

[41] More than any other politician, Churchill was at the center of creating the modern map of the Middle East after World War I. David Fromkin, *A Peace to End All Peace: The Fall of the Ottoman Empire and the Creation of the Modern Middle East* (New York: Henry Holt, 1989). For the role of oil in this period and region, see Yergin 1991, *op. cit.*, Part II.

[42] As quoted in Yergin 1991, *op. cit.*, p. 183.

After a detour through independence movements, that is where matters appear to have returned after the end of the Cold War, with the United States now playing the role of Britain then. The first use of poison gas use on the Kurds, "strongly" encouraged by Winston Churchill in 1919, was by the British in the mid-1920s, carried out by a Labour Party government.[43] Saddam Hussein's use of poison gas in the 1980s, during the Iran-Iraq war, was abetted by the United States, when present-day Secretary of Defense Donald Rumsfeld was the Reagan administration's U.S. special presidential envoy to the Middle East, with raw materials for chemical weapons and "dual use" items" reportedly being provided by British, German, and U.S. companies.[44] There are differences between then and now, of course. Among them, imperial aims are now being pursued in the context of Third World dictators, notably Saddam Hussein and Kim Jong Il, who are confronting the weapons of mass destruction of the global powers with their own ambitions and/or capabilities for wielding such weapons. More hopefully, unlike at the start of World War I, the people of the West are now far less likely to go off to war with illusions about a last great war, a war to end all wars, or songs on their lips. In fact, a substantial anti-imperialist movement is already building.

Milton Friedman

The theory that connects capitalism to freedom has been famously expressed in *Capitalism and Freedom* by Milton Friedman, who has defined the subject for the modern champions of unfettered capitalism. Freedom — the ability to make choices in personal, religious, economic, social, and political life — cannot extend to everyone in his view:

> Freedom is a tenable objective only for responsible individuals. We do not believe in freedom for madmen or children. The necessity of drawing a line between responsible individuals and others is inescapable, yet it means that there is an essential ambiguity in our ultimate objective of freedom. Paternalism is inescapable for those whom we designate as not responsible.[45]

---

[43] The British aim was to control of the region and the oil it was (rightly) thought to contain. Winston Churchill, as president of the Air Council, and in the context of suppressing a rebellion in Iraq, wrote in 1919: "I do not understand the squeamishness about the use of gas. I am strongly in favour of using poisonous gas against uncivilised tribes." As quoted in "The Churchill You Didn't Know," *The Guardian*, November 28, 2002. Available at http://www.guardian.co.uk/g2/story/0,3604,849122,00.html. For a chronology of Iraq, including the poison gas use, see "Iraq: A Century of War and Rebellion" (London: Practical History, May 2000). Available at www.geocities.com/CapitolHill/Senate/7672/iraq.html.

[44] Michael Dobbs, "U.S. Had Key Role in Iraq Buildup: Trade in Chemical Arms Allowed Despite Their Use on Iranians, Kurds," *Washington Post*, December 30, 2002, p. A1.

[45] Friedman, *Capitalism and Freedom* (Chicago: University of Chicago Press, 1982), p. 33.

Friedman does not tell us specifically to whom the word "we" refers in his phrase "we designate" just as President Bush left the "our" in the phrase "our freedoms" undefined. But since Friedman explicitly appeals to a paternalistic framework, the reader might suspect that the phrase refers to those who might, according to some defined criteria, play a modern, global version of the role of the *paterfamilias* in the Aristotelian or Augustinian household.

The issue of who is responsible and who is not surely deserves a treatise, but I will nonetheless take it up briefly here. Let me first say that I can agree with Friedman on some of the concepts he sets forth. Responsibility and freedom do have a relationship. Further, babies are manifestly not free and cannot be held responsible for their actions. Human beings become free and responsible (or not) in the social process of growing up. Some of his examples are also unexceptionable. Visiting violence upon one's neighbors is not responsible, for instance. Friedman notes that "[t]here is little difficulty in attaining near unanimity to the proposition that one man's freedom to murder his neighbor must be sacrificed to preserve the freedom of the other man to live."[46]

But other examples may be more difficult for votaries of global capitalism. For instance, should the uncounted men from the West and Japan who travel far and wide to brutalize children sold into the international sex trade deserve be designated as "responsible" and allowed to cross international borders with little or no restriction on their mobility? Or should they be jailed for statutory rape or sexual assault instead, which was the opinion of a French judge in October 2000 regarding the activities of a French sex tourist in Thailand?[47]

Friedman also takes up the problem of pollution, which creates adverse "neighborhood effects" as for instance when someone pollutes a stream and "in effect forc[es] others to exchange good water for bad."[48] Indeed, taking inspiration from Einstein, one should extend this spatial idea of neighborhood effects to the time dimension, because visiting ill-effects upon future generations is also irresponsible. This leads to some difficult questions. For instance, should those who are steering the Earth towards likely massive and irreversible climate change, be designated as irresponsible? If so, who should make the designation? Should curbs on fossil fuel consumption, the

---

[46] *ibid.*, p. 26.

[47] "Sex Tourist Gets Seven Years," October 20, 2000. Available at http://news.bbc.co.uk/1/hi/world/europe/980337.stm, viewed on December 28, 2002. At his trial the man apologized to the girl for stealing her childhood.

[48] Friedman 1982, *op. cit.*, p. 30.

main source of greenhouse gases be imposed? How and by whom? And should the principal polluters play the planet's *paterfamilias*?[49]

Madness presents ticklish problems as well. It is generally recognized that there are instances of people who are violently delusional, who are dangerously insane, and whose freedom of action must be curbed by society to the extent that is necessary to protect its other members (and perhaps also themselves). Since not all insane people are prone to violence, it is not from madness as such, but from *delusional violence* that society needs protection (though not only from delusional violence).

There are further complications. If we are to make progress towards the realization of the Jeffersonian idea of a unitary morality for people, "whether acting singly or collectively," the notion of the connection between freedom and responsibility must be extended to collectives of human beings. Moreover, much of the violence that has resulted in the restriction of the freedom of people has emanated from political, economic, and military institutions. How are we to judge whether the violence of collectives of people (organized as the state, church, corporations, social clubs, and the like) is sane and responsible, or delusional, and therefore mad, deserving of restrictions on freedom of action? Under what circumstances does collective responsibility fade into irresponsibility, thereby requiring restraints on freedom?

Given the parlous, violent state of the world, these are urgent questions. But they have deep historical roots. Imperialists have sought to justify genocide, murder, and conquest by portraying their victims as infantile, irresponsible, uncivilized, unfit, or even insane. Surviving Native peoples have been put under the "paternal" authority of those who have slaughtered their brothers and sisters, for instance. Let us note that the state of society or civilization of the victims is not here in question. The issue here is whether a civilizational structure in which genocidal violence, treaty breaking, and slavery played such large roles can be regarded as responsible today. No reasonable or responsible process can visit the sins of the fathers upon the sons. But we can surely ask whether the hallmarks of the political-military-economic culture persist in the ruling system and to what degree they dominate it.

---

[49] Neighborhood effects in the time dimension often raise issues far more complex than climate change, for which there is now very substantial evidence. For instance, the widespread introduction of genetically engineered plants in agriculture has the potential for disrupting ecosystems in ways we do not know how to assess. Theoretical considerations indicate that the very methods of assessing the short-term equivalence of engineered food grains to natural ones may lead to harm that is impossible even to discover until the damage is irreparable. For a theoretical account of the risks of genetically engineered crops, see Arjun Makhijani. *Ecology and Genetics: An Essay on the Nature of Life and the Problem of Genetic Engineering* (New York: Apex Press, 2001).

Specifically, is there a delusionally violent component to ideas such as "Manifest Destiny" that have been used to rationalize genocide in the past, which continue to hold sway today? And if there is, does it share similarities, with the delusional violence of, say, the suicide bombers of al Qaeda? Or is it mainly non-delusional, in search of material gain at the expense of others, in a manner that would be deemed morally reprehensible in the Jeffersonian sense that I have quoted? Or is it a mixture of the two?

U.S. "exceptionalism" seems to represent just such a mixture. It has been clothed in various mixtures of God, country, Christianity, free markets, and civilization and has been present in various guises well past the period when Europeans overspread the continental United States, into the period of the Cold War, and now into the War on Terror. Consider one fairly recent example, the military coup in Chile. Henry Kissinger, then President Nixon's National Security Advisor, thought the Chilean people irresponsible for leaning leftward. In a quote that was censored by the C.I.A. in a book about that agency, he reportedly said in 1970: "I don't see why we need to stand by and watch a country go communist because of the irresponsibility of its own people."[50] So when they voted for Salvador Allende, they were condemned to a paternalistic coup, which took place on September 11, 1973. Like the supposed U.S. government "paternalism" towards Native Americans, the Chilean coup extinguished freedom for millions. It led to governmentally sponsored murder of thousands.

It is natural therefore that while some think that Henry Kissinger is the essence of modern responsibility (for instance, in November 2002 President Bush appointed him to chair the commission of inquiry into the crimes of September 11, 2001),[51] there are others who believe that there is sufficient evidence for him to be tried as a criminal for actions undertaken in his official capacities.[52] And he is only the most prominent U.S. representative of a potentially rather large group of people about whom such divergent views can be held. Friedman's restriction of freedom to "responsible people" is of no help in understanding how its universality might be limited, unless we have a clear idea of how to determine whether someone is responsible or not and the process by which the determination should be made. The Nuremberg trials of the Nazis provided a good beginning, which

---

[50] Seymour M. Hersh, "Censored Matter in Book About C.I.A. Said to Have Related Chile Activities," *New York Times*, September 11, 1974.

[51] He resigned before the commission started work, because he did not want to make public the names of his clients.

[52] Christopher Hitchens, *The Trial of Henry Kissinger* (London, New York: Verso Books, 2001).

was institutionalized in 2002 as the International Criminal Court. But the United States, which presided over the Nuremberg trials, has refused the jurisdiction of the International Criminal Court; in fact, it is actively undermining the Court.[53]

As another example, one might consider the states that are parties to the Nuclear Non-Proliferation Treaty. Of the 188 parties, five are nuclear weapons states, twenty-three are non-nuclear allies of the United States in NATO. Japan and Australia are also non-nuclear allies of the United States.[54] Most of the other 158 are Third World countries that are often on the receiving end of advice (or worse) from the various institutions, like the CIA, IMF, and the World Bank, that serve as the collective *paterfamilias* of global apartheid. Yet, apart from Iraq and North Korea, which have violated the NPT, the main violators of the NPT are the nuclear weapons states, who are obligated to get rid of their nuclear weapons but show no practical intention of doing so. On the contrary, the United States, the most powerful and influential of them, has become a leader in violating its NPT commitments, adopting policies that are often diametrically opposed to its obligations.[55]

If the possession of power is not a proof of virtue, then one must conclude that the violating parties should all be deprived of freedom of action in the nuclear arena by those who have been in strict compliance. By rights, NPT enforcement should be led by countries like South Africa, which gave up its nuclear arsenal and joined the NPT as a non-nuclear state in the context of the end of apartheid. Or by New Zealand, which has affirmed that its alliance with the United States can be maintained only if the latter respects New Zealand's non-nuclear laws and principles. The responsible thing to do would be for the United Nations to empower countries that are in strict compliance with their non-proliferation obligations and have demonstrably renounced nuclear weapons to provide the policing power, should it be needed, to support the verification and disarmament actions of the International Atomic Energy Agency to carry out an agenda of a global nuclear roundup of weapons and weapons-usable materials, whether that concerns North Korea, Iraq, the United States, China, Russia, or any other declared or non-declared nuclear weapons state. At the same time, countries that refuse to subscribe to the International Criminal Court should be ruled out of leadership roles in enforcement actions.

---

[53] Deller, Makhijani, and Burroughs 2003, *op.cit.*, Chapter 9.

[54] India, Israel, and Pakistan, all nuclear weapons states, are not parties to the NPT.

[55] Deller, Makhijani, and Burroughs 2003, *op. cit.*, Chapters 2, 3, and 4.

But the present reality is that the most powerful country in the world, the United States, the only country that has used nuclear weapons to incinerate cities, insists on the right to police the world, essentially without restriction, even as it relegates observance of its own treaty obligations to the status of political convenience.[56] That is an indication that the moral state of the world today is the polar opposite of the Jeffersonian ideal of a single code of morality for people "whether acting singly or collectively."

A large part of Milton Friedman's edifice of associating capitalism with freedom is constructed on a liberal dose, so to speak, of capitalist mythology, not global economic, political, and military reality. In capitalist mythology, free individuals meet in a marketplace. Natural equality among these individuals is implicit. Capitalists generally own small, competing companies, though monopolies are sometimes possible. Milton Friedman's book, *Capitalism and Freedom*, contains no discussion of imperialism, nuclear weapons, genocide, modern slavery, the use of chemical weapons during World War I.

In Friedman's mythological world of *Capitalism and Freedom*, armies are really only for defense. Multinational corporations with revenues larger than most countries' gross domestic products that can hire private armies (to say nothing of hiring governments) do not exist. Imperialist-created famines do not exist. Partitions of countries and regions resulting from divide-and-rule politics or other imperialist conveniences do not exist. Nuclear threats by capitalist states for the control of the oil resources of others do not exist. CIA coups or Schools of the Americas, where ruthless dictators and torturers are trained, do not exist.

Thomas Friedman, a *New York Times* columnist and advocate of commercial globalization, has written with greater realism. He has noted that multinational corporations depend on U.S. military muscle:

> The hidden hand of the market will never work without a hidden fist — McDonald's cannot flourish without McDonnell Douglas, the builder of the F-15. And the hidden fist that keeps the world safe for Silicon Valley's technologies is called the United States Army, Air Force, Navy and Marine Corps.[57]

A retired U.S. general, Smedley Butler, was even more colorful in 1930s, when he made the connection between corporate interests and the military machine:

---

[56] *Ibid.*, Chapter 10.

[57] Thomas L. Friedman, "A Manifesto for the Fast World," *New York Times Magazine*, March 28, 1999.

I wouldn't go to war again as I have done to protect some lousy investment of the bankers. There are only two things we should fight for. One is the defense of our homes and the other is the Bill of Rights. War for any other reason is simply a racket.

...

...I spent thirty-three years and four months in active military service as a member of this country's most agile military force, the Marine Corps.... And during that period, I spent most of my time being a high class muscle-man for Big Business, for Wall Street and for the Bankers. In short, I was a racketeer, a gangster for capitalism.

...

I helped make Mexico, especially Tampico, safe for American oil interests in 1914. I helped make Haiti and Cuba a decent place for the National City Bank boys to collect revenues in.... I helped purify Nicaragua for the international banking house of Brown Brothers in 1909-1912... In China I helped to see to it that Standard Oil went its way unmolested.

During those years, I had, as the boys in the back room would say, a swell racket. Looking back on it, I feel that I could have given Al Capone a few hints. The best he could do was to operate his racket in three districts. I operated on three continents.[58]

The pattern has persisted. During the Cold War nuclear weapons were alerted on several occasions in the context of U.S. assertion of power and dominance in the Third World.[59] In one case, U.S. nuclear bombers were sent to Nicaragua two months before the CIA-sponsored coup in Guatemala, with a corporation, United Fruit, being the intended beneficiary of this employment of nuclear and covert action muscle.[60] The results of this use of power have been catastrophic for the people of Guatemala, especially its indigenous people. Consider just one massacre. The government's soldiers came in 1982 to the village of Sacuchum, on a mountain-

---

[58] Smedley Butler, as quoted on the Web at http://www.fas.org/man/smedley.htm. Butler, a Quaker, won two Congressional Medals of Honor. In 1933, after the election of Franklin Delano Roosevelt and the enactment of his first 100 days program, some business elites offered to finance Butler if he would agree to lead a military takeover of the United States. He refused and went public. A brief account, with sources, "An American Coup d'État?" by Clayton E. Cramer, is available at http://home.iprimus.com.au/korob/fdtcards/Butler.html. Butler also wrote a book, *War Is a Racket*, whose text is available at http://library.uncwil.edu/faculty/gulasg/racket.htm.

[59] "A Chronology of Nuclear Threats," *Science for Democratic Action*, vol. 6, no. 4 & vol. 7, no. 1 combined issue, October 1998. Available at http://www.ieer.org/ensec/no-6/threats.html.

[60] Barry B. Blechman and Stephen S. Kaplan, *Force Without War* (Washington: Brookings Institution, 1978), p. 48 for the nuclear aspect. The other aspect is discussed in briefly the book.

top. They robbed the villagers, raped about twenty women, and took 44 men with them. They cut out their tongues, and slit their throats, and killed them all. Later they killed eight more. Fifty-two women lost their husbands; over one hundred children their fathers. The newspapers announced they were guerrillas who had died in combat. There were, of course, no authorities to whom such a massacre could be reported, for the authorities had perpetrated it. The first time they were able to tell the story was to a U.S. author, who made their terror known to the world in 2002.[61]

This was, and is, called "pacification" – the peace of global capitalism for those who are yet denied the recognition of their humanity in the world. In 1999, President Clinton acknowledged that the military dictatorships resulting from the 1954 CIA-supported coup (See Chapter 1 of the following essay) had killed vast numbers of people in Guatemala. He apologized for *de facto* U.S. complicity in the murders,[62] which has apparently closed the matter. There will be no judicial processes to hold the complicit accountable. At the same time, without any discernible fuss or sense of self-consciousness, the United States has continued to call for *ad hoc* tribunals to judge others accused of similar crimes. None are from the wealthy side of global apartheid (though it is apparent that there are crimes enough to go around from all sides of it), vitiating a promise made at the trials of Nazis in Nuremberg that the international law being created there would apply equally to all.

There have also been crises over oil involving the implicit threat of nuclear weapons. The very first U.S.-Soviet military crisis after World War II, was over Iranian oil, controlled then by a British oil company (the Anglo-Iranian Oil Company) and desired by both the United States and the Soviets, at a time when the United States had a nuclear monopoly. Other oil-related nuclear crises have also occurred, such as the Iraq-Lebanon crisis of 1958 and the Persian Gulf War of 1991.

Violence at home

Let us set aside the violence that those who have designated themselves the arbiters of global responsibility have inflicted on others and consider that which they have inflicted on themselves even as they have gath-

---

[61] Daniel Wilkinson, *Silence on the Mountain: Stories of Terror, Betrayal, and Forgetting in Guatemala* (Boston: Houghton Mifflin, 2002), pp. 199-216.

[62] Charles Babington, "Clinton: Support for Guatemala Was Wrong" *Washington Post*, March 11, 1999. p. A1. Available at http://www.washingtonpost.com/wpsrv/inatl/daily/march99/clinton11.htm. Also, Douglas Farah, "Papers Show U.S. Role in Guatemalan Abuses," *Washington Post*, March 11, 1999. p. A26. Available at http://www.washingtonpost.com/wpsrv/inatl/daily/march99/guatemala11.htm.

ered into their countries the resources of the world. How shall we assess the responsibility of the conduct of European leaders during World War I, of Europeans and Americans during World War II, of widespread support or at least sympathy and understanding for Hitler in the 1930s? For instance, in 1937, Winston Churchill said of him: "One may dislike Hitler's system and yet admire his patriotic achievement. If our country were defeated, I hope we should find a champion as admirable to restore our courage and lead us back to our place among the nations."[63] Henry Ford's Nazi sympathies were so strong that he was honored with a Grand Cross of the Supreme Order of the German Eagle, accompanied by a personal note from Hitler in July 1938.[64]

How shall we assess the idea that, according to their own analysis of deterrence doctrine, Europeans and Americans and Soviets needed tens of thousands of nuclear weapons aimed at one another to prevent themselves from going to war again? The slaughter of World War II apparently did not provide enough deterrence. The threat of visiting total destruction upon themselves was apparently necessary for that. Even that did not ensure peace. Rather it caused the export of war by the West and the Soviet Union

[63] As quoted in "The Churchill You Didn't Know," *Guardian* 2002, *op.cit.*

[64] It was Hilter's recognition of the fact that Ford had published a virulent anti-Semitic pamphlet *The International Jew, a Worldwide Problem* in 1921, even before Hitler wrote *Mein Kampf.* A quick summary of the issue is in: Carlin Romano, "How Henry Ford Hoped to Mass-Produce Hatred of the Jews," *Philadelphia Enquirer*, April 4, 2002. Available at http://www.philly.com/mld/inquirer/entertainment/books/2995894.htm, viewed on 28 December 2002.

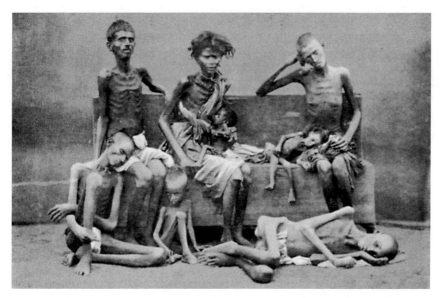

Victorian values as experienced by Indian families in a time of drought and food export from India to Britain in the 1870s. Some parts of India are experiencing these same values today of global capitalism under the rule of Indian elites.

Photographs courtesy of Mike Davis

to the Third World — the so-called "proxy wars" in which millions were killed so Europeans could have peace at the edge of the nuclear abyss. This might perhaps be considered as a nuclear extension of the intra-European great power standoff of the Victorian era in which non-Europeans were killed or starved by the tens of millions — genocide of Native Americans, famines in the colonies, with 30 to 60 million people dead from famines in India alone.[65] That European peace ended in World War I.

---

[65] Mike Davis. *Late Victorian Holocausts: El Niño Famines and the Making of the Third World* (London, New York: Verso, 2001).

Or consider what is, in the larger scheme of violence, a small but very telling example because it is up close and personal, with its very own Kodak moment.[66] During the 1950s and early 1960s, the period of atmospheric nuclear weapons testing in Nevada, the U.S. nuclear weapons establishment knowingly (since 1953) allowed the milk supply of the country to become contaminated with radioactive iodine-131, present in fallout. It did nothing to help protect the milk supply of the country. The result was to put children across most of the country at risk, irradiating their thyroids. Concerns raised in the late 1950s about the effects of fallout on children by some independent scientists were brushed aside in the name of national security.[67] During the same period, in response to the threat of a lawsuit from Kodak, whose film had become fogged due to contamination of packaging material by fallout, the Atomic Energy Commission supplied secret fallout data to the photographic film industry so it could take action to protect its products.

When the government published its maps of radioactive hot spots in 1997, after years of delay, the hot spots were dotted all across the continental United States. The highest doses in the worst hot spots were to farm children who drank goat's milk and were estimated at up to 2,000 rad to the thyroid, a level comparable to the worst exposed children from the infamous 1986 Chernobyl nuclear reactor accident. The U.S. government has been appropriating money to the follow-up of Chernobyl children, but until the time of this writing, it has not done anything to locate or inform the worst exposed people in the United States.

Moreover, the United States government located the test site in Nevada knowing that it would rain fallout on the country. In 1997, the U.S. government estimated that iodine-131 in testing fallout from that site alone would cause between 11,000 and 212,000 thyroid cancers in the United States. In 2002, a Centers for Disease Control and Prevention draft feasibility study indicated that testing in the Marshall Islands and the Soviet

---

[66] This brief account is based on Pat Ortmeyer and Arjun Makhijani, "Worse Than We Knew," *Bulletin of the Atomic Scientists*. vol. 53, no. 7, November/December 1997. Available at http://www.thebulletin.org/issues/1997/nd97/nd97toc.html. For the government study of milk contamination see National Cancer Institute, *Estimated Exposures and Thyroid Doses Received by the American People from Iodine-131 in Fallout Following Nevada Atmospheric Nuclear Bomb Tests* (Bethesda, Maryland: NCI, 1997). Available at http://rex.nci.nih.gov/massmedia/Fallout/index.html. For an analysis of the health and environmental effects of nuclear testing more generally see Institute for Energy and Environmental Research and the International Physicians for the Prevention of Nuclear War, *Radioactive Heaven and Earth: The Health and Environmental Effects of Nuclear Weapons Testing In, On, and Above the Earth* (New York: Apex Press, 1991).

[67] A 1960 University of California engineering alumni magazine editorial quoted in Chapter 2 of From Global Capitalism to Economic Justice provides an example of rationalizing harm to children. The editorial was reprinted in *California Engineer*, v.68, no.3, March 1990, p. 23.

Union also created hot spots in the continental United States.[68] The best estimate for the total number of U.S. cancers (with large uncertainties) due to radiation doses received until the end of the last century is about 80,000, with 15,000 to 20,000 of them estimated to be fatal.[69]

The United States is not an exception. Every nuclear weapons state has first of all harmed its own people in the name of national security.[70] Only the United States has had the open and democratic culture, fast eroding, to make sweeping, though still partial, acknowledgements of the damage. Despite the deceit, cover-ups, and worse (including human experiments on children and pregnant women[71]) nuclear weapons establishments around the world are still able to continue to wear the mantle of national security without too close a questioning of their motives and their legitimacy.

Borders

The view of the poet Yevgeny Yevtushenko, expressed in the excerpt of his poem that he kindly allowed me to reproduce in this book, is a direct challenge to the view of Francis Fukuyama discussed in Chapter 1 of the following essay. For the latter, the end of history is already here, since human beings have already developed the form of society, western capitalism and the associated political democracy, to which everyone can aspire. For Yevtushenko, human history will not even begin until borders have been abolished because these borders have become central to the definition of our identities. Armies and border guards stand in the way.

It is evident even upon casual inspection that armies and border guards have become among the important defining features of people's identities as human beings where nationalism is most strong – that is where people identify most with the military power of the state and the separation it provides from others. This is perhaps most transparent in the United States, which as a society where the vast majority of people have immigrant roots, still defines immigrants as "aliens" and where the common identification

---

[68] Centers for Disease Control and National Cancer Institute, *A Feasibility Study of the Health Consequences to the American Population of Nuclear Weapons Tests Conducted by the United States and Other Nations* (Atlanta, GA: CDC, 2002). Available at http://www.cdc.gov/nceh/radiation/fallout/.

[69] Institute for Energy and Environmental Research, *Fact Sheet on Fallout Report and Related Maps*, February 28, 2002. Available at http://www.ieer.org/comments/fallout/factsht.html.

[70] Arjun Makhijani, Howard Hu, and Katherine Yih, eds., *Nuclear Wastelands: A Global Guide to Nuclear Weapons Production and Its Health and Environmental Effects* (Cambridge, MA: MIT Press, 2000). Includes an Afterword, briefly updating 1995 ed.

[71] Eileen Welsome, *The Plutonium Files: America's Secret Medical Experiments in the Cold War* (New York: Dial Press, 1999).

of the term "alien," whether fearsome or pleasantly exotic (but always strange), is the subject of myth and Hollywood movie-making.

I have argued in *From Global Capitalism to Economic Justice* that the essential character of nationalism that was formed in the West in the process of the development of capitalism as a whole, including the imperialism that is integral to it, is very similar to racism. The one central difference is that the borders of racism are micro-borders, usually having a social and economic geography within states. But the role of police and armies has not been much different. The police power of the states comprising the United States was used to catch and deport escaped slaves back to their supposed owners. Friction over the practical exercise of these powers was a factor in the high emotions that put abolitionists and southern slave-owners in conflict in the prelude to the Civil War.

Maria Jimenez, director of the Borders Project of the American Friends Service Committee, has noted the role of national borders in the global economy in a manner that evokes the policed restrictions on slaves. The following observations are from an unpublished paper she shared with me:

> Erecting borders for international labor makes it difficult for large numbers of workers to leave areas considered "favorable" for the establishment and expansion of transitional production units such as the assembly plants....Sustaining regulatory schemes that guarantee control and the inequality of mobility is essential for this strategy of high profits and low wages. For that reason, the use of armed force, border policing agencies, including the military, and institutional violence are [a] necessary aspect of the global economic structure to enforce compliance with immigration and border control policies. In fact, the combination of global economic development, military integration, and the denial of rights of displaced populations, domestically and internationally, reproduce a de facto system of slavery for marginalized economic and social sectors, particularly the international migrants.[72]

It is, therefore, not only Stalinist borders, about which Yevtushenko and Solzhenitsyn[73] wrote so eloquently, that keep people in. The borders of global apartheid, designed to keep the poor out of the regions where the

[72] Maria Jimenez, "Mobility, Human Rights and Economic Development: Lessons of the International Mexican Migrant Experience and United States Immigration Policies," undated, but from the mid-1990s, unpublished draft personal communication, quoted with permission.

[73] Alexandr Solzhenitsyn, *The Gulag Archipelago: 1918:1956*, 3 vols., (New York: Harper & Row, 1974). The author also authorized a one-volume version, abridged by Edward E. Ericson, Jr., published in 1985 by Harper & Row and reissued as a paperback by Perennial Classics, in New York, in 2002.

wealth of the world has been accumulated, are also effective in keeping people in the low wage areas to which global capitalism has confined them. This reality is most starkly on view along with U.S. border with Mexico. In maintaining these exclusionary and confining borders, the cooperation of the political and business elites across the borders of states is essential, though some intra-elite tensions do result, as for instance between the governments of Mexico and the United States.

Border transactions between Third World and capitalist countries are not between equals. Indeed, one of the expressions of the hierarchy of capitalism is in the inequality of states and their governance. [74] In theory the system of states is supposed to consist of equal sovereign states, a concept dating back to the 1648 Treaty of Westphalia that ended the bloody Thirty Years War in Europe. In reality, sovereignty in internal matters is a substantial reality only on the dominating side of global apartheid. Indeed, the very context of the establishment of sovereignty by European states between the fifteenth and the nineteenth centuries occurred entirely in the context of imperialism and the gathering up, largely by force, of resources from around the world into Europe and its extensions.

While there are some Third World states that have large elements of internal sovereignty, most of them have some facets of sovereignty internally, so long as they are subject to the dictates of the military and financial structure of global apartheid. If they do not, they risk violent attempts to crush them, as the examples of Vietnam, Mozambique, Angola, Nicaragua, and others have shown.[75]

Examples abound of the subjection of the internal sovereignty of such states to their ability to serve the economic structures of global apartheid. Once-favorite dictators like Marcos of the Philippines, Mobutu of Zaire (Congo), "Emperor" Bokassa of the Central African "Empire" (a former French army officer), and Suharto of Indonesia, appointed, supported, or

---

[74] Many people in the United States believe that if Third World countries ask for foreign aid (often thought of as handouts), the United States has a right to dictate the terms. They also tend to believe that U.S. foreign aid is far larger than it actually is. Yet, the $15 billion or so per year that falls under that legislative rubric is spent mostly on strategic military alliances and as leverage in broader political and economic arenas (as, for instance, pressure to fall in line with U.S. policies on the International Criminal Court). Much of it is military equipment often used, among other things, for repression. Much of the rest works largely as a tool for transferring money from working people in the United States to select corporations (via contracts and compulsory purchasing rules) and to elites in the Third World, where it entrenches dependence and corruption. It would be far better to abolish "foreign aid" and put in place the financial and developmental policies discussed in the next essay (Chapters 10 through 12). And as regards humanitarian and natural disasters, there are far more equitable and less politically vulnerable ways for addressing them than government-controlled "foreign aid."

[75] China is not discussed in this essay. It is discussed in Chapter 7 of the next essay.

nurtured by global capitalism found, to their chagrin, that they can be unceremoniously deposed one way or another when they are deemed no longer useful.[76]

The marriage of the armed power of the state with the financial power of corporations in the context of the free flow of capital and goods and the restricted flow of workers is antithetical to human equality and freedom. It also leads the world in a direction that is the opposite of the one needed for the achievement of a system of governance, from the local to the global, that will ensure that the moral code that is expected of individuals, for instance, in the form of respect for the life of one's neighbors and for future generations, also applies to human institutions, especially the most powerful ones, governments and corporations.

The juridical foundation of such a goal has mostly been created, at least in theory, in the course of the struggles around the world over the last two and a half centuries for freedom and equality and against slavery, colonialism, male domination, and intense economic exploitation. In other words, today human beings are considered, in theory, to have equal rights. Most of these legal instruments date from the last half of the twentieth century, when the freedom movements in Asia and Africa achieved a measure of success and imperialism as an ideology came into disrepute. But, as Jimenez points out, none of these declarations, including the Universal Declaration of Human Rights,[77] assert the right to global mobility for the world's people:

> It is still accepted in international laws, norms and values that a nation-state can positively discriminate, treat differently and restrict rights of those not accepted as citizens.
>
> As to the human right of mobility, it may be worth noting that indigenous people of this [Western] hemisphere enjoyed and exercised this right before the European conquest. There are other examples—the movement of many peoples to Mecca provided an interchange of ideas that led to technological advancement. Even the most massive movement historically—the European to the Americas led to advancement in technology and even the basis of modern concepts of democracy and freedom.

---

[76] For an interesting report on human rights and intervention that raises some questions about the Westphalian system, but not about the economic and military issues at the center of global apartheid, see *The Responsibility to Protect: Report of the International Commission on Intervention and State Sovereignty* (Ottawa, ON: International Development Research Centre, December 2001). Available at http://www.iciss-ciise.gc.ca/report-e.asp.

[77] The text of this 1948 declaration can be found at http://www.un.org/Overview/rights.html.

> It is restrictions to mobility through the use of force that is inherent in subduing, controlling and integrating populations into strategies of economic exploitation of labor forces. It was use of military force that obligated native populations in North America to be confined to reservations and in Latin America, to encomiendas. It was the use of military force that led to the enslavement of the African population that led to the economic growth of the conquering elites. The use of military force is a tacit indication of the high priority placed by the elites in their quest for dominance and wealth.[78]

This lack of juridical standing for a right of mobility across borders has large implications for the majority of the world's people. For instance, Article 23 of the Universal Declaration speaks of workers' rights such as "equal pay for equal work." But, while the right to earn equal pay for equal work is now recognized in many countries at least in theory, the inequality of pay across borders is still legally permitted – indeed, it is often promoted and trumpeted as a "comparative advantage."[79] As another example, consider the right to asylum. It was the one practical route to escaping the oppression of being forced to stay inside borders. But it has eroded considerably, since its anti-Soviet, anti-communist ideological usefulness for capitalism is almost done. In the absence of a global right of mobility, the Declaration's recognition of a right of people to leave their countries or to seek asylum has become, for the oppressed in global capitalism, the equivalent of the fabled law that equally forbids the rich and the poor from sleeping under bridges.

Borders are also being used in the War on Terror. Whether by design or not, the U.S. government's conduct of that war fits in with Manifest Destiny ideology. The fact that the terrorists who committed the mass murders of September 11, 2001, were visitors to the United States under various false pretenses has been used to create a perpetual war and a vast "homeland security" bureaucracy. It has tended to create an indiscriminate taint on the foreign-born including students, immigrants, Arabs (of all religions), and Muslims. It is a dangerous approach which implicitly, at least, fails to recognize that a home-grown European-American terrorist like Timothy McVeigh, who had a great deal of ideological and racial company in the

---

[78] Maria Jimenez, comments on a draft of this essay, personal e-mail communication, December 2002.

[79] David Ricardo's theory of comparative advantage, now nearly two-hundred years old, is based on such drastic simplifications and has so many essential omissions that it has even less correspondence to the real world than Milton Friedman's largely mythological discourse on capitalism and freedom. A critique of this theory is beyond the scope of this essay.

United States and Europe, might have a considerable amount in common with foreign-born terrorists.[80] Instead, terrorists of European-American and Christian background become exceptions, people who have gone astray as individuals, like McVeigh or the children who massacred their schoolmates at Columbine High School in Colorado, and unlike the vast majority. In contrast, stereotyping is the basis of the dragnet of spying, arrests, imprisonment without charges, deportation, and other violations of human rights of people, especially Muslims and Arabs, which are coming to typify the War on Terror.[81]

The approach is not only dangerous to freedom; it is counterproductive. It ignores or downplays facts and realities that are central to a reduction of terrorism risks and to the enhancement and spread of freedom, including the following:

- the search for terrorists is a one-in-a-million search in which the engaged and free participation of people around the world and the full diversity of people in the United States is needed;

- one-in-five children in the United States lives in a family with at least one foreign-born person, so instilling fear in the foreign-born, rather than providing security and inspiring free cooperation through respectful conduct, tends to inhibit the flow of potentially vital information;

- the prosperity and even the functioning of the U.S. economy, from strawberry fields to Silicon Valley to universities and hospitals to chicken factories to research and development laboratories in large corporations, depends on immigrants;

- threats of war are likely to cause the relatively strong to arm themselves, the weak to become more resentful, and allies to become bewildered, alarmed, and possibly uncooperative.

The counterproductive nature of the War on Terror is plain to see after more than one year. Osama bin Laden and several of his top lieutenants are still at large.[82] The perpetrator(s) of the anthrax attacks in 2001 in the

---

[80] For information on various U.S. hate groups, see the Web site of the Southern Poverty Law Center, http://www.splcenter.org/splc.html.

[81] Michael Moore's brilliant film, *Bowling for Columbine*, about the high school killings, attributes the gun violence in U.S. culture largely to racially-tinged panic-mongering in the media. Yet, the urge to panic-mongering and its acceptance and success may have deeper roots in the persistence of the panic prone aspect of White settler and slave culture.

[82] Barton Gellman, "In U.S., Terrorism's Peril Undiminished," *Washington Post*, December 24, 2002.

United States is also not in custody. Pakistan is less stable than before, unable and/or unwilling to keep its promise to end cross-border infiltration into India. The governments of two of its four provinces are now under the control or strong influence of Islamic fundamentalists, a first in Pakistan's history. They are, by and large, opposed to the U.S. military presence in the region. The risks of a negative spiral of violence getting out of control to include the use of nuclear weapons by either governments or terrorist groups are higher today than at any time since the Cuban missile crisis, as witness the Kashmir upheaval that has kept South Asia closer to the edge of the nuclear abyss since May 2002.[83]

The urgency of the search for Osama bin Laden and anthrax-man has receded, taking a back seat to the preparations for war in Iraq. The U.S. military presence in the region is now vast and deep, extending from in Uzbekistan in Central Asia to Djibouti on the Horn of Africa and Diego Garcia in the heart of the Indian Ocean.[84] These realities, in the context of constant saber-rattling and muscle-flexing by the United States, are increasing antagonism towards the United States from Korea to Canada, just when the United States needs cooperation and understanding the most.

Iraq, Iran, and North Korea are all in crises, with the political position of those who wish to possess nuclear weapons stronger today than it was before September 11, 2001. A nuclear confrontation, at least in words, is emerging between North Korea and the United States, implicitly involving South Korea and potentially Japan. To make matters worse, the North Korean nuclear weapons establishment may have secured technology to make highly enriched uranium from Pakistan, connecting the two most active nuclear weapons hot spots in the world.

The grave and possibly growing risks of war and terrorism of mass destruction are a poor return for the deep wounds that the War on Terror has inflicted on freedom and privacy, on constitutional traditions of the rule of law at home and abroad, and on the best immigrant traditions of embracing individuals of all nationalities dedicated to making their way in the world though hard work, competence and enterprise. A dispassionate overview might conclude that many or most of the high-priority elements of the War on Terror make little sense as an anti-terrorist enterprise. The elements that would be most effective in curbing terrorism — internation-

---

[83] For a brief history of the Kashmir issue as well as an approach to the resolution of the conflict see articles by Arjun Makhijani and Admiral L. Ramdas (respectively) at www.ieer.org.

[84] Vernon Loeb and Bradley Graham, "Rapid Buildup in Gulf on Horizon," *Washington Post*, December 20, 2002. Central Asian and South Asian bases are in addition to those shown in this article.

al police action in conformity with humanitarian law, negotiation (for one must often negotiate with criminals as part of the process of arrest and of stopping crime), provision of security to the affected immigrant communities so that innocent members of these communities would cooperate wholeheartedly, are all notable by their near-total absence. But the War on Terror does fit much better with an imperial aim of creating a vast military presence for controlling, among other things, the most important oil and gas resources on the planet. [85]

Universal Freedom and Global Democracy

Ultimately, the assertion of freedom from the barrel of the gun has yielded wealth on a royal scale for a very few (as it generally has in the history of civilization) and modest wealth, or at least a decent standard of living (depending on one's definitions of those terms), for perhaps a sixth to a third of the world's population (a new achievement of technology combined with worldwide extraction of raw materials and energy). The limited, highly conditional freedom that this has brought for a minority exists mostly behind high walls of fear, whether these are the Lead Curtains to keep immigrants out of the capitalist countries, or the gated communities of Brazilian millionaires commuting by helicopter because they are too afraid to drive.

But for over half a century, this system has put the world at risk of a nuclear-tipped collective suicide, where it remains. The United States, Russia, Britain, France, and China have been joined by Israel, India, and Pakistan. North Korea has nuclear ambitions and Iraq had them. Nor is the irresponsibility of nuclear armaments confined to states. Osama bin Laden has laid claim to the same prerogatives of mass destruction, even though his organization may not yet have the capability for doing it with nuclear bombs.[86] But his principles are no different than those of modern states. He

---

[85] A comparison between the problematic War on Terror and the successful approach of Charles Moose, police chief of Montgomery County, is useful. Chief Moose led the team of many police departments and investigative agencies, including the FBI, to successfully pursue and capture, with the help of the public, sniper suspects who terrorized the Washington metropolitan area with a series of murders over three weeks in October 2002. But he had no aims other than public protection and justice and earned the trust of a united public by the integrity with which he approached the difficult and dangerous job. He also understood that even in the midst of the terror and the murders, it was essential to negotiate with the murderers so that they might surrender more quickly, even while keeping the police forces under his command armed for self-defense and the defense of the public. For some of his messages to the snipers see, "Chief Moose's Messages to the Snipers," *CBC News*, October 23, 2002, available at www.cbc.ca/news/features/sniper_messages.html.

[86] In a May 1998 interview with ABC reporter, John Miller, Osama bin Laden claimed the right to use nuclear weapons by referring to the killing of women and children by the United States during the bombings of Hiroshima and Nagasaki. Available at http://www.pbs.org/wgbh/pages/frontline/shows/binladen/who/interview.html.

is claiming for a non-governmental collective the prerogatives that have allowed states to kill with little to check them except other, more powerful, states that can kill more efficiently. After all, official military strategists of air warfare conceived it as an instrument for terrorizing populations and governments into submission.[87]

Jeffersonian ideas about freedom and equality have inspired the world from Harry Truman to Ho Chi Minh. But they have been overwhelmed by the ideology of power and greed – by the slave-owning side of Jefferson. This champion of freedom was a firm believer in the superiority of the White man. Despite his scholarship in the languages and culture of American Indians, the policies he espoused and promoted have caused him to be regarded as a "planner of cultural genocide, the architect of the removal policy, the surveyor of the Trail of Tears."[88]

Jefferson is then the quintessential character in the American drama of freedom. Anthony F.C. Wallace has noted that "[t]he fascination with Jefferson has grown, perhaps, because he embodied some of the major dilemmas of American culture – fault lines in the national character where differing views on how to share the spaces of the world grind together."[89] That the United States government's military capabilities are at the center of the system of global apartheid represents the dominance of the unhappier side of Jefferson. Perhaps foreshadowing that fate, Tom Paine, the more thorough votary of freedom in that era, died a pauper in New York City and was buried in New Rochelle, New York, nearly alone and forgotten in the land whose Declaration of Independence he inspired.[90]

The hopes created by the freedom struggles of the twentieth century were, by its end, suffocating in global apartheid. The love that Gandhi and King and Mandela showed for their oppressors has not been sufficient to rescue the oppressors or the rest of world from the jaws of hatred, violence, or even the peril of self-destruction, much less put them on the path of universal freedom. Gandhi and King focused their efforts on the moral restraints that the oppressed must observe in order to create a process that was sound enough to lead to freedom without the prison of hatred. But how are these moral restraints to be applied to the oppressors — to those who

---

[87]   Jack Colhoun, "Strategic Bombing." Available at   http://www.ieer.org/comments/bombing.html. Viewed on October 31, 2002.

[88] Anthony F.C. Wallace, *Jefferson and the Indians: The Tragic Fate of the First Americans* (Cambridge, MA: Harvard University Press, 1999), p. vii and ix.

[89] *ibid.*, p. viii.

[90] Foner 1993, *op. cit.*

control and ensure the maintenance of the dominating structures of global capitalism?

Consider the lessons of the global struggle against South African apartheid. That struggle was led first of all by South Africans, most importantly by South African Blacks led by Mandela and the African National Congress. But the economic, political and military fissures in the system were large enough to allow powerful global support in that struggle. It is unclear whether the struggle could have been won without it, or whether the forces of apartheid might simply have carried on and completely destroyed the country, including themselves.

The anti-Vietnam war struggle in the United States was sparked first of all by the resistance to U.S. intervention by the people of Vietnam. Without that resistance, there could not have been the reaction to that resistance in the United States both in the form of more force and the movement against the use of force. The final phase of the collapse of support for that war in the United States came when Daniel Ellsberg was inspired by a war resister getting set to join his colleagues in jail. Randy Kehler had a picture of Gandhi behind him when he made the historic speech that was the direct trigger for Ellsberg's release of the Pentagon papers.[91] Of course, Gandhi was, in a way, only coming home, because one of Kehler's U.S. antecedents was Thoreau who went to jail to protest the U.S.-Mexican War in the nineteenth century heyday of Manifest Destiny. Thoreau's war resistance was a source of inspiration for Gandhi.

The struggle in both countries against the U.S. war on Vietnam resulted in greater freedom in the United States, among other things. The publication of the Pentagon papers by the *New York Times* and the *Washington Post* led to a historic Supreme Court decision expanding the right of the public to know and the press to publish. The complex chain of events that began then also led to the enactment of the Freedom of Information Act, which provides the right to obtain government documents to a degree unprecedented in the history of great powers (though not among all countries). These events were also of a piece with a long tradition of a thirst for freedom in the United States going back to the agrarian dreams of Jefferson and Tom Paine's anti-royalist, egalitarian convictions. They brought the freedoms promised in the first amendment of the U.S. constitution to greater reality than ever before and permitted, among other things, the public to force open the dark corners of the nuclear establishment.

---

[91] Ellsberg 2002, *op cit.*, p. 270-273 and photograph section.

In stark contrast to this free-spirited aspect of U.S. political culture, militarist nationalism, which is again coming to the forefront, is a principal ideological force in the maintenance of the borders of global apartheid. Those borders define the dominant nationalities, which are the global equivalent of Whites in South Africa. It follows therefore that those borders must come down as a matter of right, or rather as an assertion of human rights, in the struggle for global democracy, just as the internal racial and physical political borders had to come down in South Africa to overcome apartheid there. In other words, if enduring freedom and peace are not divisible then it is essential that a global right of mobility be made a basic human right in an economy and society that is irrevocably global and that people all over the world join in the assertion of such a right.[92] That does not mean that people will actually migrate in vast numbers. But they must have the right to do it. People must be able to move and live and work as the circumstances in life allow them.

In a world that aspires to freedom, the walls of global apartheid must come down as surely as the Berlin Wall had to come down to end Soviet communism. It will take a global struggle in the tradition of Gandhi and King and Mandela to create a direction in which freedom will be universal rather than exclusionary, violent, and self-defeating. For this struggle to be successful, it will be necessary for the people of the West (economically and politically defined)[93] to shed their allegiance to the nationalism that identifies them with the military arm of the state, even if it may deliver oil and a plethora of goods made with cheap labor in the short-term. Despite the many struggles for freedom and equality that followed, the job begun by Tom Paine and the workers and peasants in France who supported the insurrection of the slave brothers and sisters in San Domingo remains unfinished. Militarist nationalism stands in the way. It must become as disreputable as racism.

The right of global mobility cannot be realized overnight; nor will it be realized separate from other aspects of the struggle for peace and justice. But the formulation of a right to global mobility, made very clearly in recent years during work at the U.S.-Mexican border by Maria Jimenez of the American Friends Service Committee, is an essential part of the strug-

---

[92] In theory, societies might opt for autarky, in which case they may also close their borders. That possibility is very remote from reality today for nearly the whole of the world's population. Besides, positing autarky does not relieve us from addressing the question of what happens in case of genocidal human rights abuses in such cases.

[93] Broadly, the people of the Organisation for Economic Cooperation and Development (OECD) countries.

gle against corporate-centered globalization and for a people-centered globalization that we call global democracy. [94]

Richard Falk has articulated the legal aspect of the struggle against global apartheid brilliantly in his book *Predatory Globalization*. The world community, including its governments, regarded South African apartheid as a crime against humanity. There was an international treaty that codified that crime and detailed its particulars. One might then ask, why should global apartheid not be similarly regarded? If assistance to South African apartheid, though legal under South African law, was regarded as a crime under international law, then why should national laws that confine the poor to the global equivalent of apartheid-created "*bantustans*" be regarded any differently? After all, as Falk points out, Article 28 of the Universal Declaration of Human Rights entitles everyone in the world "to a social and international order in which the rights and freedoms set forth in this Declaration can be fully realized."[95] When seen in this way, I believe that the demand for a right of global mobility in a system of global apartheid is a demand to end global segregation – it is essentially the world counterpart of the ending of violently enforced segregation in South Africa and the United States not so long ago.

When one reviews the results of the twentieth century freedom struggles in India, South Africa, and the United States, a crucial problem about the application of Gandhian principles becomes evident. While love is necessary for universal freedom and equality, it is not enough. The most important and enduring piece of evidence is this: The love of mothers has not been enough to prevent men in their collectivity and as individuals from becoming oppressors of women.[96]

Or consider the political sphere. It is manifest, for instance, that the love that Gandhi advocated for and showed to the British was not enough to prevent divide-and-rule politics, much less did it persuade the rulers of Britain to tear down the walls that still keep out from Britain the heirs of the people that British imperialism impoverished. Instead, those walls are higher and more militarized today; they are an expression of global

---

[94] Jimenez, *op. cit.*

[95] Falk 1999, *op. cit.*, pp. 22-23; International Convention on the Suppression and Punishment of the Crime of Apartheid. Entered into force July 18, 1976. Available at http://www.unhchr.ch/html/menu3/b/11.htm.

[96] I owe this insight to Annie Makhijani. In the same conversation quoted at the start of Chapter 13 of the next essay, she told me that understanding the dynamic of this problem – how men, loved by their mothers, become the oppressors of women – is the key to understanding how to create a society in which it would never be a tragedy to be pregnant.

apartheid. This outcome was perhaps foreshadowed by Churchill's 1931 comment on Gandhi, at a time when Gandhi was trying to convince Indians to love the people of the occupying power even while trying to achieve freedom from their imperial institutions:

> It is alarming and nauseating to see Mr Gandhi, a seditious Middle Temple lawyer, now posing as a fakir of a type well known in the east, striding half naked up the steps of the vicere-gal palace, while he is still organising and conducting a cam-paign of civil disobedience, to parlay on equal terms with the representative of the Emperor-King.[97]

How the exercise of a more stubborn, loving, and successful non-violence can create a process by which the powerfully armed will give up their instruments of terror and the exploitative economic system in whose service that official terror is exercised is an unsolved problem in the struggle for global democracy.

The seeds of the solution, are, I believe, to be found in Martin Luther King's hand that was extended to the people of Vietnam and the world in the last year of his life. On April 4, 1967, he joined his historic leadership of the struggle for civil rights in the United States with the struggle against the U.S. war on Vietnam (known as the Vietnam War in the United States and the American War in Vietnam). Further, he said that he "was increasingly compelled to see the war as an enemy of the poor and to attack it as such" because the military machine was a vast drain on resources in essential conflict with human needs at home. And he also declared his solidarity with the people of Vietnam:

> And as I ponder the madness of Vietnam and search within myself for ways to understand and respond to compassion my mind goes constantly to the people of that peninsula....the peo-ple who have been living under the curse of war for almost three continuous decades now. I think of them too because it is clear to me that there will be no meaningful solution there until some attempt is made to know them and hear their broken cries.
>
> They must see Americans as strange liberators. The Vietnamese people proclaimed their own independence in 1945 after a com-bined French and Japanese occupation, and before the Communist revolution in China. They were led by Ho Chi Minh. Even though they quoted the American Declaration of

---

[97] As quoted in "The Churchill You Didn't Know," *Guardian* 2002, *op. cit.*

Independence in their own document of freedom, we refused to recognize them. Instead, we decided to support France in its reconquest of her former colony.

Our government felt then that the Vietnamese people were not "ready" for independence, and we again fell victim to the deadly Western arrogance that has poisoned the international atmosphere for so long....

....

After the French were defeated it looked as if independence and land reform would come again through the Geneva agreements. But instead there came the United States, determined that Ho should not unify the temporarily divided nation, and the peasants watched again as we supported one of the most vicious modern dictators — our chosen man, Premier Diem. The peasants watched and cringed as Diem ruthlessly routed out all opposition, supported their extortionist landlords and refused even to discuss reunification with the north. [98]

A year later, in a piece that was published posthumously, he declared his solidarity with the people of the world and called for a "revolution in American values." In it, he made an indictment of militarism that rings true today of the War on Terror:

It seems glaringly obvious to me that the development of humanitarian means of dealing with some of the social problems of the world – and the correlative revolution in American values that this will entail – is a much better way of protecting ourselves against the threat of violence than the military means we have chosen. [99]

This revolution in values is occurring in corners that have not yet had much amplification from the megaphones of modern media that daily broadcast the threats of war that are loudly made. For instance, Peace Brigades International uses the higher profile of citizens of capitalist countries to protect people in war zones in places like Colombia and Chiapas.[100]

---

[98] Martin Luther King, Jr. "Beyond Vietnam: A Time to Break Silence," speech delivered at the Riverside Church, New York City, April 4, 1967. Available at http://www.hartford-hwp.com/archives/45a/058.html.

[99] Martin Luther King, Jr., "A Testament of Hope," in *A Testament of Hope, The Essential Writings of Martin Luther King, Jr.*, edited by James Melvin Washington (San Francisco: Harper & Row, 1986), p. 323.

[100] See the Peace Brigades International Web site at http://www.peacebrigades.org/.

There are efforts to try to create a standing Peace Force and to oppose the untrammeled militarism of many governments.[101] Traditional non-violence efforts continue in communities and countries around the world. A fine statue of Gandhi in Tavistock Square in London attracts respectful attention still to his life and ideas (as he did in person in his day in that city), as well as flowers, Churchill notwithstanding.

There are millions of families with roots in more than one country and more than one continent. Many of them bridge the divide of the global apartheid, including the greatest physical boundary in that structure, the U.S.-Mexican border.[102] For some, this is a source of fear. For the struggle against global apartheid and for global democracy, it is a source of hope. A global women's movement, a global environmental movement, and a movement against corporate dominated globalization are all reaching across the divide of global apartheid. Workers and family farmers are organizing across borders. Large U.S. labor unions are dropping or have dropped their anti-immigrant positions of not so long ago. Despite the U.S. government's hostility to the Kyoto Protocol to reduce greenhouse gas emissions, the State of California has adopted standards that will lead to curbs on carbon dioxide emissions. In November 2001, the people of San Francisco voted for a ballot measure that authorizes "the city to issue $100 million in revenue bonds for renewable energy systems, including wind and solar power" in a move that is seen not only as protective of the environment, but also as a vote against looming oil wars.[103]

Argentina, Bolivia, Brazil, Chile, Paraguay, and Uruguay have agreed to greatly increase mobility rights for all their citizens, [104] without raising more barriers against mobility of others, in stark contrast to the anti-immigrant walls of global apartheid that have been going up in Europe in the process of its internal integration. Such struggles and activities carry the

---

[101] For information on this "peace army," conceptualized during the 1999 Hague Appeal for Peace Conference, see http://www.nonviolentpeaceforce.org/.

[102] For an account of the repression and violence against people at the border, in the face of a commercial treaty that allows oil and the products of labor to cross freely, see Christine Kovic, et al., *Human Rights Abuses in the El Paso/Ciudad Juárez Border Region: 'Behind Every Abuse is a Community.'* Available at http://www.afsc.org/border/abuseretp.htm. Viewed on November 1, 2002.

[103] Dean E. Murphy, "For Solar Power, Foggy City Maps Its Bright Spots," *New York Times*, November 24, 2002. Information about the solar energy voter initiative is available at http://www.votesolar.org/. For more information on decentralized energy systems, see the Web site of the Institute for Local Self-Reliance, http://www.ilsr.org.

[104] Larry Rohter, "South American Trading Bloc Frees Movement of Its People," *New York Times*, November 24, 2002. p. 4. A two-year residence time is required for legalization of status from temporary to permanent residency. There is not a common citizenship as yet.

seeds of the delegitimization of global apartheid in the same way that hands across borders converted South African apartheid from being viewed by some as a gift of God to an unacceptable social and economic system even by most South African Whites (though by no means all of them).[105] But still, despite these indications of a direction, the practical structure of the struggle to successfully and fundamentally shift the power equation so as to create a path for the elimination of global apartheid still remains to be elucidated.

The International Criminal Court, and the principle of the rule of law based on justice, freedom, and equality, may provide one focus for that struggle. On April 11, 2002, the treaty establishing the International Criminal Court got the minimum number of ratifications to go into effect. While the U.S. government is flouting its own best traditions and undermining the treaty, just the fact of its existence and the reality that it recognizes war crimes against women as crimes against humanity, are immense triumphs for freedom and equality. For the first time, there is an international legal instrument based on the idea that everyone from the poorest peasant woman to the most powerful head of state are equal before the law. Were this court to become truly universal in its jurisdiction, without ifs, ands, or buts, it could be a huge step towards a juridical system that would embody the Jeffersonian idea that there must be "one code of morality for men whether acting singly or collectively."

Finally, the movement against corporate globalization is often criticized by those in power as not having alternatives to the international financial arrangements of the IMF and the World Bank. They have not looked hard enough. They are being thrown up in grassroots struggles around the world, from Argentina and Brazil to India and Bangladesh. They might also want to look at successful local currencies that have been created, for instance by people in Ithaca, New York, and other towns. They might read San Francisco's resolution regarding the water rights of the people of Bolivia. And if they want a practical alternative to the global financial and monetary arrangements of IMF-World Bank system that would allow for freer movement of people, while reducing the incentives to migrate and helping make trade more open and equitable at the same time, they can find it in the next essay.

---

[105] Goodwin and Schiff 1992, *op. cit.* There are still right wing extremists who are unreconciled to the one-person-one-vote electoral democracy of South Africa. Some of them are engaged in terrorist attacks.

FROM GLOBAL CAPITALISM TO ECONOMIC JUSTICE

To my father,

Dr. Bhagwandas G. Makhijani,

whose smile healed his patients

as much as his medicine

FROM GLOBAL CAPITALISM
TO ECONOMIC JUSTICE

An Inquiry into the Elimination
of Systemic Poverty, Violence
and Environmental Destruction
in the World Economy

Arjun Makhijani

The Apex Press

New York and London

1992

Published by The Apex Press, an imprint of the Council on
International and Publc Affairs, 777 United Nations Plaza,
New York, NY 10017, USA (212/972-9877) and 57 Cale-
donian Road, London NI 9BU, UK (01-837-4014)

Library of Congress Cataloging-in-Publication Data

Makhijani, Arjun
    From global capitalism to economic justice : an inquiry
into the elimination of systemic poverty, violence and
environmental destruction in the world economy / Arjun
Makhijani.
        p.   cm.
    Includes bibliographical references.
    ISBN 0-945257-41-4
    1. Capitalism. 2. Imperialism. 3. Distributive justice.
4. Comparative economics. 5. Environmental policy.
6. Economic history—20th century. 7. Democracy.
I.   Title.
HB501.M28   1992
330.9'04—dc20   91-36571
                                                        CIP

British Library Cataloguing-in-Publication Data

A catalogue record for this book is obtainable from the
Library.

Cover design by Janette Aiello
Typeset and printed in the United States of America

TABLE OF CONTENTS

PREFACE

The purposes of this book are:

- to analyze present-day economic systems;

- to present a vision of the economic aspect of a system which would engender justice, peace and environmental harmony;

- to discuss initiatives that people can take individually and collectively to help move us toward that vision.

For the sake of readability and brevity, I have tried to paint an impressionistic picture. This is necessarily a limited and intellectually incomplete exercise which raises as many questions as it answers. It is meant to do that; no effort of this magnitude can hope do more within the constraints of time and resources in which such a project inevitably finds itself.

The main question that has preoccupied me here is the structure of the capitalist economy in its diverse expressions from the local to the global. In our economic world, millions of children die for lack of simple things; in that same world, we have wretched excesses of consumption and waste as well as immense military expenditures. How but by the daily use and threat of force can the rich have stables of cars and jets and villas around the world, not to speak of such absurdities as hanging live lions over a private swimming pool in Bombay for tingling amusement, or serving lion steak at a party in Texas while millions starve?

The rich, who are amused by these modern circuses, and those who desire to join them, need an economic structure of exploitation so that accumulation and expenditures can be unlimited. They also need a military structure extending from the local to the global, since they must, at least subconsciously, be seized with a fear of meeting the same fate at the hands of the poor as Louis XVI and Marie "let-them-eat-cake" Antoinette, or at least of losing the money and property used to satiate themselves as the poor starve. The principal conclusion here is that the the structure of the world economy is in most essential ways like that of apartheid in South Africa—a kind of global apartheid.

I have also focused more on capitalism than on socialism, in part because the latter has practically ceased to exist as an economic system apart, and because of my own limited familiarity with the details of the evolution of centralized socialist economic systems.

Another goal of this effort has been to discuss parts of a program around which people might engage in common struggle to overcome the structures which relentlessly reproduce violence and immense inequalities. Despite differences and important tensions necessarily present due to the immense disparities in the realities of the daily situations in which people find themselves, there is ample room for that common struggle. In the destruction of the global environment and by the continued threat of nuclear annihilation, we are all dispossessed. What is the use of a Mellon or du Pont fortune if there is potential, literally, for the future itself to be annihilated? That itself should provide the impulse to unite those having the comfort of air conditioning with those facing shortages of fuelwood.

In global apartheid, the hungers, the desires, the tears and the joys of those who are dispossessed do not register as parts of the economic system. Indeed, in a real sense, the system does not recognize the humanity of the poor and the marginalized people. The process by which we rid the world of the economic depravity and wretched excess is surely the same one by which we organize to end the suffering of the children who die of want and that of the parents who must bury them. That will be the process by which the "peace" of today—the child of terror when it exists at all—will be replaced by a peace in which neighborliness and friendship can flourish and in which we can overcome the remaining conflicts without resort to force or the threat of force.

A considerable amount of theoretical, historical and mathematical work, scattered over fifteen years, has preceded this effort. Almost all of it is unpublished. Among these efforts: a theoretical and historical critique of Marx's theory of value; an analysis of monetary crises in twentieth century capitalism with emphasis on the collapse of the German monetary system after World War I and the origins of the crisis of the dollar during the 1965-1980 period; an analysis of the debt crisis and its relation to the dollar-dominated world monetary system; a paper on restructuring the international monetary system (with Robert S. Browne, published in *World Policy Journal,* Winter 1985-86) and included as an appendix in this book; and an analysis of Reaganomics and alternatives to it. I would be happy to accommodate the curious with more details about this work.

A word about the my use of terms. I use the term capitalism in its global sense, since it has always been a global system and has evolved as a global system. Thus, the term capitalism here includes both its local and its global aspects. "Capitalist countries" is defined as including those countries which are the members of the Organization for Economic Cooperation and Development, more often loosely referred to as the "West," which play a role on a global scale similar to that of Whites in South Africa. The term "Third World" refers to countries which are within the capitalist system, but which have been the objects of imperialist exploitation in various ways. It derives from an analogy with the "Third Estate" during the French Revolution, consisting of a mixture of classes (capitalists, peasants, workers) who were relatively powerless compared to the feudal and ecclesiastical ruling classes.

This book was essentially finished in mid-1990 and I have made only minor changes and added a couple of sections since that time. Due to the rapidity of events, the collapse of centralized socialist government in the Soviet Union and the many changes in Eastern Europe are not fully reflected here. But the fact that basic changes in the text were unnecessary despite a rapidly changing world has made me more confident that the analysis underlying the visions for a more just world economy is basically a sound one.

Arjun Makhijani
Takoma Park, Maryland
June 1991

ACKNOWLEDGEMENTS

My work on economics was unstintingly and lovingly supported over the many difficult initial years by my wife, Annie; my parents, Gopi and Bhagwandas Makhijani; my sister, Pushpa Mehta, and her husband Sunder; my sister, Sheela Sipahimalani, and her husband Suresh; and by Annie's family, especially her brothers Bernard and Jean-Pierre LePetit and Jean Pierre's wife, Francoise. I also owe a great debt to Kaluram Dhodade and his fellow organizers in Maharashtra, India, who taught me about the exigencies of the life of the rural poor in India and about how difficult, tortuous and long is their struggle to organize for a modicum of economic justice in the face of the threats and actual exercise of violence. My first mentor in economics was the late agricultural economist Raj Krishna, who in the early 1970s spent many patient hours explaining to me many basics about the problems of employment and of agriculture in rural India. I also want to especially thank Eleanor LeCain, Lisa Honig and Victor Honig for supporting my work in its earlier phases.

I would like to thank the Exploratory Project on the Conditions of Peace (EXPRO) which originally sponsored this work. An excerpt is to be published in a forthcoming EXPRO volume. I owe special thanks to EXPRO's founder and mentor, W.H. Ferry, who has been associated with my other enterprises, including a 1986 essay on Reaganomics and alternatives to it. Among other things, I have enjoyed the privilege of a fruitful correspondence with him which helped clarify the direction of this work. He also sent me many materials which were directly useful and which led me to resources which have been indispensable. I recommend his clipping service unreservedly.

Despite the immense claims upon his time and emotional energies made by his war-tax resistance struggles with the U.S. government, Randy Kehler gave a great deal of himself to this work. Indeed, he has helped to shape its direction. The momentum of my own writing, driven by a great many years of work mentioned above, had been to treat this as a comparison between capitalism and socialism. It was Randy's gentle but very firm persistence that convinced me that that question is less relevant than the larger one of how we can create a system in which peace, environmental harmony and economic justice can co-exist. So in a very essential way, this work is a collaboration between the two of us, although I take responsibility for the specifics because I was the one to write them down.

I want to thank Suzanne Aaron, Deanne Butterfield, Sheila Collins, Dietrich Fischer, Bob Irwin, Beth Jacklin, Diana Kohn, Marina Lent, Liane Norman, David Orr, Colleen Roach, Mark Sommer, and Julia Sweig. They helped in various ways, providing comments, editing suggestions and spirited collegial discussion over the course of the project. Amanda Bickel became the spontaneous critic and editor-in-chief of the essay, as I ran into considerable difficulty organizing the material and in deciding what to include and not to include. Special thanks for editing are also due to Michael Shuman. I also want to thank Paul Ekins, Bob Borosage, Grace Boggs, Julie Schor, Jennifer Smith and Robert S. Browne for their reviews and comments, which provided many useful insights. I also want to thank Robert S. Browne and the *World Policy Journal* for permission to reprint the paper, "Restructuring the International Monetary System," in the Appendix. Special thanks are also due to Ward Morehouse and his fellow workers at The Apex Press, where this book received final editing and preparation for publication.

The term "global apartheid" comes from an essay of the same title by Gernot Kohler that Bob Irwin brought to my attention. The terms and the concepts "war system" and "peace system," denoting social, economic, political, cultural and military systems that reproduce the conditions of war and peace respectively, are these developed by EXPRO. Of course, as with all the other aspects of this work, I take responsibility for the contents of this book and the way in which I have developed these and other ideas.

PART I

THE WAR SYSTEM

Doctor I M F
neatly shod, comes early
down dusty village roads
in his white coat.

Quickly he measures and formulates.

"Take this bitter medicine,"
says he, forcing down her a dose of
anti-body marked DEVALUATION.
"It will make me well."

Chapter 1

INVITATION TO HISTORY

Understanding current economic arrangements in the world requires an evaluation of the two predominant economic systems we have experienced in recent times: capitalism and centralized socialism.

In normal times, an effort to evaluate these systems might be an unusual and brash enterprise. One indication that these are not normal times is that so many people are doing it these days. Most are pronouncing capitalism the victor. For instance, Robert Heilbroner recently declared:

> Less than seventy-five years after it officially began, the contest between capitalism and socialism is over: capitalism has won. The Soviet Union, China, and Eastern Europe have given us the clearest possible proof that capitalism organizes the material affairs of humankind more satisfactorily than socialism. . . . The old question "Can capitalism work?," to which endless doubting answers have been given by critics, becomes "Can capitalism work well enough?," which is quite another thing.[1]

So heady is this rush to proclaim victory that a senior officer in the U.S. State Department, Francis Fukuyama, has dusted off his Marx and

---

1 Robert Heilbroner, "The Triumph of Capitalism," *The New Yorker*, January 23, 1989, p. 98.

3

Hegel and given them a capitalist twist which has been much reproduced and rebroadcast:

> ... what we may in fact be witnessing is not just the passing of a particular period of postwar history, but the end point of mankind's ideological evolution and the emergence of Western liberal democracy as the final form of government. Borrowing the vocabulary of Hegel and Marx, it may be the end of history.[2]

Marx foresaw a prolonged struggle before any blissful state would be visited upon humankind. Fukuyama has proclaimed that it is practically here: "The egalitarianism of modern America represents the essential achievement of classless society envisioned by Marx." Any remaining inequalities, even those that have grown, are merely an aberrant "legacy of a preliberal past."[3] In this analysis, not only is capitalism being declared the victor in economic terms, but democracy is seen as being inherently associated with it, so that democracy and capitalism are seen as inextricable elements in an overall victory for humanity.

But what are the criteria by which centralized socialism and capitalism are being evaluated? What, in fact, is the extent of capitalism as an economic system? If it includes the U.S.A. and Japan and Germany and France, does it not also include the places from where these countries draw their resources and their cheap labor, where they have their markets for surpluses and from which they draw huge interest payments—countries like Mexico, Brazil, Indonesia and Zaire? Does it not include those children who toil twelve hours a day for twenty cents an hour and have no toys so that children half-way around the world can have a plethora of them?

Does democracy encompass corporations in which workers have no freedom of speech about the conditions of their lives and work except upon peril of losing their jobs? Does it take into account the helplessness of communities left destitute when plants are shut down and corporations move away, without so much as a by-your-leave? Can the reality of Johannesburg be understood separately from the reality of Soweto?

The reality of capitalism is much broader and more troublesome than its ideologues allow. Its islands of wealth are set in seas of pover-

---

2   Francis Fukuyama, "The End of History? As Our Mad Century Closes, We Find the Universal State," *Washington Post,* July 30, 1989.
3   Fukuyama, *op. cit.,* p. C2.

ty. Given the immense economic misery which exists amidst plenty, the huge military expenditures that governments of the world still feel obliged to make and the terrible environmental destruction, the most important questions are not related to the narrow "contest" between centralized socialist countries and the capitalist countries. Rather, we need to understand both systems as they have operated in human and ecological terms, so that we can learn from their successes and failures.

As a practical matter, I have focused on capitalism because it is by far the dominant economic system today. Indeed, it is practically the only one. Centralized socialism as an economic system apart has practically ceased to exist. In Eastern Europe and the Soviet Union, the corresponding political institutions are also disintegrating or under severe stress. Even in China where the political structures of centralized socialism are still in place, the economic system becomes more and more integrated with capitalism. It is largely to China that corporations shifted the factories for making stuffed toys with cheap labor as wages began to rise in South Korea.

We also need to understand the internal forces which have produced so much violence in centralized socialism, as well as the forces which shaped the economic and military "contest" between capitalism and socialism. That is because a great portion of the economic reality of the world, including immense armaments production and other military expenditures has been directly or indirectly driven by that conflict. I have not addressed these issues thoroughly here, but only to the extent necessary to put the evaluation of capitalism in some perspective and to draw lessons for arriving at the principles on which an economically just system can be based.

Economic Characteristics of a War System

How can we describe the overall structure of an economic system? Only a small and distorted portion of it is expressed in the monetary terms which are the stuff of textbooks and economic statistics. Additional aspects are expressed in terms of the various indicators of quality of life, such as life expectancy or literacy or the availability of medical care. Yet even these do not capture the larger context in which the economic system operates; nor do they address the forces which sustain that context.

The term "war system" describes the principles and the dynamics which have produced war and violence and exploitation so relentlessly in human history, not least in the history of the last couple of centuries during which human destructiveness has been organized and institutionalized to an unparalleled degree. From imperialist conquest to the gas chamber, from concentration camps to nuclear weapons, to the needless economic deaths of 500 million children since the Second World War, which is often described as a period of peace, there is ample evidence that violence in the present-day world is as endemic as it is systemic.

Since violence in its various aspects—economic, military, environmental, political and cultural—has been so prevalent and recurrent, my working hypothesis is that the essence of the present-day global system can be captured in the phrase *"war system."* By war system we mean an interrelated set of mutually reinforcing institutions, policies, practices and values that function as an organic whole for the purpose of domination, exploitation and control.

The war system is a robust one which has defeated strenuous efforts on the part of people to bring about real peace and create a world in which cooperation and justice prevail. Many of its most obvious and horrible aspects are most graphic when countries are actually at war. But the war system is also at work during the periods considered peaceful. The war system goes on whether we characterize the time as "peace" or "war," generating violence and poverty and pollution as its principal products. Whether or not there is actual armed conflict, *the war system relentlessly reproduces the conditions of war.*

The obvious and necessary alternative to such a system is an equally robust and dynamic *peace system* which, despite tensions and conflicts, will produce and maintain the conditions of peace. The principal product of such a system would be the peaceful and just resolution of conflict, the restoration of the natural environment to health and vigorous pursuit of social justice within and among all countries.

The system of nuclear weapons production and testing provides a microcosm of many aspects of the war system. It has been remarkably similar in the U.S. and the Soviet Union and, so far as we can determine, in the other nuclear weapons states as well. It has been conceived and run in secrecy, often in violation of civilian laws. It has polluted a great many areas of the Earth for many generations to come. It has produced disease and death among many who have been exposed to radiation from fall-out. It has usurped financial resources for deadly projects largely at the expense of those who could least afford it. It has created sufficient weapons to destroy the Earth by intent or accident -- all in the name of national security and safety. We live in the midst of violence, thirty minutes from the abyss of utter destruction.

The war system calls this peace. Long ago, a philosopher noted the hypocrisy of the kind of thinking, which goes by the expression "national security" today, when he observed: "When the nations speak of peace, the drums of war are already rolling." In our own time, Winston Churchill was even more blunt. Peace, he noted, is the child of terror.

Peace and war merge into each other in a war system. A war system is one in which violence and the threat of violence are constants of daily life and are part and parcel of political repression and economic exploitation. It is a kind of permanent war among people and between people and the environment.

By that broad definition, the war system is hardly new; indeed, it is as old as civilization. Its core has been an economic system, controlled by rulers of cities, which exploited the majority of people in the city and country, and which cared little for the health of the Earth which sustains us all.

The economic aspect of the war system generates vast inequalities, oppression and exploitation. The property and riches that result are protected from the powerless, the exploited and the poor by violence and ever-present threats of violence. In turn, the control of guns creates new possibilities for oppression and exploitation. Thus, the system feeds on itself, reproducing violence, inequalities and environmental destruction.

Violence also pervades daily life in other ways. Social and economic divisions create many conflicts among the oppressed themselves. Moreover, oppression and exploitation tend to be reproduced at smaller and smaller economic units, right into the heart of the family. As a result, violence and the threat of violence take a great many forms—from threats and violence against women in the home, to guns in the streets, to threats and actual use of weapons of mass destruction. Thus, we are concerned not only about war and peace in the conventional sense, but also with the question of the economic aspects of the war system which reproduces violence and the threat of violence at all levels.

We focus here on capitalism—the economic aspect of the war system—that dominates the world today and which has created immense riches and immense poverty. Socialism, whatever its ambitions and whatever the fears it inspired among capitalists, has never been close to dominating the world as an economic system. Indeed, military pressure and destruction which capitalist countries have brought to bear upon socialist countries have seen to it that even when these countries have been militarily powerful, their economic influence outside their (collective) borders has generally been small, and never decisive.

Here are some of the characteristics and consequences of the capitalist economic system which reflect its war-like, violent nature:

1. Despite the fact that we live in a world which is only a few minutes away from the threat of total destruction by nuclear war, governments still spend a trillion dollars a year on the production, deployment and use of armaments that could trigger a nuclear war.

2. Twelve to fifteen million children die every year of malnutrition and easily preventable diseases, amelioration of which would require resources amounting to no more than those spent on armaments in a week or two. A surfeit of goods and vast wastefulness co-exist with immense deprivation and poverty.

3. We are destroying the Earth and depriving future generations because of the very ways in which the present economic system operates: it puts a higher value upon present consumption and discounts away the value of resources to future generations.

4. Because the economic system values only that which has a monetary price, nurture as well as nature are effectively excluded from the economic calculus. Thus, for example, the unpaid work of women is entirely discounted.

5. For hundreds of millions of young people who are in the monetized work force today, or who are about to enter it, there is little hope of meaningful jobs at decent pay. As a result, violence and conflict are becoming endemic to everyday life in huge parts of the world, including substantial areas in the wealthy capitalist countries.

6. The economic system disconnects the humanity of producers from that of consumers, so that price, value and quality of goods are separated from the conditions under which the producers must labor to produce goods as well as from the environmental consequences of production. This is particularly true of production for export in the Third World.

7. The economic system subordinates product safety and product quality to considerations such as profit.

8. Physical and other barriers to the movement of people have proliferated while resources and capital move ever more freely around the world. In fact, most people, notably those in the Third World, have become less and less mobile in the sense of being able to travel and move as they want, given the system of state control of movement through passports, exit and entry visas, and militarized borders. At the same time, the means of increased mobility, especially through more and more rapid and costly air travel, make it possible for a minority to be more and more mobile. This inequality of mobility is a part of the maintenance of larger economic inequalities.

9. The mobility of capital puts communities at the mercy of large corporations, given their relative share of economic and political power.

Violence underlies each of these characteristics. For instance, the non-monetized labor of women is ignored in the economic calculus because they are economically powerless and subjugated at home. When women themselves are treated as property, then their labor goes simply to the owner and does not accrue to them. Thus, the economic subjugation of women deriving from this situation is bound up with the broader problem of women's oppression, which includes the threat of violence against women. It is readily apparent that to the extent they have been successful in their struggle to overcome their subjugation, their labor too has become a part of the economic calculus.

Similarly, the reckless use of resources evident in the production of shoddy goods and due to planned obsolescence produces great profits. But such a system of production depends on the availability of cheap resources and cheap labor and an essential disregard for future generations. Most of that cheap labor is in the Third World where it is kept in thrall by the daily threat and use of force. These are part and parcel of the vast system of inequalities which is maintained by the use and threat of force today.

While all these related and mutually reinforcing characteristics that make up the war system apply to capitalism, many also apply to centralized socialism. In addition, some problems stem from the conflict between these two systems. For instance, while some of their military

expenditures have been driven by factors and conflicts internal to both
the capitalist and centralized socialist systems, much of it has been
driven by the conflict between them. One of the underlying causes of
that conflict comes from the basic antagonism of the capitalist powers
towards revolutionary governments that came to power with considerable popular support for redistributive justice and for the expul-
sion of the imperialist powers.[4]

In light of these human realities, it is not hard to see that declarations of capitalist victory over socialism, to say nothing about the "end
of history," are premature. In New York City's Harlem, the life expectancy of young African-American men is lower than that of young men
in Bangladesh. And infant mortality in New York City as a whole was
13.3 per 1,000 births, considerably higher than in Shanghai where it
was 10.9 per 1,000 births. Fukuyama's view from Foggy Bottom (where
the State Department offices are located) is fuzzy and does not extend
very far. A short distance from the State Department, children are being
abandoned by mothers stricken by hopelessness, poverty and drugs.
Many of these children are dying for lack of funds for social services
and medical care. Meanwhile, the same distance in another direction, a
military bureaucracy spends more than half a million dollars a minute
preparing for war, polluting the environment, and aggravating ill-health
and other forms of social distress in the United States and around the
world.

---

4   I exclude the former Eastern European governments when using the term
    "revolutionary governments," but include them in the terms "centralized
    socialism" or "bureaucratic socialism" for evident historical reasons. There
    was considerable leftist sentiment in Eastern Europe after the Second
    World War, but the governments installed there were, by the end of the
    1940s, more a product of Soviet occupation than internal political trends.
    This distinguishes them from governments in other socialist countries,
    such as the Soviet Union, China, Cuba or Viet Nam.

Chapter 2

THE COLONIAL DYNAMIC OF CAPITALISM

The successes of capitalism tend to be judged in terms of the conditions within capitalist countries alone. But the reality of the capitalist economy has always been far larger. The tradition of European colonial exploitation began with capitalism and, in diverse ways, continues to this day, with the active participation of elites in the Third World. A violent, turbulent and destructive economic history lies at the root of present-day inequalities and violence.

From the Iberian quest for gold in Africa and the Americas to the vast expansion of lands the Europeans occupied into the present century, the economic "lifeline" of capitalism has run outside the boundaries of Europe. Today, one often hears that it runs through the Persian Gulf. As a grim reminder of the reality of that assertion, the United States government dispatched almost half-a-million troops to "defend" Saudi Arabia, where religious and gender discrimination and other flagrant violations of those human rights claimed as inalienable in the U.S. not only abound but are enshrined in law. The Bush Administration waged a war against Saddam Hussein's regime supposedly to restore the government of Kuwait, which not long ago suppressed its own Parliament and financed a large portion of Saddam Hussein's Iraqi military build-up and manufacture and use of chemical weapons. Then, after the devastation of Iraq, primarily at the hands of U.S. military forces, the U.S. government allowed the same Saddam Hussein, whom it had earlier reviled as a Hitler, to resume control of Iraq with immense amounts of armaments, enabling his government to commit immense atrocities against civilians. The underlying goal is control of vast oil resources of the Persian Gulf region.

Contrary to both capitalist and Marxist theory, capitalism has never had a purely internal dynamic. The marginalization of vast areas and the impoverishment of large numbers of people have been integral to its accumulation of glitter and riches. Exploitation of the many has accompanied the development of "liberal democracy."

Third World Exploitation by Capitalism

A few contemporary examples demonstrate the persistence of Third World exploitation within the global capitalist order.

The Volta Aluminum Company in Ghana

The raw material for aluminum—bauxite—is produced mainly by a few Third World countries (as well as Australia and Canada). It is refined into alumina. The alumina is smelted into aluminum ingots by electrolysis, which is very energy-intensive. One large aluminum ingot production plant, called the Volta Aluminum company (Valco), is owned by two multinational corporations, Kaiser and Reynolds. It is located at Tema in Ghana, near the Akosombo dam.

The Akosombo dam was built with a World Bank loan soon after Ghana's independence in 1961. It was to be an exemplary manifestation of Ghana's modernization and independence. It also happened to be a project of great interest to Kaiser Aluminum and Reynolds. Most of the electricity was to be dedicated to the production of aluminum by Valco.

The dam flooded roughly two million of acres of Ghanaian land, much of it forested, creating Volta Lake. The flooding displaced large numbers of people, many of whom were not properly resettled. The huge lake divided the country North-to-South making transportation difficult and costly. Soon schistosomiasis, a debilitating parasitic disease that had been little in evidence before, and "river blindness" became endemic around Volta Lake.

Valco, in the meantime, received some of the cheapest electricity in the world. The contract was guaranteed and the government could not change the price. (However, in a modern version of noblesse oblige, the company did increase the rate it was paying from a quarter of a cent per kilowatt hour in the 1960s to half a cent in 1982.) The electricity had to be delivered or else there would be stiff financial penalties.

As Ghana's own electricity needs grew, it could not take more electricity from the dam. It had to build far more costly hydroelectric and fossil fuel generating stations. The situation became stark in energy terms in the early 1980s when Ghana was selling a huge amount of electricity on a firm basis to Valco for only $14 million while importing oil equivalent to the same amount of energy for $180 million, although the oil was used mainly for transport and not for electricity generation.[1]

While Valco paid only one-half cent per kilowatt hour for firm power, most other industries and the people of Ghana paid four to sixteen times as much for unreliable and interruptible power. Normally, firm power is much more expensive than interruptible power. In the same period, moreover, Kaiser, Reynolds and other multinational corporations were paying much higher and rising prices for electricity in Europe, Japan and the United States. Table 1 shows comparative electricity tariffs for different categories of consumers in Ghana in 1982.

Table 1
APPROXIMATE ELECTRICITY TARIFFS IN GHANA, 1982

Sector:	Cents per Kilowatt Hour
Valco	0.5
Mining Sector and Textile Mills	0.7
Residential	2.0 to 4.0
Small Light and Power	5.0 to 8.0
Large Light and Power (industrial tariff)	2.5 to 4.0

---

1   We calculate this based on the thermal input it would take to generate the same amount of energy at the rate of 11 million joules per kilowatt hour (electrical). The energy in a barrel of oil costing about $32 per barrel (1982 price) amounts to 5.5 billion joules. Most of Ghana's oil imports are for the transport sector. Some oil is used for electricity generation as well. The current (mid-1991) price of oil is about $20 per barrel.

Valco's profits in Ghana under these favorable operating conditions were immense. Based on 1982 prevailing prices of aluminum, and operation of the plant at 80 percent capacity (four potlines out of five), my estimates of Valco's operations in Ghana for 1982 are shown in Table 2 (each figure is rounded to the nearest US$5 million).

Table 2
AN APPROXIMATE ANALYSIS OF
VALCO OPERATIONS, 1982

	In Million US$
Income:	
Ingot sales @ $1,700 per metric ton	270
Expenses:	
Costs of Alumina	60
Costs of Electricity	15
Interest and Depreciation	15
Wages	10
Shipping	20
Total Expenses	120
Pre-tax Profit	150
Taxes and Payments	25
After-tax Profits	125

Note that this is not the profit actually reported by Valco. The profit reported by Valco is based not on economic considerations, but on the legal stratagem that Valco never owns the alumina, or the aluminum, but is only paid a fee for processing them for its shareholders, Kaiser and Reynolds. This allows for manipulation of revenue and expenses through the technique of transfer pricing of internal transactions between Valco and its corporate owners. Thus, the reporting of profits is correspondingly distorted. In addition, management fees and charges paid to a subsidiary of its principal shareholder, Kaiser Aluminum, are deducted by Valco and are not shown here.[2] (The profits of Kaiser and

2   Fui S. Tsikata, *Essays from the Ghana-Valco Renegotiations,* New York: United Nations Centre on Transnational Corporations, 1986. The post-1982 data on Valco are drawn from this source unless otherwise stated.

Reynolds fluctuated from year to year due to variations in production and aluminum prices.)

While Kaiser and Reynolds have reaped large profits in Ghana, the costs to the Ghana itself have been substantial. Loan repayments on the dam were on the order of $10 million per year. The revenue which Ghana lost due to underpriced electricity, relative to prices in Europe and Japan for aluminum production, was roughly $50 million per year. Additional losses to the economy arose from the necessity of supplying uninterrupted power to Valco, and disrupting domestic production instead. Further, as noted, the costs to Ghanaians for electric power were higher than the cost to Valco.

Along the way, short of foreign exchange, Ghana fell into debt. To fill the exchange gap, cocoa was cultivated on an ever wider scale, taking up large amounts of land. Gold, bauxite and other extractive export-oriented industries were developed or expanded. They consumed more electricity. Thus, oil consumption was increased, as were foreign exchange bills, debts, pollution and greenhouse gas emissions.

If one included all the quantifiable costs, including loss of production, the costs of diseases, underpricing of electricity and the like, the annual losses to Ghana might well amount to several hundred million dollars. These direct costs exclude significant items such as an industrial structure skewed toward exports to pay for foreign exchange losses from additional imports and debt payments.

This situation persisted for about two decades. Since 1985, after three years of hard negotiations, assisted by the U.N. Center on Transnational Corporations, Ghana achieved a considerable improvement in the terms of electricity sales to Valco, with an increase in the power tariff to about two cents a kilowatt hour.

Japanese Timber Imports

The Valco story is not exceptional. Let us consider briefly the Japanese "economic miracle." It is true that hard work and inventiveness have contributed to Japan's economic position in the world today. But there is much more to the tale than can be seen on the screen of a high-definition TV.

Japan has practically no resources. It imports most of its raw materials and much of its food. Moreover, some of the food which is considered "domestically produced"—fish—is the product of a systematic pillage of vast areas of the world's oceans.

Japan also uses up vast areas of land in other countries. Some idea of how much land area Japan uses beyond its borders can be inferred from the statistic that until the early 1970s, lumber was Japan's second largest import after oil. The largest amount of timber came from Southeast Asia. According to Jon Halliday and Gavan McCormack:

> In 1970, 42 million cubic meters of timber were imported . . . an increase of 16 per cent over the previous year's demand. . . . What is particularly important about lumber is the pillaging of South-East Asia's forests has a devastating effect on the lives of millions of poor peasants throughout the area, and utterly negative . . . often irreversible, effects on the whole ecology. One of the biggest uprisings in Taiwan in the early period of Japan's occupation there was triggered off by Mitsui's devastation of huge forest areas on the island.[3]

A decade later, at the end of the 1970s, the situation had not changed. Daniel Nelson noted the following in 1979 in the *Financial Times:*

> In six countries . . . —Afghanistan, Bangladesh, Sabah, Pakistan, Thailand and the Philippines—it appears that the annual increment of commercial species is being overcut.
>
> The fastest rates of growth in production since 1960 have been in Malaysia, particularly Sabah (600 percent), Indonesia, (400 percent) and Philippines (100 percent). This growth is directly related to the rapid development of the Japanese market for imported logs.[4]

Japan continues to be the largest importer of tropical hardwoods in the world. In 1988, it imported seventeen million cubic meters of tropical hardwoods in various forms. About two-thirds of this came from Malaysia, where enormous areas of rainforest have been destroyed.

The amount of forest area destroyed in Southeast Asia over the past few decades has been in the millions of acres. This destruction continues today, as Japanese and other corporations tear down irreplaceable tropical forests to plant quick-growing trees for the production of disposable paper wipes and disposable chopsticks.

The operations of some Japanese corporations range not only into Asia, but into Latin America's Amazon forest. Besides timber opera-

---

3   Jon Halliday and Gavan McCormack, *Japanese Imperialism Today,* Middlesex: Penguin, 1973, pp. 69-70.
4   Daniel Nelson, "Asia Must Plant More Trees," *Financial Times,* April 1979.

tions, Japan has participated in encouraging and aiding Brazil to grow soybeans for export, especially after the U.S. ban on soybean exports during the time of skyrocketing soybean prices in 1973. Brazil is now the world's second largest soybean exporter. This has contributed to pressures on land in Brazil, and hence to the destruction of the Amazon rainforest. Since the late 1970s, about twenty million acres of Amazon rainforest have been burned every year for land clearing for various purposes.

Along with the forest, the tribal peoples who live in the forest are being destroyed. The deprivation of land and forest generally amounts to cultural death and immense economic suffering, increase in diseases, dislocation and often actual obliteration as peoples.

The rape of Asian forests and their peoples as well as much other destruction are integral parts of the Japanese "economic miracle."

The Tea Trade

As another example of the varied marvels of capitalist exploitation, consider a modern version of the maxim of Victorian imperialism "buy cheap and sell dear"—the wonder of the "free market" in tea, the quintessential beverage of British imperialism. It typifies the way many primary products from the Third World are priced in the capitalist system.

The price of fine Darjeeling tea in a retail shop in Bombay in 1980 was $1.25 per pound. The wholesale price in Calcutta was about $1 per pound. Transportation costs from Bombay to Calcutta plus retailing costs and profits were thus on the order of $0.25 per pound. Transport costs to the U.S. for tea are certainly under a dollar a pound. Yet fine Darjeeling tea (such as that marketed under the Twinings label) sold for about $20 per pound. Exorbitant mark-ups on goods from the Third World relative to goods from other OECD countries are quite common. Even poor quality tea put in tea bags, which would retail for about $1 a pound in India, sold in a U.S. supermarket for $5 per pound or more. The situation did not change substantially in the 1980s.

Assuming that this pricing is typical of other capitalist countries as well, a billion pounds of tea exports in 1980 added up to about $1 billion in gross earnings for the Third World where the commodity is produced in its entirety, apart from minor packaging. Some of this was profits at the various levels of transactions that occur in India, and the rest was production costs. The contribution of the tea market to the capitalist countries' economies was, however, probably on the order of

$5 billion to $10 billion. The people who earn wages and profits from
sales of the tea in the capitalist countries could then buy $5 billion to
$10 billion of goods all over the world ("hard currency" purchases), but
the workers who grew and harvested the tea in India and Sri Lanka could
buy less than $1 billion of primarily locally produced goods ("soft cur-
rency" purchases).

The Price of Land in Japan

Consider the price of land in Japan. All the real estate in Tokyo was
worth more in early May 1990 than all the real estate in the United
States. Just the grounds of the imperial palace in Tokyo were priced
higher than the real estate in all of Florida, which is in itself not cheap.
Naturally, in such a situation, even a golf club membership is valuable—
about $1.1 million in an exclusive Tokyo club in early 1990. The way
the present economic and monetary system is structured, a Japanese
businessman by selling a golf club membership could hire and pay
1,000 workers for one year in a typical Third World factory. Bank loans
made on the basis of these fantastic real estate values are one source of
"hard currency" with which Japan buys wood from tropical forests and
other raw and finished goods. It also finances some of the U.S. budget
deficit. So something as intangible as a golf club membership becomes
"hard currency" that can buy 1,000 years of hard labor. In contrast, the
hard labor of the Third World's people can only turn into "soft currency" that cannot even buy Japanese rice or noodles, much less a ticket to
travel to Tokyo for a round of golf—quite an economic miracle.

Imperialism: A Pervasive Pattern

The brief portraits above are only a minute sampling from a long
and ugly history of exploitation which continues to the present day.
There are many others:

- Almost four decades of misery in Guatemala, begun for the sake
  of the United Fruit Company. The U.S. Central Intelligence
  Agency overthrow of the democratically elected regime of
  Jacobo Guzman Arbenz in 1954 is one of the most graphic ex-
  amples of post-World War II imperialism. The Arbenz govern-
  ment had dared to expropriate fallow land belonging to the
  U.S.-based United Fruit Company for redistribution to the poor.
  The company did not consider the compensation offered by the

Guatemalan government, which was based on the company's own evaluation of the land for tax purposes, to be adequate. It turned to the U.S. government for "help," with results which are by now well known.[5] The violent rule by the military and the death sqauds continues into the 1990s. At the same time, scores of huge mulitnational corporations continue to profit from cheap resources and labor.

- U.S. overthrow of the Iranian Government. In 1953, the U.S. government played a central role in ousting the elected government headed by Mossadegh who wanted Iran to control its own oil resources. The U.S. and British governments installed the Shah of Iran as the dictatorial head of Iran's government. He brutally repressed opposition, which became more and more confined to religious institutions. The tragic consequences of that 1953 coup, born of the European need for West Asia's oil, are still not played out.

- Beef production in Central America for export to the U.S. and its terrible consequences for the poor and for the environment. Thousands of acres of central American forest are destroyed every year in large part to create pastureland for export-beef in what has been called the "hamburger connection."[6] This destructive pattern, supported for many years by multinational banks, continues to be a major source of the environmental devastation currently occurring not only in Central America, but in South America as well.

- The destruction of vast areas of land to mining and refining of copper, uranium and other minerals in Africa, destined primarily for export to the capitalist countries.

---

5 See Stephen Schlesinger and Stephen Kinzer, *Bitter Fruit: The Untold Story of the American Coup in Guatemala,* New York: Anchor Press/Doubleday, 1982.
6 James Nations and Paul Komer, "Rainforests and the Hamburger Society," *Environment,* Vol 25, No 3, April 1983.

- The eye injuries suffered by Southeast Asian women for the sake of the electronic chip industry. In Malaysia and other Southeast Asian countries, 80 percent of the young women employed to solder gold wires onto high-tech electronic chips get eye diseases within a few years. They are laid off and disappear from the high-tech production process, and a fresh batch of young women with better than 20/20 vision is brought in. Toward the end of the 1980s, even these production lines were being closed down in Malaysia due to the search for ever-cheaper labor.[7]

A detailed and careful study of any of these subjects would reveal the same pattern of destruction of both human beings and the environment (and in fact many such studies have been done).[8] In this way, the riches that capitalism generates are not just the product of inventiveness and marvelously productive technology; they are also the product of plain, old-fashioned exploitation. From the wood veneer that makes many electronic goods look appealing, to toilet paper, aluminum, chrome, rubber and high-tech electronics, there is a great deal of destruction of nature, people, labor and land that does not show up in the monetary price of the products of the capitalist system at all. It shows up as high infant mortality and poverty and ecological devastation in the Third World. These destructive consequences often persist long after the product is in the garbage dump.

---

7   Lourdis Beneria, "Gender and the Global Economy," in Arthur McEwan and William Tabb, eds., *Instability and Change in the World Economy*, New York: Monthly Review Press, 1989, p. 254.

8   There are many studies which bring out clearly the connections between imperialism and capitalism. I mention two: Eduardo Galeano's *Open Veins of Latin America*, New York: Monthly Review Press, 1973; and Walter Rodney's *How Europe Underdeveloped Africa*, Washington, DC: Howard University Press, 1982. Ram Manhor Lohia's essay, "Economics After Marx" (in Lohia, *Marx, Gandhi and Socialism*, Hyderabad: Nava Hind Press, 1963) attempted to create a theoretical structure for this reality. Rosa Luxemburg in her essay, *Accumulation of Capital*, New York: Monthly Review Press, 1968, also discussed some of the connections and tried to organize them into a theory of the capitalist economy.

Capitalist Governments, Corporations, Third World Elites and Military Power

The preceding examples of oppression are rooted in the close relationships that exist between capitalist governments, corporations and multinational banks, and Third World elites. Exploitation would not be possible in its current form were it not for the way these groups and institutions interact and the immense financial and military power which they are able to exert. That power is an inherent part of the daily violence and threat of violence which is inherent in the capitalist economic system. Below we consider some key aspects of the ways in which these institutions maintain their positions in the world and the web of ideological justifications they use to justify the status quo.

Corporations and Capitalist Theory

Many contemporary journals and magazines as well as historical works have explored the intimate connection between capitalist governments and corporations.[9] Corporations, directly or indirectly, played a central role in every one of the examples we have discussed above. They are the principal economic vehicles which dominate the structure of production and distribution today. As such, they are, together with multinational banks, the main vehicles moving capital around the world, connecting the relative prosperity in the capitalist countries to the cheap labor and resource devastation that is going on in the Third World. There clearly are other important actors, as is discussed below, but the interlocking network of multinational corporations and the banks which finance many of their operations is the central economic one.

Multinational corporations (including multinational banks) collectively represent the most powerful economic forces in the world today.

---

9   For example, an account of U.S. corporations and military and political policy can be found in a collection of essays, edited by William Appleman Williams, *Corporations and the Cold War*, New York: Monthly Review Press, 1969. For a look at corporations in current events, one could scan the pages of the magazine *Multinational Monitor* (published in Washington, D.C.). For Japanese corporations, see *AMPO* (published in Tokyo). For the role of corporations in ozone depletion and the greenhouse effect, see Arjun Makhijani, et al., *Energy Sector Transnational Corporations and the Global Environment*, Takoma Park, MD: Institute for Energy and Environmental Research, 1990.

As Table 3 shows, annual sales of the largest corporations are greater than $100 billion, a sum which exceeds the gross domestic product of over 120 countries, including all but three of the largest Third World countries (India, Brazil and Mexico), and a number of relatively wealthy capitalist nations as well. Multinational banks control assests of hundreds of billions of dollars. Moreover, they have much more concentrated control of vast sums of "hard currency," which is generally in short supply in Third World countries. Large portions of their holdings are liquid assets or convertible to liquid assets. They can move capital around the world with the speed of computers; they can rapidly invest in or divest from communities and countries. They are responsible for the extraction of vast quantities of Earth's natural resources. They chart the course of much of the world's technological development, and they determine, to a considerable degree, the prices of large numbers of products around the world.

Table 3
CORPORATE FINANCIAL POWER: SALES VS. GNP

Corporation/ Country	Sales of MNC/GNP of Country (in billions of US$)	Corporation/ Country	Sales of MNC/GNP of Country (in billions of US$)
Brazil	$ 285.9	*Exxon*	$ 87.3
India	248.1	*Royal Dutch Shell*	78.4
Mexico	149.4	*Nissho Iwai*	72.9
Mitsui & Co.	117.0	Algeria	60.7
Korea (South)	113.1	*IBM*	59.7
General Motors	110.0	*Mobil*	54.4
C. Itoh	108.5	*Toyota Motor*	50.4
Sumitomo	103.6	*Sears, Roebuck*	50.3
Marubeni	96.1	*Hitachi*	44.7
Mitsubishi	93.3	Malaysia	30.1
Ford Motor	92.5	Ghana	5.3

Sources: Corporate figures from "The Global 1000, " *Business Week*, July 17, 1989; country figures from *World Resources 1990-1991*, New York: Oxford University Press, 1990.

Their policies are not internally restrained or guided by any logic of the well-being of the community or of the environment. They are institutions avowedly and unabashedly devoted to the pursuit of profit.

Yet capitalist theory maintains that there is no need to impose social constraints on corporations. The ideological justification is Adam Smith's hypothesis that an "invisible hand" operates in the marketplace: if individuals work to maximize their own benefit, defined as profit, communal well-being will be the inevitable outcome. This remains a powerful vein in capitalist theory, which is often used to justify decisions of governments not to intervene in corporate activities, despite the fact that the practical failure of unfettered commerce to deliver widespread well-being is obvious as soon as we look at the system in its global reality.

The operation of large industrial enterprises has resulted in the environmental devastation of vast areas and physical injury to large numbers of people. And this is quite apart from the economic oppression of vast numbers of people in the Third World as well as capitalist countries that has often accompanied uncontrolled corporate activity. Despite the fact that many corporations themselves now often admit that they cannot make improvements in the safety and environmental soundness of their operations and products unless government provides them with a "level playing field" through regulation, there is still a strong tendency to give corporations a free hand.

Throughout the world, technological decisions of immense economic and environmental import are left to the corporations to decide. Even when they are not the technical innovators, their control of capital and markets is usually decisive in what innovations actually reach the consumer. When there are environmental, health or safety problems associated with industrial production, whether they be toxic dumps or ozone depletion, those corporations that have profited from the production processes which caused them practically never pay the full costs of clean-up, if indeed they pay anything at all. For instance, a private plutonium production plant, supposedly a commercial one, built by Getty Oil near Buffalo, New York, for $26 million operated for only six years but left behind a radioactive mess that will cost taxpayers billions of dollars to clean up.

Government failures to regulate corporations adequately or hold them accountable are manifestations of the close ties between capitalist governments and the corporate world. The nexus between capitalist-country governments and large corporations (including banks) is perhaps the single most important structural element of the war system because the military, political and financial power of governments is used to protect the property and prerogatives of large corporations.

Promoting the Corporations Abroad: Capitalist Governments Intervene

Rather than leaving everything up to the "invisible hand," capitalist governments have more often been involved in actively supporting corporate activities abroad, sometimes with military force. Government interest in corporate activities expresses itself in innumerable ways from pressure to maintain high military production to an unconscionable trade in armaments, an economic reason-for-being of the Cold War.

In the last 200 years, the wars of colonial conquest in Asia and Africa, the genocide of tribal peoples in North America and Australia, and the many interventions to re-subjugate the people of Latin America have all relied on military force. A principal goal of these actions by capitalist governments has been to enable the pursuit of profit by privately owned corporations.

The exploitation of resources, environmental destruction and impoverishment in the Third World would not be possible without violence and the threat of violence. For instance, Japan's rise as a capitalist power, like that of the Europeans, was based upon imperialist expansion and cheap foreign resources. The Japanese invasion of China beginning in 1931 (which marked the onset of the Second World War as much as later European events) was economic in origin. The conflict between Japan and the U.S. that led up to the Japanese attack on Pearl Harbor also involved colonial resources, such as Indonesian oil. Japan, like the European powers and the U.S., went to war over controlling resources, labor and markets outside of its borders. Similarly, German aggression in Eastern Europe and the Soviet Union was over control of resources and cheap labor without which it could not establish itself securely as an economic and military power in Europe.[10]

The mythology of capitalism is that of the "free market" in which the "government intervention" is regarded as undesirable. In reality, governments of capitalist countries have had a central role in providing the military force which has enabled capitalism to exist at all. More than any "invisible hand" guiding the functioning of the market place where goods are bought and sold, the military hand of the capitalist state has

---

10 Arjun Makhijani, "Monetary Crises in Twentieth Century Capitalism." Unpublished paper, 1981.

been central to the economic development of capitalism.

The ties between corporate economic interests and governmental military structures have also been clear in the years succeeding World War II. As the Second World War came to a close, the chairman of General Electric suggested the creation of a "permanent war economy" to maintain purchasing power (no hesitation at government role in the market there). Those who hoped for a "permanent war economy" after World War II were looking for more than the maintenance of internal domestic purchasing power. American plans for its economic future were based on capturing the markets of Europe and former European markets in the Third World. This in turn necessitated two things. First, the Soviets with their supposed and actual antagonism to multinational corporations had to be kept out of Europe as much as possible after World War II. Second, in a Europe bereft of resources and devastated by war, the U.S. had to take over Europe's imperialist role, keeping the Third World in the capitalist orbit through economic and military influence.

In explaining post-war policy in testimony to Congress in 1944, Dean Acheson firmly linked jobs and even the rule of the Constitution in the U.S. to foreign markets:

> When we look at the problem of [of full employment] we may say that it is a problem of foreign markets. . . . [Y]ou could fix it so that everything produced here would be consumed here. That would completely change our Constitution, our relations to property, human liberty, our very conceptions of law . . . and nobody contemplates that. Therefore you must look to other markets and those markets are abroad.[11]

These considerations were at the heart of the U.S. strategy of containment, spelled out in National Security memorandum NSC-68, which has guided post-war policy to a successful conclusion for capitalism. This policy had two prongs. One concerned maintaining an international system conducive to the pursuit of American economic political and ideological goals. The other was aimed specifically at the Soviet Union and its assumed determination to achieve global domination. To quote the NSC memorandum directly:

---

11 Dean Acheson, congressional testimony in 1944, quoted by William Appleman Williams in "Large Corporations and American Foreign Policy," in Williams, ed., *Corporations and the Cold War*, New York: Monthly Review Press, 1969, pp. 95-96.

Fostering a world environment in which the American system can flourish . . . embraces two subsidiary policies. One is a policy which we would probably pursue even if there were no Soviet threat. It is a policy of attempting to create a healthy international community. The other is a policy of "containing" the Soviet system. These two policies are closely interrelated and interact on one another.[12]

The way in which United States military power and corporate economic interests were to be maintained was by violence and the threat of violence. Deterrence did not mean merely preventing an equally armed Soviet Union from attacking the U.S. It meant the superior assertion of U.S. power to keep the Soviet Union out of areas in which the U.S. or other capitalist powers exercised dominance. The theory behind NSC-68 provided for violence directly against the Soviet Union and in the Third World.

In the context of arguing for broader military capabilities than those for all-out nuclear war, NSC-68 revealed the U.S. definition of deterrence in the immediate post-World War II period (until about the mid-1960s): "The only deterrent we can present to the Kremlin is the evidence we give that we may make any of the critical points [in the world] which we cannot hold the occasion for a global war of annihilation."[13]

There we have the essence of a war system: the readiness to annihilate everything if one cannot win on one's own terms.[14]

An ideology in which U.S. power, based on nuclear weapons and the economic power that it supported, was a great "good" for both the U.S. and theoretically the rest of the world, which was heavily influenced by U.S. intellectual and cultural as well as economic and politi-

---

12 National Security Council Memorandum 68, as cited in Thomas Etzold and John L. Gaddis, *Containment: Documents on American Foreign Policy and Strategy 1945-50*, New York: Columbia University Press, 1979, p. 401.

13 *Ibid.*

14 There exists voluminous literature on the shaping of U.S., nuclear policy and its relation to foreign policy and corporations. Some examples are: Konrad Ege and Arjun Makhijani, "Nuclear War Is Not Unthinkable: For the Pentagon It's an Option," *CounterSpy*, July/August 1982; Arjun Makhijani and John Kelly, "Target Japan: The Decision to Bomb Hiroshima and Nagasaki" (unpublished in English; published in Japanese by Kyoikusha under the title *Why Japan?*); and Gar Alperowitz, *Atomic Diplomacy: Hiroshima and Potsdam*, New York: Penguin Books, 1985. See also Williams, ed., *Corporations and the Cold War, op. cit.*

cal institutions after World War II. The persuasive power of the media and Hollywood also played a role in this global domination as well as the direct economic influence of the military-industrial complex.

Consider the University of California at Berkeley, a leading center of science teaching and research. It gave the respectability of academia to the making of the atom bomb during the Second World War so that scientists would have a comfortable ambience and not have to salute the head of the project, General Groves. After that war, it has continued to run the laboratories where later generations of nuclear weapons have been designed, receiving vast funds from the government for that purpose.

The text of an April 1960 editorial from its magazine for engineering alumni illustrates how deeply the war system can insinuate itself into society, particularly those corners where direct economic interests prevail. It is a remarkable document of the war system. We quote it in full:

> The ultimate aim of the Soviet Union and China is the Communization of the entire world, by force of arms if necessary. Our defense, and thus the defense of the free world, is based on atomic and hydrogen weapons. Nowhere on the defense perimeter around the Soviet Union and China are there sufficient conventional forces to even slow down a Communist conventional aggression. Thus, any agreement on our part to refrain from using nuclear weapons would amount to unilateral disarmament. Not only would we lose our ability to retaliate against a Soviet nuclear attack on the United States, but more important, our ability to fight "brush fire wars" would be seriously weakened; and the "brush fire war" is considered a more likely means of Communist aggression than an all-out attack.

> The Korean conflict demonstrated two things that are pertinent here: our inability to make any headway against a vastly more numerous, though poorly equipped army, which is no less numerous today and better equipped; and the ability of both sides in the conflict to observe limitations on their strategy. We refrained from bombing their bases in Manchuria, they refrained from bombing our bases in Japan, Okinawa, and the Philippines. Therefore, there is no reason not to expect both sides in a future "brush fire" war to keep the nuclear weapons used within tactical limits.

> The increase in radiation one receives from fallout is about equal to the increase one receives from cosmic rays when moving from sea level to the top of a hill several hundred feet high. This nevertheless

increases genetic and pathological damage, though to a degree not
great enough to be measured statistically. It means, though, your
babies' chances of having a major birth defect are increased by one
part in 5,000 approximately. Percentagewise, this is insignificant.
When applied to the population of the world, it means that nuclear
testing so far has produced about an additional 6,000 babies born with
major birth defects.

Whether you choose to look at "one part in 5,000" or "6,000 babies,"
you must weigh this acknowledged risk with the demonstrated need
of the United States for a nuclear arsenal.[15]

This extraordinary editorial from a university alumni magazine
shows an equal readiness to sacrifice children in the United States as
well as those around the world, all in the service of the wielding of the
greatest weapons of terror yet invented. The ability of "both sides to observe limitations" and not destroy each other with nuclear weapons is
used as a reason to use weapons of terror on weaker countries.

As partial explanation for these horrifying views, it is interesting to
note that the economic interest of the laboratories run by the University
of California was and is most closely tied up with the design of nuclear
weapons and therefore in the testing that is associated with the proving
of those designs. Hugh Gusterson, a Stanford University Anthro-
pologist, studied the nuclear-bomb designers of Lawrence Livermore
Laboratory in California and found that their rituals around nuclear
bomb design and testing strongly resemble tribal rituals and are used to
create the bonds of community among the scientists.[16] The essential
difference, of course, is that the rituals of tribal people revolve around
the sustenance of life and the regeneration of nature which makes it possible; the rituals of the bomb designers and testers revolve around the
celebration of instruments of mass destruction and death, the ultimate
symbols and reality of the war system.

The ties between economic and military interests in the capitalist
countries are many and complex, and they have been justified in many
ways. The military and economic subjugation of the vast majority of
people in Third World countries by capitalist country governments and

---

15 An April 1960 editorial in the *California Engineer*, reprinted in *California
Engineer*, Vol. 68, No. 3, March 1990, p. 23.
16 Hugh Gusterson, "Rituals of Renewal Among Nuclear Weapons
Scientists," Center for International Studies, Massachusetts Institute of
Technology, Cambridge, February 16, 1991.

corporations remains one of the most brutal aspects of the war system.

Subjugation at Home: Military Power
Within Capitalist Countries

The close relationship between corporations and governments in capitalism, which has, in various ways, persisted and dominated the world economy from the East India Company to Krupp, General Motors and Mitsubishi, has had one continuing feature: capitalist country governments have been the prime protectors and guarantors of the property and prerogatives of corporations which are organized for profit. The military power of the state is not only important for the interests of capitalist powers abroad. It is also important domestically.

The inequalities and impoverishment occasioned by the pursuit of profit in the capitalist system are so immense that the threat of armed force and its use have been needed to create and maintain that system. Moreover, the control that most people, including relatively well-paid workers in the capitalist countries, have over their economic existence is so small relative to the decision-making and financial power of corporations, that forceful, armed protection of the property and prerogatives of corporations has generally been necessary, both within capitalist countries and internationally. The State may use military force to break a strike and enforce the prerogatives of the property owner. It does not usually come to the aid of the worker who has unjustly lost his job with the same force or alacrity. However, in the capitalist countries, the direct use of force has slowly (although erratically) declined over the past century and a half, due to the local gains made by workers' struggles. There have been periods of severe regression in some capitalist countries, notably following loss of imperialist profits and colonies, as with Germany between the two world wars.

An essential purpose of armed forces (including police forces) has been to protect the power and property of the rich and the corporations against the poor. The poorer the majority of the population and the greater the internal class differences, the more militarized and violent this protection tends to become.

Subjugation Abroad: Military Response to Revolt
and Revolution in the Third World

Military subjugation within Third World countries has changed in form since the end of direct colonial rule. Revolts and revolutions in capitalism have been centered in precisely these areas that were the most relentlessly and violently impoverished by capitalist practice. Not that these always took the same form or that they were always successful. But from peasant revolts to nationalist movements, they have been a constant feature of capitalist history over the past century and a half. Key actors in these struggles have been the people rendered utterly propertyless by capitalism, the truly impoverished "with nothing to lose," the landless rural workers, poor peasants (whose property is often at the mercy of moneylenders), unorganized workers in small industry and the unemployed in the Third World.

The first phase of these struggles (and the imperialist reaction to them) resulted in three broadly different outcomes:

1. Socialist revolutions in which nationalist, Marxist and Leninist ideas were joined in uneasy theories, ideologies and practice. These generally occurred when resistance movements were confronted with wars, or violent internal repression, as well as the impoverishment produced by imperialism.
2. Nationalist movements of varying intensity in which local ruling classes (capitalists, bureaucrats, landowners) secured political independence from imperialist rule, but where economic connections to imperialism remained strong, as, for example, in India, Ghana and Algeria.
3. More or less pliant regimes or puppet governments put in place by imperialist rulers to avoid more nationalist or leftist governments. Such pliant governments were imposed at the point of the U.S. gun in many of the countries in Latin America which achieved independence from Spain and Portugal in the nineteenth century.

Although struggles for independence from colonial rule stemmed from a desire to reduce oppression, that has not been the general result for the majority of people in the Third World, who continue to be both poor and oppressed. Violent repression of the people in Third World countries remains very strong. It works to maintain the prerogatives of local elites and, in many cases, also of multinational corporations and banks operating in the Third World. Immense and growing class divisions have allowed a common purpose to emerge between the military structures of repression in the Third World and the protection of local and foreign corporate property. These phenomena occur to a large extent irrespective of whether Third World countries are ruled by elected or non-elected governments. Today, not only are the armed forces of the capitalist countries engaged in the service of capitalism; they have, in effect, been joined by most of the armed forces of the Third World.

Nationalism and Racism

The military subjugation of the economically deprived by the privileged, both between countries and within them, is an essential expression of the capitalist war system. The naked use of force to maintain inequalities and exploitation is not how capitalism is "marketed," however, either nationally or internationally.

For many years capitalism was sold domestically as anti-Communism, clothed in God and Country. Such propaganda was made easier by the violent reality of the repression under Stalin, but it was only the newest form of old rationalizations. Before there were any socialist countries, similar policies of economic exploitation were clothed in arguments of extending the benefits of European civilization to the "backward" peoples of the Third World. Exploitation was sold as the "White Man's burden." Domestically, the use of force by some groups to oppress others has been touted as the maintenance of law and order, as the romantic image of the conquest of the West, as scientific progress and as racial superiority.

Here we consider two ideologies commonly used to justify oppression: racism and nationalism. In most capitalist countries, nationalism is overall a "respectable" ideology. Racism is not. Yet the ways the two are used to justify oppression are very similar.

The global reality of capitalism, as opposed to its mythology, is that, as an economic system, it is similar to South Africa in its dynamic and divisions and in its violence and inequalities.[17]

The essential facts of apartheid and the global economy are similar. There are even similarities in the history of the political-economic alignments between capitalist countries in their relations with the Third World on the one hand, and racial alignments in South Africa on the other. In South Africa, the two main groups of Whites—the English and the Boers—fought a very bitter and violent war (the "Boer War"). But

---

17 The earliest publication that I have come across, which explores the parallel between capitalism and South Africa, is an essay by Gernot Kohler, *Global Apartheid* (Working Paper No. 7), New York: World Order Models Project, 1978.

right after it, they compromised to establish common dominance over the non-white people of South Africa. There was an analogous result in global capitlism after two world wars. In exchange for markets, an open door for U.S. capital and bases for Cold War military strategy, the U.S. became the military guarantor of a continued flow of cheap resources and labor to Germany and Japan (as well as other capitalist countries), providing precisely what the Nazis and Japanese militarists had sought to obtain through war. Thus, despite tensions resulting from trade, employment and other issues, capitalist countries as a group have tended to act in a similar manner in their economic policies and behavior toward the Third World.

The South African system of pass laws is reproduced on a international scale by the system of passports and visas by which mobility is easy for a minority and difficult for a majority. This reality is graphically illustrated by the difference between the heavily policed U.S.-Mexican border and the quite open, non-militarized U.S.-Canadian border. Similarly, the elimination of borders in capitalist Europe proposed for 1992 goes along with a hardening of the European border to people from the Third World. As one official of the European Economic Community recently said: "The principle of free movement within the [EEC] region is built around having solid external borders, so the internal frontiers cannot come down until measures are taken to secure the external borders."[18]

The European governments are trying to prevent people from the Third World from settling on their continent. The cheap labor, markets, land and resources of the Third World are welcome, and extracted by force if necessary. Trade is imposed by international rules of "free trade" and free capital movement and International Monetary Fund "conditionalities." But the people are not free to move.

South Africa like the capitalist countries can also be said to have a "liberal democracy"—but only for a small portion of its population. Similarly, with the global capitalist system, liberal democracy prevails mainly in the capitalist countries, excluding the vast majority of the people in the system who live in the Third World. Even the statistics match—the same divisions of White and non-White; similar differences of income; similar differences in infant mortality; similar expropriation of land and resources; similar rules giving mobility to minority and robbing it from the majority; and the similar immense and forcible mar-

---

18 EEC official quoted by Alan Riding, "Rifts Imperil Europe's No-Border Plan," *New York Times*, April 16, 1990, p. 19.

ginalization of a vast number of people not involved in any essential way in the monetized economy, but who are ruled and daily oppressed by it. And within each community, many kinds of divisions exist, including those of class and gender.

Table 4 shows how remarkably similar some of these social indications are in capitalist countries and the Third World on the one hand and in the White and non-White South African.

Table 4

**COMPARISON OF THE CAPITALIST ECONOMY
WITH SOUTH AFRICA, 1975 – 80**

	Capitalist			South Africa		
	OECD*	Third World	Total	White	Non-white	Total
Life Expectancy (in years)	75	55	60	70	55	60
Infant Mortality per 1,000 births	15	110	85	20	120	100
Maternal Mortality per 100,000 Live Births	10	600	450	N/A	N/A	N/A
Daily Supply of Food Calories per Person	3,100	2,100	2,400	N/A	N/A	2,600

*   OECD countries include western, northern and Southern Europe (except Yugoslavia, Albania and Turkey), Japan, and Australia and New Zealand. These countries are often designed as "the West" despite the obvious geographical absurdities.

All figures are approximate and rounded. N/A = not available.

Sources: World Resources 1988-89, Basic Books, 1988; South Africa statistics estimated from this and other sources.

The similarities between apartheid and Third World oppression do not stop with their social impact. The *ideologies* which support the two systems are also roughly parallel. In order to rationalize exploitation, characteristics of inferiority are ascribed to the dominated peoples, which sets up the dynamic of racism. Both racism and nationalism as an oppressive force have arisen as ideologies out of the economic demands of the capitalist system. The nationalist ideologies used to justify capitalist imperialism, the ideologies of "oppressor nationalism," are as much as excuses for exploitation as the racism that is used to justify oppression in South Africa.

Both race and nationality strongly manifest themselves in the social interaction of the dominating and the dominated; they are not phenomena internal to a particular group. "White" is defined by "Black" much as "Black" is defined by "White," for as soon as "Whites" are out of the context of that social setting, then they themselves take on diverse characteristics. A peasant in Brittany is Breton when confronted with a Parisian, French when confronted with a German and European when confronted with a Russian, but White in the face of a Moroccan or Algerian or Senegalese. The one principal difference is that oppressed races and nationalities tend to internalize the attitudes of their oppressors, while the reverse is not true of the oppressor races and nationalities.

The strength and passions associated with these identities are volatile and dependent, in part, on a person's assessment about economic prospects of his or her particular group relative to the others. In the case of racism and oppressor nationalism, the ideologies generally come to be shared by the working people of the dominant nationality to a great extent, despite the evident larger interest in solidarity that they might have with workers of other races. It is a social and economic reality that the poor and oppressed standing at the door of relative privilege can be quite prejudiced and ready to do violence to protect it. For example, overt racial prejudices are often strongly held by White European and U.S. blue collar workers.

In this analysis, there is little social difference between the operation of racism and nationalism as an oppressive force. The difference is rather one of political-military descriptions. Oppressor nationalism involves political-military boundaries (which define countries) over which a nationalist group claims exclusive privileges, while racism does not explicitly involve political-military boundaries. Since racial dynamics can give rise to desires to establish separate countries, there is often a fluid relationship between nationalism and racism.

Of course, despite the critical similarities between oppressor nationalism and apartheid, there are also many differences. Some stem from the reality that South Africa is set within the overall context of global capitalism and some from the fact that in South Africa the Whites and non-Whites live within the boundaries of the same country. Thus, while the overall analogy is useful, important aspects of both oppressive systems need to be addressed separately. But it is plain that violence is inherent both in global capitalism and in South African apartheid, and that a principal motive for both is economic exploitation.

Chapter 3

MONETARY IMPERIALISM

A principal aspect of the economic subjugation of Third World, as it has evolved in the twentieth century, centers on the functioning of the international monetary system. Since the end of formal colonial rule, one of the harshest realities which Third World countries have had to deal with is the international monetary system dominated by the U.S. dollar. This has meant that economic problems internal to the U.S. can be exported, at least temporarily, to other areas of the world. For example, for many years the U.S. government inflated the world economy to cope with economic problems at home. The printing of money by the U.S. and other capitalist powers creates world inflation because these are "hard" currencies which can be exchanged for goods all over the world. In contrast, when a typical Third World country prints money, it only creates local inflation because its currency is not easily convertible.

The U.S. began its strategy of global inflation in 1965 to wage both the war on Viet Nam and the "War on Poverty" in the U.S. The U.S. expanded its inflationary policies in response to the increase in oil prices of the 1970s by simply printing more of its "hard currency" to pay for oil. To varying degrees, other capitalist powers followed the U.S. lead in expanding money supply. As a result, world prices of goods and services of the capitalist countries increased rapidly. By this process, capitalist countries were able to transfer the burden of increased oil prices back to the Third World, including both oil-importing and oil-exporting countries. Although the cumulative oil import bill of the OECD countries increased by $1.5 trillion between 1973 and 1982, they had, as a group, balance of payments surpluses over the period, and not deficits.[1] Many Third World countries, both oil importers and oil exporters, became seriously indebted during this period. In many cases, this was also due to the corrupt transfer of capital out of their countries by Third World elites.

By 1973, inflationary policies had caused the end of the gold-based dollar system through which dollars could be exchanged for gold at a fixed rate. By the end of the 1970s, unabated inflationary policies almost caused the collapse of the international monetary system based on the dollar.

It was at this point, in October 1979, that President Carter called in a conservative banker, Paul Volcker, to raise interest rates, squeeze workers at home and abroad, reduce inflation and, most importantly, increase the value of the dollar. High simultaneous real interest rates and a high dollar increased the real value of Third World debt suddenly and enormously. The people of the Third World were being asked to pay far more than they had ever contemplated so that the dollar-dominated international monetary system could be saved and domestic growth in the U.S. could resume with low inflation. This was to be based in part on cheap foreign manufacturing labor and ever-cheaper resources.

By 1984, increasing imports resulted in a high U.S. trade deficit. The debt crisis appeared to be threatening the monetary system anew. Many in Congress became concerned. The Reagan administration sent in Beryl Sprinkel—then Undersecretary of the Treasury in 1984 (he went on to become the Chairman of Reagan's Council of Economic Advisors)—to explain the situation to members of Congress and to calm their fears. He did so in these words: "The debt crisis is, to a large extent, an indirect result of our success in curing inflation and revitalizing the American economy."[2]

In the face of this reality, why do not the governments of the indebted countries form a cartel, threaten to renounce the debt and col-

---

1 Arjun Makhijani, "Oil Prices and the Crises of Debt and Unemployment." Unpublished draft report prepared for the International Labour Office, Geneva, 1983.
2 Beryl Sprinkel, congressional testimony of March 29, 1984, as reported in the *Washington Post,* March 30, 1984.

lapse the banks in an attempt to get a better deal, as has often been suggested?

One reason is that control by the capitalist countries of the trading and financial system can be translated into effective threats. For example, R.T. MacNamar, also a Deputy Secretary in the Reagan administration's Department of the Treasury, put it in this delicate way:

> A repudiation takes place when a borrower unilaterally renounces responsibility for some or all of his debt obligations. Under such circumstances, the foreign assets of a country that repudiated its debt would be attached by creditors throughout the world; its exports seized by creditors at each dock where they landed; its national airlines unable to operate; and its sources of desperately needed capital goods virtually eliminated. In many countries, even food imports would be curtailed. Hardly a pleasant scenario.[3]

On another occasion, MacNamar was even more blunt: "Have you ever contemplated what would happen to the president of a country if the government couldn't get insulin for its diabetics."[4]

But there is also another reason, and it is probably more powerful. The rich in the capitalist countries and the rich in the Third World have, over the last several decades, developed mutual interests that can be and often are far stronger than the interests the rich in the Third World may have in common with their own poor. As Susan George has described in some detail, a good bit of Third World debt was due to the flight of capital from Third World to banks in the U.S., Switzerland and similar havens.[5]

Even after the onset of the crisis and the immense suffering that "IMF medicine" has brought to vulnerable segments of the populations of the indebted countries, the outflow of capital, and the corruption that it represents, have continued. When a journalist asked a Mexican policy-maker why they did not form such a cartel and threaten the stability of the banks to make the U.S. pay attention, he asked rhetorically: "Where do you think I have my money?" The intensely corrupt relationship between the government in Zaire and the French and U.S. governments is another well known example.[6]

---

3   R.T. MacNamar, quoted by Susan George, *A Fate Worse than Debt: The World Financial Crisis and the Poor*, New York: Grove Press, 1988, p. 67.
4   R.T. MacNamar, quoted by George, *op. cit.*, p. 68.
5   George, *op. cit.*
6   See, for example, George, *op. cit.*, Chapter 7.

The traditional bond between the rich across boundaries of countries, expressed in the old days by the intermarriage of royalty, is in some ways closer today due to the way the financial system operates and the way in which riches are stored—in the banks, bonds, stocks and real estate of capitalist countries. For corporations based in the capitalist countries, these connections make control of Third World resources much less difficult than it otherwise would be.

The transfer of capital from the Third World to the capitalist countries is not all due to corruption and greed. The instability and impoverishment engendered by repeated devaluations required by the International Monetary Fund have produced such instability in the value of many local currencies that most working people, and even much of the middle class, face constant erosion of purchasing power. As a result, large numbers of people convert their money holdings into dollars and other "hard" currencies, often on the black market. Thus, a vicious circle is set up in which capital flight and instability feed on each other, so that every significant aspect of the monetized economies of Third World countries becomes dominated by foreign exchange considerations.

In many countries, the instability has become so severe that the local monetary systems have been essentially destroyed, and even transactions within countries happen in dollars. It is not possible for shopkeepers or farmers or traders to buy and sell using currencies with an utterly unpredictable day-to-day value. The resultant understandable and common flight to the dollar is destroying one more important aspect of independence of Third World countries from imperialist institutions. A similar process is also going on in many formerly socialist countries, although its economic origins are different in many respects. This process has given rise to a new noun—"dollarization"—which means the replacement of a local currency by the U.S. dollar. This occurred in Nicaragua in the 1980s, even though the Sandanista government was the object of economic warfare by the Reagan administration, in Argentina and, in varying degrees, in several other Latin American countries. When it occurs, much of the remaining economic independence is destroyed.

The results of these manipulations of the international monetary system and the value of the debt has been catastrophic for most debtor countries. The polices of the International Monetary Fund, often called prescriptions, were supposed to have cured the disease of debt. But for the Third World they have aggravated it. There has been the pain of increasing poverty, unemployment and suffering. Yet for all this, the debt has not declined; it has increased. In 1982, when the debt crisis was made official, Third World debt totaled about $500 billion. In 1989, it was about $1.2 trillion. The patient is not only suffering more; she is a lot sicker.

But the banks, which had the greatest exposure to Third World loans, have had enough time to avert any danger of collapse (at least so far as Third World debt is concerned) by setting aside loan-loss reserves and diversifying portfolios. Many of them also made immense profits in loan fees by loaning more money to the Third World, which was paid right back as service on existing loans. During most of the 1980s, the Third World provided a net inflow of capital on the order of $50 billion a year to the capitalist countries. The International Monetary Fund has not reevaluated the theories or fundamental defects in its prescriptions, as a more rational approach to the problem would demand. Why should it? The patient may be suffering and sick. But the doctor is doing quite well, thank you.

Chapter 4

THE DYNAMIC OF CAPITALISM
WITHIN COUNTRIES

The expressions of capitalism within countries, that is within the specific political-military units which form governments, are basically different within the capitalist and Third World countries. In the former, rising levels of material consumption enabled the majority to rise out of poverty, even though the course was erratic. There the struggles of working people for higher pay and better working conditions resulted in success for many, even though these successes were biased heavily toward the male gender of the dominant ethnic and racial segments of the populations of these countries.

In the Third World, the situation has been different. Third World elites have generally done little to improve overall living conditions within their countries. In contrast to the capitalist countries, greed and the pursuit of riches have often pulled Third World elites in a direction opposite to nationalism and domestic economic investment. In the Third World, misery, low wages, high unemployment, high marginalization and great internal regional and class differences are the economic realities which underlie continuing and severe regional, religious, ethnic and other social conflicts.

The Capitalist Countries

In spite of the massive export of poverty and exploitation to the Third World over the last 200 years, and despite the amassing of immense wealth, the problems within the capitalist countries persist. In many ways, divisions which are characteristics of the differences between capitalist and Third World countries also exist within capitalist countries, although in the latter the oppressed ethnic groups are minorities.

This too is not a new reality. The problems of unemployment, of low wages, of racial discrimination and exploitation, and of gender-based discrimination are longstanding. But after about three decades of amelioration of many of the problems since World War II, they have since again become more severe. Homelessness abounds in the U.S. Large parts of northern England have become populated by the chronically unemployed, with practically no hope for the youth of meaningful jobs. East Germans at first were embraced with nationalist fervor by West Germans—unlike the immigrant Turks (among others) who build the Mercedes Benzes which many West Germans have and East Germans want. There has been an increase in racism among Germans on both sides of the now-defunct Berlin Wall. It is not much different in other capitalist countries, several of which have seen the rise of racist and anti-immigrant groups and political parties.

In the United States, about a fifth of the children live in poverty, and over thirty million people have no medical insurance. The problems of households headed by single women have increased as they struggle to cope, but wages for most of the jobs available to them (when they are there) are low. In 1989, median annual income in families headed by women was about $13,600, while the comparable statistic for men was $25,000. Median annual income for families headed by Black women was only $9,300. Median figures mean that fully half of these families are living below these incomes. And there are about 10.5 million families headed by women in the United States. Instead of being aberrations, as Fukuyama claims, inequalities have been growing in the United States; they are also becoming more entrenched in a particular pattern, with the poor concentrated among families headed by women and among Black and Hispanic people.

In fact, large numbers of people, especially among African-Americans, have become utterly marginalized, confined to ghettos not only of poverty but of unemployment and hopelessness, where violence rules and people must daily struggle to recreate their humanity in the face of misery. In 1989, fifty-eight children died of violence in Detroit, home of that marvelous symbol of capitalism, the American automobile. Fifty-three were African-American; five were White. Forty-six were shot; four were stabbed; three were beaten; two drowned; two starved; and one burned.[1]

Guns and drugs have destroyed entire communities. Yet the sales of guns continue unabated and practically unchecked. A new "war on drugs" is announced. More money is spent. Much equipment is procured. Many jails are filled. Indeed, so many jails are filled that it has become a lucrative venture for capitalists. In many states of the United States, even jails have been "privatized." Corporations take charge of prisoners for a fee. Thus, a class of corporations with a direct interest in maximizing the number of incarcerated people, or least keeping it above certain minimums, has been created in a country which now has the largest prison population in the West.[2] And the trade in drugs and guns goes on.

All of this is par for the capitalist course. The values of greed and violence that animate the sales of guns and all manner of armaments are essentially those that make possible an equally deadly traffic in drugs. The one may be legal and the other not. But the social result for millions of people who are affected adversely by the traffic in arms as in drugs is much the same.

In brief, for large numbers of people who suffer racism and sexism in the capitalist countries, living conditions more closely resemble those in the Third World than that of the majority of Whites in their own countries. These problems are generally underlain by the increases in the severity of class divisions, with the rich becoming much richer and the poor becoming poorer. At the end of the 1980s, real industrial wages in the U.S. had fallen to 84 percent of their peak in 1972.[3]

---

1   Lenora Byes, "It's Time for a Look in the Mirror," *Save Our Sons and Daughters Newsletter* (Detroit), Vol. 4, No. 2, February 5, 1990.

2   Drug Policy Foundation, *Biennial Report: 1988 & 1989,* Washington, D.C.: The Foundation, 1989, p. 4.

3   U.S. Department of Labor Bureau of Labor Statistics, *Supplement to Employment and Earnings,* August 1981, July 1984, June 1985, August 1989; and *Employment and Earnings,* March 1990, Washington, D.C., cited in Lucinda Wykle, Ward Morehouse and David Dembo, *Worker Empowerment in a Changing Economy,* New York: The Apex Press, 1991, p. 33.

Large corporations have played a major role in creating this situation in the U.S., as they have in Third World countries. Guided by the search for profit, they have often exploited workers in "company towns." They have fought environmental and safety controls and fought efforts to provide workers with basic economic protections. Even well-paying jobs may be two-edged swords. Many of the high-paying industrial jobs are in the weapons industry. There people must daily confront the reality that present high wages may expose them to deadly chemicals and radioactive materials. They must choose between jobs with decent pay and their own long-term health.

Because of their capital mobility, corporations have been able to hold communities and workers at ransom by threatening to move to areas with lower wages and fewer restraints on their polluting activities or on health and safety practices. The rise of infrastructure like roads and electricity in the Third World has meant that corporations could easily export manufacturing there, pay far lower wages for labor that was more productive in terms of equal units of cost and all but ignore health and environmental standards.

So long as workers are prevented from organizing effectively, and so long as the corporations can threaten to move out of organized areas, this job blackmail will continue. Union-busting has become the norm. Over the last decade and a half, it has become clear that wages will tend to be stagnant or go downward and unemployment will remain high in the capitalist countries, so long as the oppressive conditions remain endemic in the Third World. Take, for instance, this lovely reminder of financial muscle from David Packard, the chairman of Hewlett-Packard company, who was speaking vigorously in favor of opening the Diablo Canyon nuclear power plant located on an earthquake fault in California:

> If the Diablo Canyon [nuclear facility] is not brought on stream this year, our company will clearly have to re-evaluate its decision to build a major facility in Roseville [California]. . . . Our company's current plans call for the creation of 15,000 to 20,000 additional jobs in the decade of the '80s. These jobs will be lost to the state if energy problems force us to divert this growth outside California.[4]

Through the power of capital mobility, the misery that exists for

---

4   David Packard, quoted by Richard Kazis and Richard Grossman in *Fear at Work*, New York: Pilgrim Press, 1982, p. 52.

many within the capitalist countries is inexorably tied to the misery that exists for most in the Third World.

The Third World

Within Third World countries, barring a few with relatively small populations, there has been no relief from economic suffering for the majority of people. Not only has the condition of landless workers, poor peasants and artisans worsened, but tribal peoples, who in the times before imperialism were independent of monetized economies, have seen their lands, freedom and their very societies and cultures destroyed. This process goes on to this day, with tragic human and environmental consequences.

Political independence provided in some cases only a brief respite from the process of economic subjugation. The connections of Third World elites to imperialist countries, the ideology of large-scale industrialization as "progress" (the frequently tragic results of which are illustrated by the case of the Akosombo dam in Ghana discussed above), the power of multinational corporations, heavy military spending, the deliberate and often violent subversion by the capitalist countries of moves toward economic independence—all have joined to create the dismal economic reality in which 40,000 children die each day of malnutrition and the easily preventable diseases that arise from it.

Among the strongest forces perpetuating Third World misery are the divisions that exist between races, genders, religions and classes within Third World countries. Many kinds of severe conflicts, some directly economic (relating to land, employment and wage issues) and some around social and political issues (ethnic, religious and regional divisions), have become widespread. These conflicts are often fanned by segments of local elites or political parties, in a manner quite similar to the divide-and-rule policies which were practiced by imperialist rulers of the Third World.

Third World elites tend to place a variety of personal and class interests before building their own societies as nation-states. In general, the "nation-state," as labeled in the capitalist industrialized countries, does not exist in the Third World. Indeed, the whole premise of "nation-building" has been based on a false premise that the experience of the capitalist countries could be repeated in most, if not all, Third World countries. This cannot be done precisely because the Third World as it exists today is a part of the experience of capitalism. National unity in the capitalist countries is based, in part, on fragmentation of social structure in the Third World. That fragmentation means considerable internal turmoil and a lack of substantial cohesion across classes which characterizes nationalism in the capitalist countries.

The overall dynamic since independence has been the closer integration of the controlling classes in the Third World (landlords, capitalists, and the governmental and military structures which together protect property rights) with international corporate and financial structures. Elites across boundaries have cooperated, despite their tensions, to keep wages low, to prevent the rise of powerful unions which would demand better wages and living conditions, and to prevent the redistribution of land and the associated means of production to the people who work it. There have been precious few exceptions, and most of these have been due to the long, persistent and militant demands of people in the face of considerable odds and repression (see the example of Kerala in Part II).

This cooperation between ruling classes in Third World and capitalist countries has not been without its conflicts and tensions. These tensions have manifested themselves in various ways. For instance, Third World governments have, from time to time, tried to assert some economic independence, demanding a New International Economic Order. Another important example was the formation of the Non-Aligned Movement. But overall these impulses have been much weaker than the political will which Third World elites have displayed in keeping wages low in the Third World, and workers and peasants in their place—dirt poor.

Chapter 5

THE ECONOMIC ACTIVITY OF WOMEN

The study of economics as well as economic policy has long focused almost exclusively on monetized activity. The people who work by looking after children, fetching firewood and water, caring for the sick in their families, cooking and cleaning, and maintaining homes and clothing are not treated as "economically active," by mainstream economists and therefore as "unproductive." These "unproductive," uncounted laborers are primarily women and older children.

For instance, James Mill wrote it was "pretty clear" that the interests of women who did not appear in the marketplace with money could simply be included with those of men and hence "struck off without inconvenience."[1] Adam Smith's "invisible hand" which converted self-interest and greed into the common good operated only in the monetized marketplace, peopled by men. The hand that cooked was to be guided by perfect altruism. It was, as Nancy Folbre and Heidi Hartman have pointed out, simply a way to ignore the contribution of women to economic life and "leave the question [of gender inequalities] beyond the purview of economic analysis."[2]

---

1   James Mill, quoted by Nancy Folbre and Heidi Hartman, "The Rhetoric of Self-Interest: Ideology, Gender and Economic Theory," in Klamer, McCloskey and Solow, eds., *The Consequences of Economic Rhetoric*, Cambridge: Cambridge University Press, 1989, Chapter 12.
2   Folbre and Hartman, *op. cit.*

Yet no economy can function without the kinds of work that have traditionally been done by women—cooking, gathering fuelwood, bearing and nurturing children, fetching water, maintaining homes—whether this work is monetized or not. Much recent scholarship has shown that the amount of non-monetized work that women and children do is comparable to and often greater than all work in the monetized sector, especially in the Third World.

Marilyn Waring has noted that, in contrast to the demonstrably essential work that women do, which is uncompensated and uncounted, a man doing nothing but awaiting an order to fire a nuclear missile (and presumed, according to the military code of conduct, ready to kill his partner if he does not do his part of the job when the order comes) is regarded as both "economically active" and "productive."[3]

The mainstream of economic thought in both capitalist and socialist countries has focused on monetized activities, even when they are violent and destructive, while ignoring non-monetized work, although this continues to be essential to the functioning of the formal or monetized economy.

Further, a considerable amount of monetized work by women is undervalued. When monetized activities are counted, these are valued at prevailing wage rates. The wage paid to the worker measures the "value added" by the work. But we note that women are generally paid less than men for the same work, or work that requires comparable training and skill. Thus, women's productivity is undervalued. Those who are not paid at all are effectively defined as "unproductive"; those who are poorly paid are effectively defined as "less productive." For instance, in economic statistics secretaries are deemed less productive than truck drivers and nurses less productive than doctors, not out of any utilitarian rationale but simply because truck drivers and doctors make more money per hour. Comparisons of productivity across regional and national boundaries are even more skewed by such monetary measures.

The near-total focus of traditional economic theory and policy on monetized activity at prevailing wage rates affects a much wider scope of economic activity than is realized. This is because the sale and purchase of commodities generally does not represent the work it takes to derive utility from that commodity over its useful life. Food must be

---

3   Marilyn Waring, *If Women Counted: A New Feminist Economics*, New York: Harper & Row, 1988, Chapter 1.

cooked, shirts washed and ironed, homes maintained. For instance, over the useful life of a shirt, the non-monetized labor may be much larger than the labor time it took to make the shirt.

The examples can be quite easily extended beyond the realm of household work. For instance, transportation systems and the arrangements of housing and work locations are generally designed with little regard to people's travel time because that time is non-monetized. The result is detrimental not only for the individual who must fight traffic jams, but also for the quality of the air, the amount of petroleum needed to enable cities to function, the expenditures on roads and so on. Yet the failure to count the labor of a large portion of the population—consisting mainly of women and children—still stands out as one of the most glaring failures of the present system of economic accounting.

Monetary measures like Gross National Product (GNP) have utility in capitalist economic systems as measures of monetized activity on which profit can be determined in a systematic way. Monetized profit cannot be determined from non-monetized activity, and so it appears irrelevant from the point of view of production, sales and circulation of commodities, and of capital. And profit is the principal driving force of capitalism.

The failure to count non-monetized labor is not a problem of capitalism alone. Socialist systems, while not geared explicitly to profit, have also ignored non-monetized labor. The underlying goal of socialist economic organization of the bureaucratic variety appears to be parallel to profit: the maximization of material output—numbers of shoes, tons of steel and coal, and oil and toilet paper. Only recently has it come to be realized that rolls of toilet paper produced may not be such a good standard-of-living indicator if the toilet paper feels like newsprint. The result of such policies have been unpleasant for consumers and disastrous for the environment. Here again, women have been major victims of the system. Because it was not monetized, time spent in lines (primarily by women) was considered of little importance until it became a political issue.

Failure to count non-monetized work has had profound social consequences in terms of the relationships between women and men. In many societies, women's economic dependence has subjected them to the dictates of male-dominated society, depriving them of the right to make the most basic decisions about their own well-being.

Thus, for women in many capitalist countries as well as in socialist economies, stepping into the monetized economy has been critical in improving their status relative to male family members and members of society generally. But in a war system, this can have ironic consequences. A woman can now sit next to the man waiting for an order to fire a nuclear missile and be counted as productive. There are many other problems as well. Single mothers are by far the most impoverished segment of U.S. society. Women's work continues to be undervalued and underpaid and children remain primarily the responsibility of their mothers with no adequate provision for child care.

As Lourdis Beneria, who has studied the role of women in the world economy, notes:

> On the one hand, the feminization of employment implies an increase in women's income-producing activities, which might result in greater autonomy for women, in gender decomposition and a higher degree of equality between the sexes. On the other, these changes are based on inequalities that are likely to persist stubbornly, precisely because they are instrumental in the current functioning of the global economy.[4]

Women's increased involvement in traditionally "male" areas, i.e., in currently monetized activities, has in some respects led to more exploitation rather than less. Women are now often expected to be active in a monetized economy that does not compensate them adequately for their work and yet fulfill traditional duties in the non-monetized economy. When they are unable to do so, the result often is alienation of child-rearing, because fathers generally do not fill the gap left by working mothers.

Similar problems, with somewhat different roots, also obtain in Third World countries. Here, too, there has been a feminization of poverty. According to Ben Wisner, who has studied the problems of poverty in Africa extensively:

> The poorest households in Africa are those headed by women. In many countries the proportion of female-headed households is as high as twenty to thirty per cent. . . . Even when they have not faced famine, they have had to work harder and harder with shrinking resources for their families. . . .[5]

---

4   Lourdis Beneria, "Gender and the Global Economy," in Arthur MacEwan and William K. Tabb, eds., *Instability and Change in the World Economy*, New York: Monthly Review Press, 1989, p. 255.

5   Ben Wisner, *Power and Need and Africa*, Trenton, NJ: Africa World Press, 1989, p. 18.

One reason for the large number of single female-headed households is that the miserable economic situation of many Third World families has sent many husbands and fathers away from their families in the villages in search of paid work in the cities and abroad. The need both to take care of children and to do traditionally "male" work at home, combined with inferior social status and earning power, makes it very difficult for women to support their families. The benefits women may find in such a situation in terms of control over their lives are generally outweighed by the difficulties of day-to-day survival.

The failure to take women's work adequately into account is a reflection of sexism in society generally, and in the economic system specifically. The failure to value fully both the monetized and non-monetized work of women seems a worldwide phenomenon which has not yet been overcome in capitalist, socialist or Third World economies—despite some steps in the right direction in some countries. This is a problem which must be solved if the war system is to be truly overcome. In fact, the relative value that an economic system places upon nurture, without necessarily monetizing it, may be one of the best indicators of progress toward a peace system.

Chapter 6

CAPITALISM AND DEMOCRACY

It is often suggested that political democracy is a natural corollary of capitalism and that the two are closely intertwined. While the general political aspects of the history and reality of democracy are beyond the scope of this book, I will briefly discuss the supposed connections between the two.

In fact, the association between capitalism and democracy is generally based on a rather narrow examination of them, confined to certain historical periods and geographic locations. The larger reality of capitalism has been worldwide and is associated with imperialism, racism and poverty. Capitalist country governments, which proclaim democracy at home, have routinely set up and supported the most murderous and repressive regimes, waged war on liberation struggles and subverted and destroyed people's revolutions by military and economic pressures. They have also subverted democracy and circumscribed it at home when convenient. During World War II, even as Churchill proclaimed he was fighting for the freedom of Britain, he vowed not to preside over the liquidation of the British empire, and jailed freedom-fighters in India. When imperialist profits have declined, as with Germany between the wars, the capitalist powers have jettisoned political democracy for the most vicious and violent regimes, to come back reincarnated as democracy when cheap foreign resources are restored. It is quite remarkable how imperialists can undergo rapid reincarnations from militarists and Nazis to votaries of political democracy when profits are restored.

A principal thesis of this chapter is that capitalism and democracy are as related in the global economy as they are in South Africa. In capitalism, as in South African apartheid, there is oppression and political subjugation for the many and a conditional "liberal democracy" for the few.

The Third World Countries

Let us look at Third World countries first. In many countries, essentially military regimes, which are armed, trained and/or supported by the capitalist powers, still govern. The roots of many of these regimes go back to colonial days. As we have already discussed, the internal class divisions in the Third World are very strong. The differences of income are so great and the extent of the poverty is so wide that physical repression is the norm. The violation of human rights has generally been far worse in the Third World than in the centralized socialist countries after Stalin's death. This applies not only to regimes like Pinochet's or Mobutu's, which have been notorious for their violence. It is also true of Third World countries where multi-party voting prevails and a considerable amount of freedom of the press is well established.

India is perhaps the model country in this respect, with a well-established formalism of democracy in many areas. And, in fact, it is true that, in many respects, the human-rights situation in most parts of India has been better than in many Third World countries. Yet even in those parts, the condition of human rights for the poor and most women, poor or not, is deplorable. Here are three examples relating to the police and judicial system.

In 1978, upper-caste landlords burned and destroyed, directly or by instigating others, the homes of hundreds of thousands of Untouchables in Maharashtra over the renaming of a university in honor of one of India's greatest leaders, B.R. Ambedkar, who was also a leader of the Untouchables. No action was taken against the perpetrators.

There are annually several hundred dowry murders, in which husbands and/or in-laws murder women over demands for more dowry. Hundreds of other women commit suicide due to living conditions or terrible oppression in their in-laws' homes. Yet practically no one is ever prosecuted.

Consider Bhagalpur, a town in the state of Bihar in North India.

Some years ago it was discovered that the police were blinding prisoners (generally poor people) by poking their eyes with needles or pouring acid into them. No one received any serious punishment.

These kinds of incidents and crimes are repeated every week, every month, year-in and year-out in places called democracies. The reality is that the poor and most women live not only in economic privation but also in fear of violence, with no practical hope of judicial redress. The two are systemically related, for it is, in large measure, the threat and the reality of violence which has kept the economically oppressed from rising up against their oppressors.

Three or four million children die in India every year of hunger, poor water supply and malnutrition-related diseases, even as India exports food. This is possible in part because the poor are repressed by ever-present threats of violence. Indeed, after independence food production in India has grown faster than population. How can a government be said to represent its people democratically when they are hungry and food is being exported? How can a country be called a democracy when a majority of its citizens may be subjected to arbitrary and criminal violence and the threat of violence to "keep them in their place"?

The situation in other Third World countries is not qualitatively different. In South Asia, as in many other parts of the Third World, slave-labor conditions continue to exist, where economic bondage and exploitation, actual violence and the threat of violence are closely linked in the most immediate way. There are millions of "bonded laborers," including children, trapped in highly exploitative work from which they cannot escape. For such persons all over the Third World, talk of democracy and the "end of history" is no more than a cruel joke.

Another aspect of the situation in the Third World applies to young people and is coming to affect the political system profoundly. Tens of millions of young people have been through schools, but the direction of investments and production has failed to create any jobs for them— let alone meaningful, decently paid work. Oftentimes the main practical result of a formal education is to turn young people away from agricultural work. For instance, in Zimbabwe, three-fourths of the students who have finished high school in the decade since independence in 1980 are unemployed. There are tens of millions of educated unemployed in South Asia, daily becoming more frustrated for lack of meaningful, if any, work.

With no hope of reasonably remunerative employment in the so-called "organized sector," many struggle to survive in poverty in the "informal sector." They face situations of utter hopelessness and are at the same time surrounded by images of wealth and consumption by the rich, which are daily reminders of the immense inequalities and the cynical greed that is at the core of the values of the capitalist economic system.

One consequence is increased violence among the poor. It is not surprising that some of these unemployed young men turn to the formation of gangs and that some of these gangs turn to the drug trade. In the Third World, moreover, many gangs are coming to have substantial influence over the activities of political parties at the base. That is contributing to increasing levels of violence in political life; it also feeds into ethnic tensions which are generally sharpened in deteriorating economic conditions. This violent behavior is also found among those who wield governmental authority. Very often the greed and corruption at the top percolates down, a tendency reinforced by poor pay at the bottom. The temptations are strong for soldiers and police officers to convert the power of their officially held guns to financial gain. In many countries, police and military forces are simply seizing what they want, wreaking havoc on already poor and vulnerable economies. The various kinds of violence melt into each other, creating grave insecurity and reinforcing poverty.

This is capitalist "democracy" in the Third World, all too often even in those countries which have multi-party elections.

The Capitalist Countries

Democratic rights within capitalist countries are generally greater than in the Third World. The modest levels of true democratic rights that prevail have been won by a hard struggle often violently opposed by governments and corporations. But even within the capitalist countries, these rights are incomplete and conditional.

For example, human rights in many capitalist countries still do not extend very far into the economic sphere. Even today, most workers in the U.S. do not have the right to criticize their employers without fear of losing their jobs. They may criticize working conditions, and their employers may fire them for it—a situation no different from that in places where authoritarianism is considerably more formalized. The one difference is that this right can be gained in the U.S. and other capitalist countries through workers' struggles in the democratic political space which does exist. Historically, for unions, it has come second to the struggle for economic benefits.[1]

It is well recognized that multi-party electoral systems, supposedly a central feature political democracy (because they allow people to "throw the rascals out" via a peaceful election), are vulnerable to subversion by the power of money.

That is why there is considerable popular disillusionment with the electoral system in many capitalist countries. That frustration is perhaps the greatest in the U.S., where the corruption of big money in politics has been legalized and institutionalized in political contributions of "Political Action Committees" and of rich individuals to electoral campaigns and political party coffers. When elections are driven by money, then the chances are that when voters do "throw the rascals out," the new faces soon become like the old, at the mercy of money on pain of losing the next election. In any case, it has become very hard to throw out the old; in recent years, well over 90 percent of incumbent members of Congress have been re-elected.

Multi-party electoral politics have a role in a democratic system, but this is far from the only, or even the main, guarantee of political freedom or of human rights. Political freedoms in capitalist countries exist *despite* the frequent opposition of the core institutions of capitalism as an economic system—large corporations (and their antecedents) and capitalist country governments with powerful military establishments linked to those corporations.

Another problem is that the arena in which democratic rights can be exercised is generally local. When people make broader connections, or when essential aspects of the system are challenged, the democratic space shrinks dramatically. The exercise of democratic rights without government harassment, intimidation or worse has generally been on condition that the core aspects of imperialism should not be threatened. These core aspects include anti-communism, maintenance of corporate supremacy at home and corporate as well as military supremacy abroad.

When capitalist exploitation has been threatened, capitalist governments unleash special institutions to spy on, infiltrate and subvert the opposition. Whether one looks to the McCarthy era of witch-hunting, the FBI's efforts to undermine Martin Luther King in the struggle for civil rights, the official attack on the Black Panthers, the U.S. government's infiltration of anti-war movements and even churches (as

---

1   Richard Kazis and Richard Grossman, *Fear at Work*, New York: Pilgrim Press, 1982.

in the case of the Sanctuary Movement to protect undocumented Central American refugees), it is not hard to establish that real freedoms are eroded by the establishment when it feels itself substantially threatened. In Britain, as in many other countries, freedom of speech is severely circumscribed in these areas by the Official Secrets Act, which makes even simple statements of fact regarding a broad range of subjects into crimes against the state.

The citizens of capitalist countries can and do protest such policies and can potentially change them—a fact which provides hope for the future. This political space exists because of the length of time in which democratic rights have been established in them. Among the people of the U.S. and many other capitalist countries, a tradition of free discourse and democracy has become solidly enough established that it is difficult for the government to curtail it, at least sharply and suddenly. This was dramatically and publicly evident in the 1988 presidential candidacy and platform of Jesse Jackson. That campaign was itself a sign of deeper yearning for peace and justice, many everyday expressions of which are found in communities throughout the U.S. in the movement against intervention in Central America, the Sanctuary Movement, the nuclear disarmament movement and many aspects of the environmental movement. The exercise of freedoms in these struggles in the U.S. often enhances the struggles for justice of people outside of it.

The connections between repression in the Third World and the repressive impulses of capitalism in the capitalist countries are in many ways exemplified by the conditions of refugees from capitalist-sponsored or -supported wars. The legal situation of El Salvadoran refugees in the United States which prevailed until about the end of 1990 illustrates both the repression and the possibilities in the democratic space in capitalist countries to gain justice through international solidarity.

In late 1989, the Central American Refugee Center reported that more than a million Salvadorans had fled their homeland to the U.S. because of their fear of death squads, government-sponsored torture and repression.[2] Yet U.S. support for the Salvadoran government—to the tune of $1 million a day in aid—continued while most human rights violations in El Salvador were essentially ignored. They were politically embarrasing. As a result, the U.S. refused to grant refugee status to Salvadorans and they lived in the U.S. in constant fear that they would

---

2   Daniel A. Katz and Sylvia J. Rosales-Fike, Mass-mailing Letter from the Central American Refugee Center, Washington, D.C., November 1989.

be captured and sent back perhaps to be murdered in their own country. However, due to constant struggles and the availability of judicial redress, and no doubt the disintegration of the Soviet Union in the geo-political background, temporary refugee status was finally granted to them in late 1990.

Many internationalist struggles, whether for peace, for economic justice or for environmental sanity, are based on increasing solidarity among peoples across boundaries. It is the broadening and deepening of these struggles that will make freedom truly indivisible. For the present, with the historic crumbling of corrupt, authoritarian and centralized structures of power in Eastern Europe and the Soviet Union there is more freedom and respect for human rights within those countries than there is within capitalism as a whole when Third World countries are included. Whether this movement in the U.S.S.R. and Eastern Europe can be consolidated and institutionalized without be-coming part of an exploitative and repressive world economic order of capitalism is among the great questions of our time.

The economic task before us is to begin a profound restructuring of capitalism. We need a structure which includes justice for those who have been cast out and marginalized today, and which respects the rights to health and safety of tomorrow's generations. We must end the per-manent state of war among the peoples of the world and between them and the Earth.

Chapter 7

CENTRALIZED SOCIALISM

Recent years have seen the disintegration of centralized socialist economies in Eastern Europe and the Soviet Union. Indeed, even before the sudden political and economic changes which have occurred in Eastern Europe and the Soviet Union in the last few years, centralized socialism was in the process of ceasing to exist as an economic system separate from capitalism. The integration with global capitalism also continues in China. But China has not experienced the same disintegration of its economy as has occurred in the Soviet and Eastern Europe, and large portions continue to be relatively unaffected in a direct way by that integration which is concentrated in a few regions of China.

The disintegration in the Soviet Union and Eastern Europe, especially during 1989 and 1990, has pointed up long suppressed problems within centralized socialism. Yet centralized socialism has also had important economic successes. We look at it briefly here for three reasons:

1. The economic accomplishments of socialism relative to capitalism as a global system have been seriously underrated.

2. It is crucial to understand how repression and violence became institutionalized in centralized socialism. The violence of Stalinism is one of the main causes of the vehement rejection

of centralized socialism in Eastern Europe and in the Soviet
Union, especially among the non-Russian nationalities.

3. It is important also to understand the similarities and differen-
    ces between capitalism and centralized socialism in terms of
    both creating a vision of an economic system based on peace
    and considering how we might build such a system from where
    we are today.

This brief assessment of centralized socialism cannot begin to address all the issues involved. Although Marxism is a formal, common
thread, there are crucial differences between the Bolshevik revolution,
which was urban and European in inspiration, and the later agrarian
revolution of China, which was largely oriented toward land and rural
areas in its vision and programs, and which has therefore never been as
centralized in its economic organization. There are yet other differences between these two and the Cuban revolution and the more recent
ones, such as those in Nicaragua and Angola. In many ways, each
revolution has had its distinctive characteristics. We will not address
these differences, although they are vital to a sound understanding of
socialist economies. The main purposes here are to understand some
aspects of the war system as it existed under socialism to establish an
approximate economic comparison between capitalism and socialism,
and to draw lessons from successes and failures of both.

Centralized socialism is not parallel to capitalism as a determinant
of the global war system and hence its role within that system is different from that of capitalism in many essential respects. Most fundamental is the fact that socialism has never been the dominant
economic system in the world. Even in Eastern Europe, which the
Soviet Union dominated militarily until recently, the methods and
results of economic control were different from those of capitalism.

In contrast to capitalism, where subjugated areas are systematically impoverished and exploited, most of Eastern Europe under Soviet
rule generally had a higher level of material consumption than the
Soviet Union. Further, socialist revolutions have had an anti-colonial
and anti-imperialist inspiration, representing a large part of the problem
that imperialists traditionally have had with socialism. This was an essential aspect of U.S. containment policy with respect to the Soviet
Union.

Here we will discuss only the Soviet Union, Eastern Europe and
China, omitting for a number of reasons other countries where Marxist

revolutionary governments were or are established. For the most part, the economic situation in these latter countries has not stabilized, often due to severe external military and economic pressures. Further, most of these countries have been continuously integrated into the world economy to a considerable extent, without an autarkic period, making an evaluation of the type presented here for the Soviet-East European case and for China problematic.

It is also important to note that the military apparatus of socialism was built in reaction to imperialist attack. In the Soviet case, this happened right after the revolution. China was under imperialist attack for decades before the revolution and, in fact, its revolution was largely shaped by the resistance to Japanese imperialism. U.S. policy has also included consistent nuclear threats to both countries. The direct threats to China decreased after the acquisition of nuclear weapons by China and the decisive phase of the Sino-Soviet split in the 1960s.

In both China and the Soviet Union, the same power which was used to defend revolutions was used to achieve internal redistribution, and later to re-establish privilege and authority over the people. A related problem has been the notion that economic and political democracy could be replaced by a "vanguard" political party. Both of these problems have been reinforced by the uncritical acceptance of large-scale industrialism as the vehicle of "progress."

This analysis of centralized socialism is based on the period when it did exist as an identifiable economic system, producing and consuming almost all of what it needed and not essentially dependent on substantial trade with the capitalist system. For the Soviet Union and Eastern Europe that period began to end in the mid- to late-1960s and for most countries had ended by about 1980. For China the erosion of the autarkic period began in the mid-1970s. Therefore, using data from the mid-1970s or a few years earlier is a reasonable way to compare centralized socialism and capitalism as economic systems when they existed largely independently of each other.

It is important to note some crucial distinctions between the Soviet Union and Eastern Europe on the one hand and China on the other. The Soviet-East European economy has essentially collapsed as a centralized system. The Chinese economy is gradually becoming integrated into the global capitalist system without undergoing a phase of collapse. Further, in China, the centralization of the economy has always been far lower than in the Soviet Union, since there has never been a phase of central control over land. In China, a considerable level of control over land has been retained by peasants through the various phases of decentralization and centralization (up to the commune level) that have characterized China's post-revolutionary history. The following comments and generalizations are limited by the essential difference that "centralized socialism" has been far less centralized in China than in the Soviet Union and Eastern Europe, a distinction which is accentuated by the fact that China has a much larger proportion of its people in rural areas and in agriculture.

Failures and Successes; Theory and Practice

The Industrial Focus

Some of the most serious failures of centralized socialism have been rooted in theory which glorified industrial infrastructure at all costs, including the costs of human initiative and development.

Marxist theory saw the future welfare of working people in the just distribution of production and the social control of the means of production. (There has, of course, been considerable argument as to the relation of social to governmental control.) The focus was on large, centralized structures which would produce a lot in a hurry and bring a decent standard of living to all. Planning would be centralized and a system of balancing supply and demand would be created through such planning. Private property was regarded as capitalist and thus undesirable, even if it had to be tolerated from time to time. The problem of individual initiative, the reality that economic and social life must continue to be centered on small-scale social institutions, especially the family, was not a part of the thinking in any systematic way, nor was it integrated into planning.

These plans for a socialist state were based on Marx's assumption that socialism would follow capitalism in England or Germany. He assumed that a huge, productive industrial structure would already be in place when the workers took control, the benefits of which could then be redistributed.

But when Marxist theory was applied to practical revolutionary situations, numerous problems emerged. Neither the sources of socialist revolutions nor the conditions with which revolutionary governments were left to operate were as Marx had predicted.

Revolutions actually happened not in England or similarly industrialized countries, but in places such as Russia and China. These countries were not only poor; they had been systematically impoverished in the process of shifts that capitalism and industrialization had introduced in the early nineteenth century. For instance, even as Marx was writing *Das Kapital*, the mechanisms of transfer of poverty out of the capitalist countries were operating in full swing.

Thus, many of the roots of the Russian revolution lay with the peasantry, which had been victimized by the capitalist imperialist system, and not solely among industrial workers. The Tsar had squeezed grain from the Russian peasant for export (mainly to Germany), in part to pay for debts incurred due to huge military expenditures. The peasants in Russia were so impoverished that they were abandoning iron ploughs for wooden ones—iron had become unaffordable—at the very time that their U.S. counterparts were increasingly using iron ploughs to improve productivity. Conditions for most workers were equally bad. On top of these deprivations Russian peasants and workers were asked to fight and die in the Tsar's wars. Revolts and revolutions followed.

The situation confronting the Soviet revolutionaries after the revolution was not one of a ready-made productive industrial apparatus. It was one of a largely agrarian country devastated by war, which was followed by imperialist invasions, "civil" wars and military threats even in the periods of "peace."

The reality of military threats and of actual intervention by imperialist powers created its own logic of building heavy weaponry, which could only come from internally developed heavy industry. The problem was severe in the Soviet Union, not only because it was attacked immediately after the revolution, but because there was no other country it could rely on for even a modest part of these requirements.

This was coupled with Marxist theory which glorified large-scale industry and industrial workers. Therefore, heavy industry became the primary focus of the new political economy, despite the fact that peasants had provided the decisive force in the making of the revolution. Indeed, there was a disdain for the peasant ("potatoes in a sack of potatoes," Marx had derisively said of them) and work on the land. By the logic of this theory, peasants could only be converted from their stubborn, non-proletarian individualism by the industrialization of agriculture. Simultaneously, agricultural labor would become much more productive. The problems generated by the lack of industrialization both in the city and even more in the countryside were compounded by a lack of theory with which to understand the revolutionary situation. Neither Marx, nor the Marxists who led the Bolshevik Revolution realized that land must be nutured and loved, and as with the rearing of children, individual and local control was essential within an overall context of social rules that ensured economic justice and ecological sense.

Although the pattern of a focus on heavy industry was not so severe in China, where there was more emphasis on rural development and light industry, it also prevailed there.

In common with other systems of economy that have been run from the cities (in other words, in "civilized" economic systems), socialist systems have generally taken resources from rural areas to build up cities. One result of this system was to blunt the initiative of the peasantry. It has also resulted in grave ecological harm to productive land in rural areas.

The industrial focus also came at the expense of the service sector. In the heavily centralized and industrialized system in Eastern Europe and the Soviet Union, there developed a situation where there was essentially no system by which the desires of the purchasers could be communicated to the producers. The producers were ruled by governmental and Communist Party bureacracies, but these institutions did not incorporate consumers' desires and decisions into their direction of the production system. Government departments produced for each other in this system of centralized planning. This, together with the emphasis on quantities of production to meet quotas, meant that the quality of goods tended to be poor, even as the variety of production was unsatisfactory.

The Issue of Individual Initiative

For such a crude system, in which many of the basic questions of economic organization were not even systemically posed, much less answered, the successes have been remarkable. The worst problems of poverty were eliminated in the Soviet Union and China, despite external military pressures and, in the case of the Soviet Union, actual extensive destruction. Yet an enduring problem within the system has been the failure to recognize the importance of individual and local initiative and incentive as a necessary positive force in any complex economic system. When individual initiative and effort were rewarded, it was only as a reluctant and temporary concession to the heritage of a bourgeois past. The role of the individual in the economy, as in much else, remained obscure, even though personality cults became the rule in the political realm.

Thus, some of the reasons for the successes of socialism were never appreciated. For example, there is considerable evidence that the economic development under socialism derived partly from their redistributive aspects, a fact which was not fully integrated into socialist thought. Redistribution gave that hope of better living conditions to hundreds of millions of people living in grinding poverty who were suppressed under prior regimes whenever they tried to get ahead or get a bigger share of society's production. A substantial portion of the growth that occurred in the production and consumption of essentials derived basically from the energy which redistribution gave to the poor and the investments of labor time which they made as a result.

Carl Riskin, who has studied Chinese economic history closely, has summed up the Chinese experience with socialism in these words:

> Finally, there is the issue of distribution. A massive redistribution of industrial and commercial capital and of land did of course occur in the early 1950s. . . . [T]he land reform redistributed some 13 per cent of net domestic product in 1952 of which peasants retained enough after taxes and compulsory sales at low prices to increase their per capita disposable income by a quarter. Land reform alone may have provided almost one-half the increase in national savings between 1950 and 1952 while still raising consumption for most peasants. To this must be added a substantial increase in public consumption in the form of public health and sanitation measures, and the provision of elementary education to increasing numbers of people.[1]

This is a startling and unusual conclusion. Redistribution in favor of the poor led to economic growth, increases in income and increases in savings. It is quite the opposite of the "trickle-down" theory at the center of Reaganomics, the prevailing capitalist economic doctrine during the 1980s, that more money in the hands of the rich would produce prosperity. The theory benefited only the rich and those in their immediate proximity who could catch the juiciest trickles first.

The failure of the socialist system to recognize this fully can be seen in its ambivalent attitude toward land redistribution. The ironic, and for the most part reluctant, result of socialist practice in regard to property has been the creation of more small-scale private property within the production system than is prevalent in capitalism as a whole. For example, there are more private property owners in Poland and China than in Brazil. This is not only a post-Cold War phenomenon. It goes back to the beginnings of socialist governments in these countries.

---

1   Carl Riskin, *China's Political Economy: The Quest for Development since 1949*, New York: Oxford University Press, 1987, p. 77.

Sometimes these changes were made against the will of the centralized socialist bureaucracies. Socialist governments came to power in countries where peasants were in the majority. Therefore, there were strong demands for a plot of land that the peasant could control, no matter how small. Even in the Soviet Union, where the city-based ideology of nationalization of land prevailed as part of the Bolshevik program up to the time of the revolution, nationalization had to give way for at least a short while to land redistribution, since it was the peasants who did most of the fighting against the imperialist invaders and the White Russian armies.

The momentum of the Bolsheviks was toward centralization, despite the interregnum of the New Economic Policy during most of the 1920s, when individual property was reluctantly accepted as necessary to maintain the system of production. The murderous, forced collectivization after 1929 represented a terrible consolidation of this trend. It undermined Soviet agriculture and the very human basis of much of the revolution. Subsequent to that, many of the material gains in the Soviet Union have come from poor labor conditions and extreme oppression of people, including minority nationalities, in the period when Stalin was fully in control (1929 to 1953).

The energy provided by redistribution in the Soviet Union could not be sustained in the face of this violence. Moreover, other forces of centralized planning worked to stifle individual and community initiative. There was no overall model of economic organization in which families and communities had a principal role. Centralized structures were enshrined in theory and bureaucratic repression operated in practice. As is well known, the bureaucracy of the Communist Party became a center of privilege, in stark contrast to its egalitarian rhetoric.

The Party also became practically the only route to well-paid positions in the economy and at certain levels to wealth, although that wealth could never be officially acknowledged. (The following joke that made the rounds during the Brezhnev era was indicative of the inequalities that prevailed and the public attitude toward them. Brezhnev, wanting to show off his wealth and villas, took his mother on an extensive tour. She showed no joy that her son had risen so high in life; instead, she looked worried. Brezhnev asked why she did not seem impressed. "I'm impressed all right," she replied, "but what if the Reds come back?") The enthusiasm and inventiveness of peasants and workers had been replaced by the sycophancy of bureaucrats.

This failure to find an effective model in which egalitarian socialist aims are compatible with individual economic initiative is not only a feature of socialist European history. It is all the more remarkable in China, which has made more efforts at decentralization in practice, and where a large portion of the gains of land redistribution have been sustained. Indeed, as Riskin has observed, China has lurched from centralization to decentralization in an effort, often violent, to find a balance:

> Yet to an economist, the striking characteristic of Maoist response to central administrative planning was its failure to put forward an alternative. While Mao objected to hierarchical and bureaucratic prerequisites of a central planning regime, he also rejected reliance on the market as an institution that inevitably encouraged the "restoration of capitalism." Full of ideas for the proper structuring of authority and participation at the micro-economic level, Maoism had virtually nothing positive to say about the fashioning of an integrated, cohesive macroeconomy . . . [I]ndeed, one can scour the literature of Maoism without finding a serious discussion of socialist macroeconomic organization.[2]

A principal theoretical failure for centralized socialism in both the Soviet Union and China has been that there has been no macroeconomic vision of organizing the economic system other than a bureaucratic and centralized one which has perpetrated authoritarianism and violence and stifled economic initiative. This inability to create a system in which human rights and political freedom prevailed has been significant, for without it there was no way in which the energy of the people could be tapped for the long haul. The failure to integrate the initiative and hopes of people on an individual level into the larger economic and political scheme and the resulting authoritarianism, which often turned to contemptuous or anarchic violence against the people themselves, have been principal problems. The violence of the state against the people in China and Rumania in 1989 are among the more recent examples of this phenominan.

The repression of people, the stifling of initiative, the installation of bureaucracies which became centers of privilege, all of these are familiar and have been publicly acknowledged throughout Eastern Europe and the Soviet Union. (It has been reported that former Rumanian dictator Ceauscesu's daughter ate off solid gold plates. Whether true or not, its believability is an indication of the great cor-

---

2 Riskin. *op. cit.*, pp. 6-7.

ruption of socialist egalitarian values produced by an authoritarian system.)

One of the most important destructive results of Stalinist repression on the economic system was the pervasiveness of fear. No reasonable or just system of economic life, much less one that relied on centralized planning, can be based on lies and distortions. Yet fear created a huge incentive to fabricate the statistics of economic reporting which is the lifeblood of planning. It appears today that considerable portions of this system fall into the venerable third category of Mark Twain's progression: lies, damned lies and statistics. The terrible problems for planning that this posed and, indeed, the impossibility of proper planning in such a context began to be realized in the mid- to late-1980s, as the fresh winds of truth and free debate began to blow.

Of course, problems within the centralized socialist systems have been amplified by external pressures, but these cannot be looked at in isolation from socialism's internal problems. Socialist theory as applied in the Soviet Union and China failed in its own terms: it could not provide, in the long-term, a successful way to organize a large and complex economic system. The successes of socialism that remain in China continue to derive mainly from the individual and local initiatives, which flowed from land redistribution, and were sustained by a macroeconomic framework of effective minimum income laws and other economic protections for hundreds of millions of people.

The Collapse of Centralized Socialism in Eastern Europe and the Soviet Union

The manner in which the Soviet Union acquired control over Eastern Europe and the immense scale of violence under Stalin form the background to the disintegration of the Soviet-East European economy. Yet they are not sufficient explanations, for the level of violence decreased drastically after the death of Stalin and considerable increases in material production and consumption continued for about two decades after that.

There were a number of factors during these decades which laid the seeds for the collapse in the past few years. In narrow economic terms, the following factors appear to have been important:

- Excessive military expenditures since the Cuban missile crisis and the Soviet decision to achieve parity in nuclear weaponry with the U.S.

- The large proportion of scientific and technical personnel devoted to military research, development and production, without an external source of such personnel. (The U.S. had an external supply due to immigration.) On the contrary, emigration restrictions were put in place in the Soviet Union partly because of shortages of such personnel.

- Linkages to the international market on terms of trade which were for the most part relatively poor.

- Concentration on investment in heavy industry for export markets (as, for example, in Poland) when relative competitiveness of even lower-wage countries and capital mobility put exporters at a disadvantage, especially in recessionary times.

- Poor development of the service sector.

- Economic desires being driven by the conspicuous consumption in the capitalist countries, and also among the very officials of governments and political parties who while professing egalitarianism and socialist virtue went after "hard currency" and lusted for capitalist cars and VCRs.

- Poor quality of consumer and capital goods.

- A lack of connections in planning and production between consumers and producers.

The capitalist powers have long sought to put economic pressure upon socialist countries, in part by forcing the diversion of resources to military purposes. For instance, as journalist I. F. Stone noted at the time, the 1957 Gaither report to President Eisenhower:

> . . . envisages stepped-up economic warfare against the Soviets. . . . It calculates . . . that if the U.S. added about ten percent to its defense commitment in terms of gross product, "the Soviets would have to raise theirs by one-third and do so in a nation already on the meagrest

ration of consumer goods."[3]

In this strategy, the capitalist powers succeeded for the Soviets did not develop a response based on minimal deterrent force to counter this pressure. Especially after the Cuban missile crisis, they decided to devote all possible efforts to securing military and especially nuclear weapons parity.

Yet the serious problems of European socialist countries stemmed from broader mistakes in economic policy. Their present problems cannot be separated from the rapid integration of the European centralized socialist countries into the world economy in which capitalist countries have access to cheap labor and resources in a large number of places. For example, it is not without some significance that the most devastated country in Eastern Europe as the system collapsed was Rumania, which was the country most open to foreign capital, and to the capitalists' *rules* for doing things. Rumania was the first Warsaw Pact country to become a member of the International Monetary Fund in the 1970s.

From the start, those who founded socialism looked to capitalist Europe as the model for what the good society would look like—less labor time, more production, more "leisure" and limitless consumption. They were aware of imperialism and its oppression of the Third World, but they neither integrated that awareness into an operational theory which questioned the success of capitalism as a highly developed and productive system, nor did they develop criteria to judge their own accomplishments in that perspective. In capitalism, the ideology of limitless profits has gone hand in hand with the ideology of limitless consumption. While the former had no formal place in socialism, the latter became its declared goal: "We will bury you," Khruschev once loudly proclaimed to the U.S., referring mainly to the sphere of consumerism.

Today, the implementation of privatization is proceeding on the assumption that capitalism actually works according to what is perceived as the U.S. or West European reality of relative plenty—without taking account of the deprivation and gross inequities both within these countries and with their Third World victims.

---

3   I.F. Stone, "How John Foster Mitty Triumphed at Versailles," in Neil Middleton, ed., *The I.F. Stone Weekly Reader*, New York: Vintage Books, 1974, p. 69.

The move away from centralized socialism is also a product of its history of violent oppression. The human aspect of centralized socialism, in which even the beneficiaries at the local level were subjected to violence, was quite different from the situation in the capitalist countries in the last two centuries or so. In the capitalist countries, the gradual export of poverty and repression to the colonies made it possible for both political violence and fear to decrease as most workers saw material improvements in their lives. The political turmoil of centralized socialism today, as compared with the stability of the capitalist countries, stems in great measure from this difference in their economic and political dynamics. Yet it is notable that some of the political and bureaucratic control measures are very similar. In the capitalist system, the movement of people, especially among those of the Third World, is controlled by passports and visas. Similar internal visas exist in centralized socialism to control and monitor people's movements.

A further tragic failure of centralized socialism has been the wholesale destruction of the environment, of the health of large numbers of people, and thus of future productive capacity. This is especially clear in Eastern Europe and the Soviet Union, where water bodies have become poisoned chemical soups, where the air has been fouled, and where even the huge Aral Sea has partially dried up. The costs arising from the damage to human health, water, agricultural land and human settlements from the Chernobyl accident could far exceed the revenues from all the electricity generated from nuclear power plants in the Soviet Union. Yet it is a sign of the fixation of large-scale industrialism, which is common to both socialism and capitalism, that the official quest for more nuclear power continues in the Soviet Union and many other countries.

Centralized socialism has turned the mechanistic aspects of Marxist theory into even more mechanistic reality. The flowering of the individual human being in society was lost as a principal goal. It was not hard to turn "Marxism-Leninism" into a religion, with as many sects as there were parties, each of which proclaimed it had the ultimate correct interpretation of the scriptures. What was supposed to have been a scientific approach to the study of society became transformed into a set of constantly changing official rituals used to rationalize inequalities, violence and oppression and to create an entire system of lies in the name of progress and the security of the state.

So today, we have the strange reality that socialist countries themselves appear blind to their considerable economic achievements relative to capitalism. The worst excesses of poverty and misery were alleviated, without creating a system of foreign economic exploitation. That has been a considerable achievement, which capitalism cannot match. But the rulers of the socialist countries set up the goal of capitalist consumerism as the standard of achievement and failed to deliver. That is the economic standard by which their own people and others have been judging them.

Chapter 8

CAPITALISM AND SOCIALISM: A COMPARISON

Monetary comparisons tell us little about the real conditions in which people live. They omit so much of the reality about human well-being as to be useless. To compare properly the relative successes of capitalism and socialism, we must therefore look at other indicators.

One indicator of well-being that is not reflected by monetary calculations is the health of the environment. But since environmental problems are endemic to both capitalism and socialism, and since an evaluation of these problems would expand the scope of this book to unmanageable proportions, we have not attempted to use quantitative environmental criteria.

What we do consider is average life expectancies and infant mortality which give a rough idea of some of the end results of economic practice in human terms. This still does not address the important problem of differences between groups within countries or between the rich and the poor. For instance, within the Soviet Union, tribal people of the North have infant mortalities comparable to many Third World countries. But although inadequate in this respect, infant mortality is one of the best indicators of the economic situation of people within a country. Maternal mortality is another.

Data on life expectancy, infant mortality and the like are subject to some uncertainty. Many have looked closely at the available information in recent years. While the exact figures may be in some doubt, for the most part, order-of-magnitude figures as reported in recent compilations of statistics give a fair and consistent picture.[1]

For the following comparison, we have taken the figures for the industrialized capitalist countries, added to them the figures for the Third World and compared this composite to the statistics for the centralized socialist system. We feel justified in doing so since, as argued throughout this book, the well-being of the capitalist countries has been inextricably intertwined with exploitation of the Third World.

The period for this comparison hase been carefully chosen. Today, socialism does not exist as an economic system apart. A considerable portion of the Soviet-East European economy is now integrated with capitalism, and has been increasingly so since the late 1960s. China has been on the same course, but for a somewhat shorter time. Thus, we have chosen for comparison a time period when these countries could reasonably be said still to be distinct economic systems. Table 5 gives the comparative figures.

---

1   There is no question that life expectancy in the socialist countries is higher than in the Third World and infant mortality is much lower. The discussion of economic problems, shortages, poor health care and so on is generally in the context of a comparison with the industrialized capitalist countries which have only a minority of the total population living under capitalism. While the exact figures are in some question and there are severe pockets of deprivation and poverty affecting millions, there is no evidence that average levels of living as expressed in infant mortality and life expectancy are like the Third World, and all available evidence, statistical and anecdotal, is against such a picture—even in 1990, when economic conditions in Eastern Europe and the Soviet Union had deteriorated considerably.

Table 5
A COMPARISON OF CAPITALIST AND CENTRALIZED
SOCIALIST ECONOMIES, 1965 (1975 for China)

	Capitalist			Centralized Socialist	
	OECD	Third World	Total	East European*	China
Life Expectancy (in Years)	70	55	60	70	65?
Infant Mortality (Deaths per 1,000)	25	130	100	30	60?
Daily Supply of Food Calories per Person	3,100	2,100	2,400	3,200	2,200
Safe Water Supply (Percent of People)**	90	50?	65?	80-90?	N/A

*   Food production in the Soviet Union may have been lower than reported because of over-reporting to avoid penalties for falling behind Plan requirements. Similarly, infant mortality may have been 25 percent higher.
**   Safe water supply figures in most countries may not reflect presence of some toxic industrial chemicals.

All figures are approximate and rounded. N/A = not available.

Source: World Resources 1988-89, New York: Basic Books, 1988.

The economic situations of the centralized socialist countries at the time they broke away from the capitalist system were at least as dismal as those prevailing in the Third World today. Moreover, these countries were devastated by war. The Soviet Union had to face hostile attach by fourteen foreign powers, and then again devastation during World War II.

When one compares economic systems, it appears to be no contest: centralized socialism for all its lines and scarcities has had lower infant mortality and better living conditions than capitalism. Regarding Chinese statistics, one should take into account the fact that two-and-a-half decades was not a long time to have achieved so much, given the enormity of the country, the extent of the poverty and destruction, which prevailed in 1949, and the complexity of its problems (2,000 percent inflation and millions of drug addicts in 1949, for example).

In contrast, capitalism has been a failure as an economic system even in its own terms, when one considers the system as a whole and not just the situation in a few countries. Far from being a consumer's paradise, the vast majority of people in capitalist economies, most of whom live in the Third World, are poor. The twelve million children, who die needlessly every year, die mainly within the capitalist economic system—that portion of it which, in Johan Galtung's words, capitalism uses "as a place to fetch or use nature and dump pollutants; as a place to use cheap labor and dump excess labor from back home (a major function of colonialism); as a place . . . to carry out research projects that could not be done at home. . . ."[2]

On the basis of infant mortality, life expectancy, food supply and safe water the "winner" between capitalism and socialism seems clear—socialism. Yet the general consensus from Deng to Gorbachev to Fukuyama is quite the contrary. The difference between the assessment that we have made and the prevailing view is that the latter is based on the desires of individuals to duplicate just one part of the capitalist system that is located in the capitalist countries—the rich part. "You only live once," as one East German going to the West put it. That was an expression of an individual's hopes based on the peculiar position of East Germans in the world today. Such hopes and desires are not based upon a recognition of the reality of the capitalist system as a whole. In their rush westward, East Germans saw the dollars and Disneyland of capitalism, and even the bananas in the markets of West Berlin, but not the devastation and the debts in the places where the bananas are grown.

Neither centralized socialism nor capitalism provides the framework for a workable and sustainable economic system. In socialism, the positive effects of redistribution are evident. Yet the failure to tap individual initiative and creativity to provide the quality and variety of goods, which people seem to want, and to do that within a political system, which resists ossification and authoritarianism, were

2   Johan Galtung, "Towards a New Economics: On the Theory and Practice of Self-Reliance," in Paul Ekins, ed., *The Living Economy*, London: Routledge & Kegan Paul, 1986, p. 100.

basic failures. In addition has been the problem of the severe damage to the environment. Freedom, plenty and equality were what socialism promised. It has not delivered, despite considerable success in alleviating most of the worst problems of poverty.

Inventiveness and Initiative

In capitalism, the inventiveness and individual energy that accompanies the prospect of profit have contributed to considerable innovation and to the translation of innovation into mass production and marketing. We have an immense array of technologies and technical knowledge, some of it terrible, some relatively neutral and dependent on context and some beneficial—necessary to understand the Earth and help restore it to health.

It is important to note that, while capitalism has been able to translate innovation into mass production and marketing, inventiveness is not only motivated by greed or profit. First, there have been considerable innovations in the Soviet Union. Sputnik was, after all, a Soviet accomplishment. Even in non-military areas, there have been advances in socialism that are noteworthy. The intensification of the use of traditional systems of organic fertilizers was an accomplishment of Chinese rural development. There have been remarkable advances in orthopedics in the Soviet Union, and also considerable theoretical accomplishments in science. Overall, however, the combination of a focus on military production and a lack of feedback from consumers has resulted in poor-quality consumer goods and a high level of dissatisfaction among the people of socialist countries. Many problems have intensified as socialist countries try to copy the capitalist countries, and as they try to integrate themselves into the capitalist system.

Even within the capitalist system, much accomplishment, innovation and initiative is linked to satisfaction in one's work and other social factors, rather than to the prospect of immense profits. In fact, most large corporations are huge bureaucracies with great inefficiencies; many have a hard time innovating.

Furthermore, the greatest accomplishments of human inventiveness and creativity were not motivated by profit. The scientific work of Einstein or Ampere or Raman was not motivated by patents and profits. Schubert and Mozart wrote musical pieces of genius that did not provide enough funds even to keep them out of poverty. Van Gogh painted prolifically, although he failed to sell his works. Money has a role in initiative, creativity and inventiveness, but it has been much exaggerated by capitalist ideologues.

Alas, much of the inventiveness in capitalism is directed toward perverse ends, such as the subversion of consumer taste, for example, through advertising. To take the one alluring photograph of a hamburger that appears in an advertisement, hundreds of hamburgers are thrown away. The apples in the supermarket might be mealy and tasteless, but they must all be waxed, shiny and ruby red. Pictures extolling strength and pristine nature, often with sexual suggestions, are used to peddle cigarettes which sap strength, cause cancer and maim fetuses in their mothers' wombs. Much of the creativity and artistry driven by money and profit is devoted to such activities. Indeed, huge portions of the economic system have been subverted in this way.

An outstanding example is the car-oriented transportation system in the U.S. Early in this century, General Motors, Firestone and Standard Oil colluded to economically destroy public transportation, especially non-petroleum-based public transit, replacing it with cars. The result has been the creation of a system in which the car is virtually required for everyday life in many parts of the country. Moreover, through advertising and promotion, cars have been transformed from a potentially reasonable means of conveyance, in many situations, to status and sex symbols that have a quite unreasonable hold on modern human desire.

Indeed, the individualistic system of monetized activity dedicated to profit promotes greed and indifference to human values in the marketplace. How such greed is to be isolated from the general culture and values of society has remained a considerable mystery which the ideologues of the pure "free market" have not explained. When savings and loan banks in the U.S. (historically focused on financing residential housing) were deregulated under Reagan, there was so much high-living, corruption and fraud in the management of these banks that hundreds became bankrupt. They are being bailed out by the taxpayers of the country at phenomenal expense.

A fitting capitalist counterpart to Ceascescu's daughter's alleged gold-plate dining was the Texas banker's dinner party, mentioned earlier, at which lion steaks were served to guests with depositors' money.

Summation

We can now evaluate Heilbroner's proclamation, "capitalism has won," because it has organized "the material affairs of humankind more satisfactorily than socialism." The facts and analysis presented here point to a conclusion different from the one arrived at by Heilbroner. For all its internal faults and violence and repression, and despite all the violence and economic pressure to which it has been subjected by the capitalist powers, even bureaucratic socialism has been able to provide for the material needs of its people better than capitalism. That the opposite conclusion is common today shows only the extent to which the awful economic reality afflicting the people of the Third World, who are the majority of people in the capitalist economic system, has been ignored.

Just as environmental destruction was for a long time ignored because it had no immediate monetized cost, those who work for low wages, who are unemployed and who work for no wages at all have been ignored. And like environmental costs, human costs often show up later. They can persist for a long time afterwards, and affect quite different people from the ones that benefit from the monetized activity in question.

Consider Bangladesh, often contemptuously referred to as a "basket case" in economic terms. Today, 90 percent of its workers are in agriculture or unemployed. But it was once the center of the finest textile manufactures in the world, in some ways the model for Lancashire. A third of its people were employed in non-agricultural occupations. Conquest by the British resulted in systematic expropriation, followed by a terrible famine in 1771. Bangladesh became useless to capitalism, once its manufacturing was destroyed and replaced by machines in other parts of the world, under the protection of British guns, taxes and tariffs.

This pattern of oppression has been perpetuated, apart from a few years of evanescent promise, under the Bangladeshi elite. Bangladesh is of little economic consequence in the world economy, producing little that is "strategic." It is of marginal significance in the world of "hard currency". Yet almost a thousand children die every day in Bangladesh from the sicknesses that poverty brings. This is a direct result of the history of exploitation and destruction which the capitalist economic system has inflicted upon the country.

In essential ways, the sicknesses from which so many children in the Third World are dying today are no different from the cancers and other diseases that are produced by the deadly accidents and emissions from the toxic dumps of long-abandoned factories. At the Bhopals and Love Canals of the world, people suffer economic privations and illnesses long after those who benefited from the economic activity have left the area for profits elsewhere. But Union Carbide of Bhopal fame and Occidental Petroleum, owner of Hooker Chemical Company which poisoned peoples' homes at Love Canal, are still making deals and profits.

The fact that the present economic calculus ignores the needless deaths of five hundred million children since World War II demonstrates that the capitalist system treats these children and the many others who have been terribly wounded as dispensable or irrelevant. That cannot diminish the horror of the reality, or the moral bankruptcy of the economic practice.

Just as it is narrow and fundamentally wrong to see environmental destruction merely as an "externality," which is incidental to the operation of a well-functioning market system, it is also wrong to see marginalization, suffering and unemployment and, indeed, hopelessness for huge numbers of people as mere "externalities" to a system that otherwise functions well.

Capitalism has separated its short-term beneficiaries from its victims both geographically and culturally through the institutionalization of oppressor nationalism and racism in a manner similar to apartheid. In socialism, the violence that accompanied large-scale industrialization was internal to the socialist countries. In capitalism, this has only been partly true. Over the last two centuries, violence in the capitalist countries has been more and more confined to wars of immense and ever-more destructive scale fought under the banner of nationalism. Routine violence has been largely exported to the Third World as have the smaller wars. Not that the Third World was free of violence before subjugation to capitalism. Capitalism was superimposed upon the oppressive systems which already prevailed in most places. These were transformed to suit the purpose of the extraction of profit.

The systematic destruction of the environment and the gross inequities and violence that prevail in the world today are the main indicators of the need for worldwide restructuring of economic life. If we look at the distribution of the consumption of resources between countries, we see that 20 percent of the world's people consume about 80 percent of the world's (monetized) resources, such as minerals, fossil fuels and diverse consumer goods, while 80 percent of the world's people consume only 20 percent of the (monetized) resources.

However, if we look closely at the Third World where 20 percent of the resources are consumed, we find that a similar pattern is repeated inside those countries. That is, within the Third World, 80 percent of the people get only about 20 percent of resources.[3] Thus, when we take national as well as class differences into account, we find that about one-third of the world's people consume 96 percent of the resources, and two-thirds of the world's people consume only 4 percent. Looked at in this way, we see that resource consumption problems and concomitant environmental destruction are being created primarily by a minority of the people, who then loudly proclaim that there are too many poor who are destroying the environment.

Both Soviet and capitalist industrialization have been violent in their own ways.[4] Both capitalism and centralized socialism have also been destructive of the environment—the very basis of biological existence. Both economic systems have have very violent histories. They have systematically ignored or downplayed the role of the family in economic life, even though the family is the focus of an immense amount of work activity and is, generally, one of the principal bases of our individual identities and social roles and hence our existence as human beings. Both systems have contributed to global environmental problems, such as the accumulation of greenhouse gases and huge quantities of toxic and nuclear wastes. But a geographical difference is evident. In socialism, most environmental destruction has happened within the socialist countries. In capitalism, much of it has been exported to the Third World.

Centralized socialism in Eastern Europe and the Soviet Union has collapsed, in part due to the people's rejection of its repressive and violent aspects, and in part based on economic hopes shaped by perceptions of the success of capitalism. Yet the accomplishments of capitalism have been far smaller and less impressive than is generally believed, because the non-monetized human and environmental costs have not yet been taken into account.

No system in which the economic and environmental failures have been as huge as those of global capitalism can be regarded as a reason-

---

3   These are order-of-magnitude figures. In some Third World countries, resource consumption figures may be even more skewed, while in others it may be less so.

4   The revolutions in peasant societies like China have had a somewhat different history of industrialization, which needs to be separately evaluated.

ably functional one which can be fixed with tinkering and technological change. Capitalism needs restructuring on a worldwide basis even as centralized socialism needed it in Eastern Europe and the Soviet Union. Moreover, the framework for the restructuring in the socialist countries needs to be changed in light of a more realistic assessment of capitalism.

We do not have an economic system which assures a decent existence for this generation with some equity and justice, which is compatible with human freedom, dignity and the protection of the environment, and which functions responsibly toward future generations. We must create one.

PART II

ECONOMIC JUSTICE AND A PEACE SYSTEM

With one hand we must resist the old; with the other we must create the new.

—Randy Kehler's rendering of
the Dutch Kabouter's "Policy
of Two Hands."

Chapter 9

PRELIMINARY CONSIDERATIONS

The violence, greed and exploitation characterizing capitalism, the violence and authoritarianism characterizing socialism and the environmental destruction characterizing them both have made people all over the world search for a "third way" between capitalism and socialism. These efforts have provided much inspiration, many successes at the local level and many failures rich in lessons.

We need to learn from the experience of socialism. How can we redistribute wealth and income in a way that creates positive economic impetus by alleviating poverty, stimulating savings and producting essential goods so as to provide a positive direction toward global economic justice?

We need also to learn from capitalism. How can the positive aspects of individual ownership as well as political democracy, which exist in the capitalist countries, be incorporated into a more vigorous and universal democracy that includes economic aspects, extends from the global to the local and also can be free of the corruption to which multi-party electoral systems are prone?

We need to complement electoral systems with more direct aspects of grassroots democracy and to integrate these with economic democracy. We have to learn how to disentangle redistribution from the creation of an authoritarian political and economic machinery, and political democracy from imperialism and oppressor nationalism.

Providing a comprehensive picture of a peace system is an immense and, in certain respects, impossible task, given our murky perspective from within the prevailing war system. The following is only a partial exploration of some principles and some practical steps toward creating a peace system economy.

The focus of the discussion here is on the transformation of capitalist institutions and practices, which dominate the global economy, for the same reasons that our analysis of the war system centered on them also. In such institutions and practices lie the keys to the war system and the keys to replacing it with a non-violent system of economic justice and environmental sustainability. These institutions and practices now dominate most of the world, and their reach is growing. The Soviet and East European economies are rapidly becoming fully integrated into the global capitalist structure, and to a considerable extent this is also true of China.

Four interlinked features of the war system stand out in our analysis of its economic dimensions:

1.   The nexus between governments (including their militaries) and large corporations (including banks) is perhaps the single most important structural element of the war system.

2.   The structure of consumption, mobility, politics and wages in the global economy has essential features which resemble the operation of apartheid in South Africa. In effect, the structure of the global political economy is that of global apartheid. Global apartheid includes systematic economic denial and discrimination. One essential aspect is the marginalization of hundreds of millions of people who play no significant role in the operation of the global economy, although that economy shapes in many ways the nature of their existence. Large numbers of marginalized people exist in capitalist as well as Third World countries.

3.   The exclusion of unpaid labor from the economic calculus, especially that of women, results in a distortion of economic structure away from the work which is essential to sustaining life.

4. Environmental destruction from the local to the global has been an integral part of both the capitalist and socialist economic systems. It arises in large measure from the pursuit of short-term ends, such as profit and material consumption at the expense of the Earth and of future generations. In other words, today we largely exclude environmental impacts from the economic calculus.

The high level of violence, poverty and inequality in the world today may change form and location, but it will persist so long as we do not have a fundamental restructuring in each of these areas. The scope of our vision, our concerns and our actions must extend from the local to the global. The economy that we live in is global, and the central institutions which dominate it—multinational corporations and banks—are also global. Therefore, no vision which covers a single country can begin to address the questions of economic justice and environmental sustainability.

Three basic kinds of questions arise when we attempt to envision an economic system based on peace:

1. What principles should underlie this economic system?

2. What economic institutions should characterize it?

3. What means and instruments of change will enable a transformation of the present economic structure to a more just and environmentally sound one? In other words, how do we get from here to there despite the fact that immense forces exist to maintain the present order of things? And what actions can individuals and communities take to help create that new order?

One may ask the last question in a somewhat different way: the present order provides considerable short-term benefits to the one-third of the population that consumes over 90 percent of the resources. This minority has a stake in the present economic and military system. Why should it give up those benefits? What does it stand to gain?

A part of the answer can be seen in the drama being played out in South Africa since the late 1980s. The conflicts which the system of horrendous inequalities engendered are so intractable and have resulted in so much violence that they made the system untenable even for the privileged minority. It is crumbling in the face of the long struggle of the people it has oppressed. In that struggle, the solidarity of large numbers of people who do not directly suffer from apartheid has been crucial.

Fukuyama may think the end of history is here. But the immense numbers of dispossessed and disinherited have only just begun writing it. The struggles for political independence of a few decades ago are now moving toward struggles for a system of economic justice and environmental sanity.

A great vulnerability of the war system stems from what it demands of those who derive material benefits from it: that they be ready to give up everything and go to war in an instant and, indeed, be ready for a nuclear holocaust. Two world wars and many ones of lesser scale, but of equally intense horror, have been waged in this century alone. Many people all over the world already find that the human costs of maintaining a war system are unacceptable, and many are already organizing against it. They have found the exchange of some strontium-90 in babies' teeth, nuclear wastes littering the countryside and the threat of instant annihilation to be an unacceptable price to pay for present comforts.

There are other factors which make the war system unattractive within the capitalist countries as well as among the Third World elite. Some of these factors relate to the fact that material benefits from the present system are not uniformly distributed among the privileged minority. Within that one-third of the world's population, which consumes almost all the world's resources, there are basic problems which cannot be addressed without steps to improve the plight of the poor all over the world.

Take the problems of drugs and the immense violence in the inner cities of the U.S., now spreading to Europe. Coca leaves are grown in Peru and Bolivia, countries devastated by the debt crisis. The poor of these countries did not create the debt crisis, yet they are suffering its effects. One way for them to overcome at least some of the economic losses they have experienced has been to grow coca. Peru and Bolivia have come to depend on the sales of coca paste and cocaine for foreign exchange (some of which is used to pay off their foreign debts). The drug "war" in the United States is unlikely to be won without taking action *both* to improve conditions for the poor in the United States and to relieve the economic crisis in the producing countries in the Third World.

Similarly, the problems of wages and jobs in Third World and capitalist countries are closely related. Corporations seek cheap, productive labor in the Third World to reflect relative productivity, but workers in capitalist countries want job security and decent wages. This is one reason that wages, discounted for inflation, have not increased in the U.S. since 1973. Indeed, the purchasing power of wages for a substantial proportion of workers has actually fallen. The immense differences of wages between countries *unrelated to differences of labor productivity* exercise a downward pull on wages. Thus, so long as wages do not rise in the Third World, to reflect relative productivity, workers in the capitalist countries are affected adversely. Many workers in capitalist countries are realizing this, and they are beginning to create pressure for a change in the current system.

Other pressures on the current world system are based in the many hidden environmental and financial costs imposed, the impacts of which have yet to be fully realized. For example, the human cost of cheap goods that are made in the Third World is very high. Elites must make substantial military expenditures both in the Third World and capitalist countries, the end of the Cold War notwithstanding, to maintain the exploitative order. Moreover, the military apparatus within the Third World and in the capitalist countries often act in concert.

There are also many environmental, economic and political costs. Under the guise of national security, weapons production, including nuclear weapons production, has poisoned the land, air and water; entire branches of government such as the Department of Energy in the U.S. (which is responsible for nuclear weapons production), have routinely broken laws, cheated and covered up, and created an immense economic burden for the present and future generations in the form of liabilities and "clean-up" costs.

Other hidden environmental costs stem from the nature of the goods produced in the Third World. Goods manufactured as cheaply as possible are cheaper to throw away than to repair, since the relative wages for repair are far higher. This not only affects the workers who are exploited. Communities in all capitalist countries are awakening to the fact that the conveniences of high-resource consumption wind up in the local landfill, threatening their environment.

Then, it is becoming increasingly clear that some kinds of economic activities—no matter where they are located—can affect the entire world adversely. The vast global environmental crisis affects even the children of the ruling classes themselves. Not even the captains of industry can escape the need for an intact ozone layer to protect them from deadly ultraviolet radiation. They have now agreed to a phase-out of ozone-depleting chlorofluorocarbons (CFCs), although not as rapidly as they could. With the threat of climate change, the benefits to people all over the world of adopting more environmentally sound approaches to production and consumption is becoming clearer to large numbers of people in the capitalist countries. In general, it is becoming increasingly difficult for the capitalist countries to separate themselves from the environmental costs they have been imposing on the Third World for centuries.

The war system imposes human, environmental and financial costs on everyone in the world. The reality of the world today is that those who have paid the most, those who have been pushed to the margin are struggling to break free. In the short term, their demands are in some conflict with those who are consuming most of the world's resources. But there is also considerable common ground between them. There is an urgent need to expand that common ground if we are to begin to heal the wounds of permanent war among people and between people and the Earth. That need is being more and more widely recognized. From the conflicts and tensions of the war system are emerging the forces and coalitions which are demanding fundamental change in the way that the military and economic arrangements of the world are presently structured.

Chapter 10

SOME ELEMENTS OF ECONOMIC DEMOCRACY

A true peace system will require a fundamental restructuring of power between the institutions and individuals that now hold much of the world's wealth and make most economic decisions—banks, corporations and other beneficiaries of the capitalist system—and those who supply most of the wealth—workers, farmers, women and communities. The extraction of profits and wealth from the labor of others and from the Earth, without representation of workers and communities and without consideration for future generations, are two of the most glaring anti-democratic aspects of capitalism. The grave inequalities of financial power and the disconnection of the humanity of those who produce from those who consume must find systematic remedy within a peace system if it is to be robust and survive the tensions and conflicts which will continue to exist.

The idea that "taxation without representation" is undemocratic has been a long-held principle which has joined economic ideas to political ones. It inspired the U.S. revolt against British rule. But the immense scale of economic deprivation in the world today is indicative of a much greater failure of representation from the local to the global. We do not have economic democracy which would be characterized by control of their economic future by individuals and communities in a manner that does not jeopardize the control of others or of future generations.

Widespread starvation in the midst of plenty, uncompensated unemployment and the flouting of the even modest standards of worker safety and environmental responsibility are not only economic problems for the present. The total discounting of non-monetized work, which is largely the work of women, is a major political as well as an economic problem. These inequalities are indicators of an undemocratic economic system in which the economically weak have no representation in the marketplace. That economic weakness translates into political weakness and often into effective deprivation of political representation. This is especially true when there is the daily presence of violence and the threat of violence in people's lives. In practice, poverty and severe economic inequality translate into a lack of political freedom.

Thus, economic justice in the redistributive sense, as well as economic democracy in the sense of accountability and effective control of people over the basic economic institutions of society, are necessary aspects of a peace system. Economic democracy and redistribution are needed at all levels, from the family and the community, to countries and the entire global economic system.

Redistribution in favor of the poor has often been regarded as inimical to economic incentive, while redistribution in favor of the rich has been regarded in recent years as favoring "growth" and hence prosperity—the rising tide that will lift all boats. These have been the principal tenets of Reaganomics and the massive redistribution in favor of the rich that has occurred in the U.S. during the 1980s. Through U.S. government leverage in international financial institutions, such as the IMF and the World Bank, these ideas have been adopted by or forced upon a number of countries. The general result in the U.S. has been that the rich have grown richer and the poor poorer. That reality has been reproduced on a global scale.

Our analysis indicates that individual incentive and redistribution in favor of the poor can be compatible. Redistribution of land in China provided the main incentive which led peasants to greater economic effort. Not only was it the leading edge of the abolition of the worst aspects of poverty in China; it was in the context of redistributive justice that drug addiction and many other social ills were abolished within a few years after the revolution.

The failure of socialist revolutions to cultivate incentives systematically does not represent a failure of redistribution, but the squelching of local initiative by the centralized socialist state and the absence of democratic political processes. The most extreme expression of these aspects of centralized socialism was the forced collectivization and mass purges during the Stalinist period in the Soviet Union from 1929 to 1953.

Redistribution in the economic sphere is not only a redistribution of income, as, for example, through progressive taxation. Just as fundamental is the redistribution of control. Land redistribution created a modicum of local control. The Japanese method of management gives some control to workers on the factory floor. Control, responsibility and accountability are all critical elements of economic democracy which require a redistribution of economic power in favor of communities, workers, families and individuals.

Redistribution and economic incentive can be combined and must be combined. What incentive is there for people who make 50 cents a day to excel and innovate? Where are the incentives for peasants whose labor is appropriated by landlords and moneylenders and corrupt government officials to invest and increase production? How can people with no hope of any employment, let alone meaningful employment at a decent wage, be creative? A large part of the problem of the global economy and the lack of initiative in it stems from the fact that there are hundreds of millions of people without any realistic hope of economic security or well-being.

The enormous energy of people to create and innovate can only be brought to bear systematically on solving economic problems if there is distributional equity and the recognition of the humanity of all within the context of the practical operation of the economic system.

Redistribution does not mean absolute equality or the abolishing of riches. It means limiting riches and abolishing poverty. The example of the state of Kerala in India discussed below shows that a strong commitment to redistribution can enhance both political democracy and improve the human economic condition immensely with very modest resources.

Some aspects of economic justice and democracy are:

1. The establishment of democratic control over corporations and other economic institutions.

2. Restructuring of the international monetary system, one of the principal vehicles of global capitalist exploitation today.

3. The establishment of ways to phase out economic activities which are endangering the Earth.

4. Land redistribution in the rural Third World.

5. Guaranteed employment at decent wages to all who want to work. The late Indian agricultural economist, Raj Krishna, used to say that if property as a source of income is protected by government, then labor as a source of income must also be protected. At a minimum, that protection implies guaranteed employment at minimum wages set to produce above-poverty-level income for full-time work.

6. The integration of non-monetized work into the economic calculus in diverse ways and the accompanying empowerment of women in the economic system.

7. The establishment of democratic control over markets from local to global to enable socially just and environmentally sound economic systems to be compatible with individual and local initiative.

Governments and Markets

The idea of a "free market," where economic transactions between sellers and buyers occur outside government control or "interference," is a part of the hoary mythology of capitalism. None would claim that such a market ever existed, but it is posited as the ultimately desirable state of affairs for an efficiently functioning economic system.

We have seen that the role of capitalist country governments has been central to the evolution of global capitalism. Today, their military power, together with that of Third World governments, protects the property of the rich against the poor. As we have noted, one aspect of the "invisible hand" of the capitalist market consists of the military power of the capitalist state.

Further, governments create money and operate the monetary system, without which there could be no complex transactions and no system of extraction of profit which is central to capitalism. The savings and loan banks in the U.S., where private corruption and greed as well as a rigid commitment to deregulation joined economic circumstances to produce massive bank failures, were bailed out by the power of government to tax the people to shore up the monetary systems. Indeed, the extent to which the money of any government circulates and commands purchasing power is one measure of the reach of that government's economic "sovereignty." It is in that sense that we can clearly see the operation of monetary imperialism today dominated by the dollar, increasingly complemented by Japanese yen and some European currencies, notably the German mark. (These may soon be joined by the "ecu," the common currency of the economic union of Western European countries.) While the reach of these currencies is global, Third World currencies only circulate locally. Some countries, like Liberia, have no currency of their own at all.

Markets as places where privately created money was used to exchange privately protected property may have characterized many feudal situations more than modern capitalism. The Bank of England was created at the end of the seventeenth century by merchants as a vehicle for making a loan to the king. It went on to become an economic foundation stone of the British government and provided the monetary basis for global capitalism dominated by British imperialism in the nineteenth century.

Governments also constitute an immense market for the purchase of goods and services, and are a major factor in determining the shape of the market. Even in the United States, where the government's role is smaller than in many other countries, federal, state and local governments account for about 20 percent of the purchases of goods and services.

Governments also own vast natural resources, including a great deal of land, large portions of the oceans off their coasts and the resources under the sea. Through the control of these resources (and royalties), they also control the conditions of production and prices of essential commodities, such as oil, agricultural goods and timber.

The conservative arguments about "free markets" usually come to a quick end when one suggests that governments stop printing money, protecting property, guaranteeing bank accounts and purchasing large quantities of privately produced goods with money obtained by taxation of the people.

The underlying argument about markets and governments is not about whether government should have a role in the economic system, but rather about what that role should be and whose interests governments should defend, and with what priorities. The current and traditional orientation of capitalist governments has generally been to support institutions, such as large corporations, which the elite and wealthy require to extract profit and control the system, while making concessions to other sections of society only when such actions do not jeopardize control of the existing system or when they are compelled to act by popular political pressure.

After all, traditional markets are institutions where money is the vehicle of economic information, conveying the desires of those who have it to those who would meet those desires. Large institutions and the rich have the decisive advantage there. Even in this sphere, private parties rely on a government-run judiciary to settle contractual and other disputes. Further, the modern marketplace has been perverted by corporations spending large amounts of money to stimulate human desires, and to market huge quantities of armaments on an unprecedented scale.

The debate about the role of government in the marketplace is therefore not one about governmental "interference" in private affairs, but about how meeting the needs and serving the economic interests of people around the world can be harmonized with those of future generations. These must become the central goals of both governmental and non-governmental economic institutions in a peace system.

Restructuring the Large Corporation

The structure of the large corporation enables it to use and manipulate resources around the world, at the same time avoiding systematic accountability to the communities in which it operates. The corporation can open a factory, make a loan, shut down a mine or move to another community or country with hardly any restraint commensurate with the effects of such actions on workers and communities. As Charles Lindblom has observed:

> It has been a curious feature of democratic thought that it has not faced up to the private corporation as a peculiar organization in an ostensible democracy. Enormously large, rich in resources, the big corporations command more resources than do most government units. They can also, over a broad range, insist that governments meet their demands, even if these demands run counter to those of citizens . . . and they exercise unusual veto powers. . . . The large private

corporation fits oddly into democratic theory and practice. Indeed, it does not fit.[1]

One reason that democratic thought has not faced up to this problem is that it has operated on the narrow compass of single countries, while large corporations have ranged the world. Further, there is a great deal of confusion in democratic thought in the context of capitalism between the notion of "freedom," as it applies to economics and to politics. In economics, "liberal" thought has stood for the right of owners of property, and hence also of corporations, to make profits in any manner they see fit (even though their property is protected by governmental military power). In political theory, freedom has connoted a democratic system in which just laws establish the rights of people with respect to governments. But nowhere are the rights of people established with respect to large corporations, which are today the main determinants of economic reality.[2]

One of the principal requirements of movement toward a peace system is that democratic control over corporations by communities, including workers, must be established. Indeed, we must question the basis on which the corporation has been granted the legitimacy from which to dominate the global economic system. In many respects, the corporation has the legal status of a human being, but it cannot be sent to jail. When it goes out of business, many of the wealthiest personnel, such as chief executive officers, often become richer by getting fat fees from the corporate carcass; at the same time, workers and communities become more destitute.

All too often, taxpayers bear the burden of cleaning up the mess. This is a large area in which there is de facto taxation without representation. It is a standing assault upon political democracy. The several hundred billion dollar savings-and-loan banking crisis and taxpayer bail-out in the U.S. is perhaps the biggest example of this kind, showing at once the undemocratic nature of the corporation and the extent to which the electoral political system has become beholden to that undemocratic institution. The crisis was caused in large measure by the

---

1   Charles Lindblom, as quoted by Gar Alperowitz and Jeff Faux, *Rebuilding America—A Blueprint for the New Economy*, New York: Pantheon Books, 1984, p. 239.
2   This thesis is further developed in David Dembo, Ward Morehouse and Lucinda Wykle, *Abuse of Power: Social Performance of Multinational Corporations*, New York: New Horizons Press, 1990.

unelected executives of savings and loan banks. But since it threatened the financial system with collapse, the political system is forced to pour in hundreds of billions of dollars of tax money to pay for the cost of poor decisions made in the pursuit of private profit.

Further, corporations are not only undemocratic institutions within the context of the economies of countries. On a global scale, there is not even a minimum system of laws or accountability by which the most egregious practices can be stopped or regulated. The accident in Bhopal, India, at Union Carbide's pesticide production plant resulted in thousands of deaths and caused tens of thousands of injuries. Yet, in this worst industrial accident in history, there was no system by which the victims could bring Union Carbide to justice, nor any arrangements for adequate interim relief from the corporation of the disaster to alleviate the suffering of the victims as the tortuous legal process wore on.

It will not be easy to bring accountability to the corporation or to create economic institutions which will enable the democratization of the global economy. Democratic control of corporations by communities and workers raises a number of difficult practical and conceptual issues. There is the problem of the prerogatives of people versus those of property: what rights should property holders have? Another practical problem relates to the global power of large corporations which makes it difficult, if not impossible, for communities to exercise effective control over corporations under the present international order. A third issue relates to the tensions between communities and workers. Large corporations operate in hundreds of communities, and the interests of workers are often tied up more with the corporate entity than with the specific community in which they may live and work.

This raises a corollary problem of the conflicts between the short-term and long-term interests of communities. The short-term need for jobs and investment, which corporations today use to their own benefit and to further their control and profits, often overwhelms long-term considerations such as environmental protection or economic security. Yet another problem is that of the tension between consumers on the one hand and workers and communities, where production takes place, on the other, in terms of the price of products and the economic and environmental conditions of their production.

Many of these conflicts stem from the vast scale of the operations of large corporations. There are many aspects to this vast scale: financial, geographical, varieties of production, scale of production, quantities produced and the reach of sales and markets. This makes for a vast disparity of power between large corporations and communities. In the context of small communities with high unemployment and poverty, corporate power is generally overwhelming. Other problems are not those of scale but of the manner of control and decision-making as it relates to communities, workers, consumers and the environment. Nonetheless, like large political units, large economic units can also be made subject to democratic control.

Mobility of Capital and of People

In capitalist theory, the mobility of capital and goods is supposed to be sufficient to equalize wages among countries so that the mobility of people has not been regarded as essential or even particularly relevant. The reality is devastatingly different. Over the past two centuries, and especially during this century, wage differences between capitalist and Third World countries have become immense. This disparity has been institutionalized by the militarized boundaries between capitalist and Third World countries.

For example, the U.S.-Canadian border is relatively secure, non-militarized and open. In contrast, the U.S.-Mexican border is a highly militarized one which separates a high income area from a low-income area, a high-wage area from a low-wage area and a relatively low unemployment area from a relatively high-unemployment area. Goods and capital are very mobile between all three countries, but people cannot easily move from Mexico to the U.S. or Canada. The U.S.-Mexican border is insecure despite being heavily militiarized because of the immense disparities in incomes and wages between the U.S. and Mexico.[3]

The U.S.-Mexican border makes communities on *both* sides more insecure. Workers in the United States suffer when corporations close up shop and leave for Mexico's lower wages and more lax environmental regulations. At the same time, Mexican workers suffer because they are paid low wages and frequently work under very unsafe conditions. Such injustice and inequality creates pressures among people in Mexico to emigrate to the United States, often under ghastly and inhuman conditions, in order to try to increase their wages and family incomes.

Global corporations insist that the boundaries of countries should be porous to goods and capital. Take, for example, the sentiments of a

---

3   Juliet Schor, "The Boundaries of Economic Systems." Paper prepared for the Exploratory Project on the Conditions of Peace, Washington, D.C., June 1990.

former chairman of IBM, Jacques Maisonrouge:

> For business purposes the boundaries that separate one nation from another are no more real than the equator. They are merely convenient demarcations of ethnic, linguistic and cultural entities. They do not define business requirements or consumer trends. Once management understands and accepts this world economy, its view of the marketplace and its planning necessarily expand. The world outside the home country is no longer viewed as a series of disconnected customers and prospects for its products, but as an extension of a single market.[4]

To corporations trying to market and produce globally with the lowest cost and the highest profit, ethnic, linguistic and cultural matters are insignificant. To real people, they are often among the most important ways they define themselves and their lives. Besides the economic costs involved in moving, people find it much more difficult to move and leave their communities than corporations do. For corporations, moving is sometimes simply a matter of transferring electronic blips in bank accounts.

Democratic control by communities and workers over corporations requires the establishment of some limitations on the mobility of capital, at least until an equivalent mobility of people is established. These limitations need not take the form of outright and total prohibitions. That would probably be undesirable. However, a minimum of accountability and responsibility should be built into the operation of any corporation in any community. The level and scale of that accountability should correspond to the scale and diversity of a corporation's activities. In addition, specific policies are needed to curb capital mobility.

Some of the policies necessary to bring a measure of accountability and responsibility to the operations of multinational corporations could be as follows:

- Full disclosure by corporations of information about *all* their operations in *each* community where they operate. This would include information about wage levels, working conditions, worker health and safety, past record of plant closures, nature of goods being manufactured (in the case of manufacturing companies) and any known adverse health and environmental effects.

---

4   Jacques Maisonrouge, quoted by Richard J. Barnet and Ronald E. Muller, *Global Reach*, New York: Simon & Schuster, 1974, pp. 14-15.

- Liability for the accuracy and completeness of the information disclosed.

- Personal criminal liability on the part of top management for certain crimes committed by the corporation.[5]

- Freedom of speech for workers in regard to health, safety, environmental and financial accountability issues—including the right of workers to address these issues publicly without threat of losing their jobs.

- Obligation to conduct a reasonable amount of research to estimate health and environmental effects of their products prior to initiating sales and liability for failure to do so.

- Establishment of minimum uniform rules of safety for products, processes and of worker safety and health, as well as global liability for failure to obey these rules.

- Taxation of stock sales in order to discourage short-term speculation, without discouraging long-term ability to raise capital for productive purposes.

- Minimum wage standards which take into account both local and global purchasing power of the wage.

- Provision of capital for front-end investments in roads, schools, sewer systems, etc. which communities must make when large corporations move in.

- Payment of costs of dislocation in terms of unemployment, lower home values, job retraining and other costs when major employers close down operations. A contingency fund for this purpose—a sort of severance fund for communities—could be set up when a corporation starts operations as a condition of allowing investment.

---

5 For an example of how this might relate to environmental crimes, see Makhijani, et al., *Energy Sector Transitional Corporations and the Global Environment,* Takoma Park, MD: Institute for Energy and Environmental Research, 1990.

- Complete financial disclosure.

- Global freedom of information rules for global corporations (similar to the Freedom of Information Act which allows people in the U.S. to get information from the U.S. government).

- Use of the best available technology worldwide for protection of environment, health and safety.

- Contribution to interim relief funds for victims of accidents and environmental clean-up after accidents based on *common standards* for all the countries in which a large corporation operates.

No single community has enough power to establish such rules and make them operational. Therefore, it will require cooperative struggle by communities all over the world, both in relatively high-wage and low-wage countries, if multinational corporations are to be subjected to a minimum of requirements of accountability, and social and environmental responsibility. One objective of such a struggle should be to establish an international agency to create and to enforce rules and regulations for multinational corporations, along with a workable, democratic process in which non-governmental organizations as well as governmental institutions have a role.

Beyond that, we also need to look at the very institution of the large corporation as a principal instrument of the global economic system. There is a case for some global economic integration, but should corporations organized for the profit of stockholders and run by managers be the vehicles for that integration as they are today? Would the policies for democratization suggested above be sufficient to change the nature of the corporation so that its productive functions could continue without the immense costs that they have so far created? These are old, nettlesome questions, set here in the context of the problem of the mobility of capital as it affects differences in economic conditions across the political boundaries of countries.[6]

6　This is a large discussion in itself, beginning with the philosophy and the principles on which corporations of all kinds (and not only the economic ones) have been created. Two relevant publications of the Center for the Study of Democratic Institutions in Santa Barbara, California, are Scott Buchanan, *The Corporation and the Republic* (1958) and W.H. Ferry, *The Corporation and the Economy—Notes Followed by a Discussion* (1959).

There are considerable obstacles to putting effective controls on corporations, which arise from the economic and military boundaries between capitalist and Third World countries. Because low-wage labor can be and is often highly productive, it is often much cheaper to make goods in the Third World and ship them to the areas of high consumption, such as the United States, Japan or Europe. Therefore, when communities in the capitalist countries try to put restrictions on corporations, such as front-end investments, severance payments on leaving, disclosure requirements or strict adherence to environmental rules, a great incentive is created for multinational corporations simply to close up shop and move their production operations elsewhere, especially to those Third World countries that have sufficient infrastructure as well as liberal rules for profit repatriation.

It is essential for communities (including workers and their unions) in the capitalist countries and in the Third World to establish real restraints on the mobility of capital around a program of well-defined mutual interest. While tensions between rich and poor communitites will continue to exist, there are substantial mutual interests in increasing wages, in maintaining security of employment and in enhancing environmental quality. Some cooperation is happening already. For instance, labor unions in capitalist countries are demanding that corporations have adequate minimum standards for wages, safety and health in Third World locations. Similarly, there are networks of tribal people, organizers and environmentalists in the Third World who have made common cause with environmentalist groups in the capitalist countries to stop World Bank loans which cause massive destruction of the environment and of local economies.

Elementary justice requires much more open borders than exist today, especially between capitalist and Third World countries. People of European origin today occupy land several times the land mass of Europe. To expand their access to land and resources, Europeans occupied North America, Australia, New Zealand, considerable portions of southern Africa and the eastern parts of the Soviet Union. This was accompanied by genocide of native peoples in North America and Australia. In addition, exploitation and considerable destruction took place in the colonies which were occupied economically for the purpose of exploitation. For instance, Bangladesh is poor today largely because it was economically and physically devastated by the British with the collaboration of local rulers. Similarly, we have discussed the role of corporations in destroying forests in the Third World. Latin America is an amalgam of the two forms of European expansion.

To shut out almost all Third World peoples in European-dominated areas from Siberia westward to the Americas, while still demanding control over and use of the world's resources, is a continuation of past injustices. We realize that opening borders cannot redress all injustices; nor are we advocating mass movement of people from South to North. Indeed, most people would rather not leave their homes and communities. However, the capitalist countries policies of excluding Third World people, at the same time insisting that they must have Third World resources through trade and movement of capital, are basically unjust and cannot be sustained within the context of a peace system. They are a fundamental feature of the war system. People who are shut out from riches and comforts derived in part at their expense will express their frustrations in many ways, including violence.

We realize that economic opportunities in the capitalist countries cannot be expanded to accommodate all the people in the Third World within the context and operation of the present economic system. Indeed, we have argued that it is in the nature of capitalism to create riches for the few and marginalization and poverty for the majority.

Opening borders is not going to change the nature of that system by itself. Nor is it something that is likely to be accomplished so long as huge inequalities persist. It is a long-term goal which, along with other goals like nuclear disarmament, provide us with a vision and a direction.

The boundaries between countries are only a part of the problem of inequalities because great inequality also exists within countries and within communities. Today, communities, whether they be cities in the United States or villages in Pakistan or India, are intensely divided by income, by ethnicity, caste, race, gender and religion, which contributes to tensions and violence within those communities. In a fundamental way, abolishing grave inequalities between countries and abolishing grave inequalities within countries is part of the same dynamic. That dynamic is in many respects in opposition to the demand of corporations for unrestricted mobility of capital and resources.

National Self-determination

Borders may, of course, have positive value for those seeking self-determination. As is well known, national self-determination, and the boundaries that some oppressed groups seek to establish to free themselves, have long had great importance in the Third World. Their significance has been dramatized recently by the events in the Soviet Union and Eastern Europe.

From an economic standpoint, socialist revolutions have represented the most radical struggles to establish boundaries against imperialism. They achieved radical restrictions on the mobility of foreign capital inward at the same time that they created more widespread ownership of private property by land redistribution. Both of these aspects arose largely out of practical necessity rather than by programmatic or theoretical design, especially in the Soviet Union.

The need for creating a global system of local self-reliance is not in contradiction with the idea of national self-determination. However, justification for tight borders is lost when national self-determination becomes a vehicle for internal exploitation and oppression. This happened in diverse ways in the Soviet Union, in its former Eastern European satellite neighbors and in most of the Third World.

Imperialism allowed the consolidation of nationalism in the capitalist countries. But, as we have discussed, in the Third World nationalism has not been consolidated. Rather, those areas that were more severely exploited tended to experience more intense internal economic divisions and strife. Other internal divisions were also exacerbated. The deliberate policies of the ruling elites, the severe competition for diminishing resources and the growing class divisions intensified internal conflict and divisions. Similarly, the violence of forced collectivization, forced labor and Stalin's purges prevented the consolidation of a Soviet nationalism despite economic gains and successful defense against external aggression.

Today, various combinations of class, gender, ethnic, religious and linguistic oppression prevail within Third World countries. In many instances, some of these conflicts also coincide approximately with geographical areas, so that they have produced demands for national self-determination that are often similar in character to the demands made during the struggles for national independence from political control by European powers.

The character of these struggles and demands is more diverse and complex, however. In economic terms, they are driven by a global system that has many layers of exploitation and deprivation. But at each layer, the struggles tend to be confined to the most visible symbols and the most immediate instruments of that exploitation, whether that be a local military garrison, a landlord or a dominant religious group. Often, they also represent the desires of local elites or incipient elites to control territory and the prerogatives of government. Frequently, these strands are mixed up, as has been the case with most independence struggles.

The establishment of new borders to throw off oppressive rule must continue to be part of the complex road toward the establishment of a peace system. Peoples cannot begin to relate to each other freely and communities cannot be self-reliant unless there is freedom from oppression, whether that be linguistic, cultural or economic.

But at the same time, borders can play only a limited and temporary role in the establishment of freedom from oppression. The establishment of borders in the struggle against national oppression is a defensive measure, the continued existence of which must be justified not only by the presence of an external threat, but also by practical progress in the reduction and elimination of other forms of oppression within those borders. This is because within all these boundaries the insistent questions of class inequalities, of the oppression of women and of the despoilation of the environment remain. In most areas, there are significant minorities whose rights are put into question by the demands of national self-determination.

Today, after several decades of experience with the results of independence movements and various kinds of governments in the Third World, we must ask more insistent questions about the long-term direction of various struggles and how they link up with the overall direction needed for a reduction in conflict and violence, and for increasing economic justice at all levels from the family to the neighborhood, the country and the globe. Self-determination, to be meaningful, cannot become a license to oppress, despoil and exploit. When it does, it loses its legitimacy.

Private Property

There has been considerable confusion in both capitalist and socialist thought regarding the question of private property in the capitalist economic system. Both have emphasized the role of private property as the institution upon which private profit is based. Capitalism has seen it as the only desirable vehicle on which to base a prosperous economy, which would be coordinated overall by an "invisible hand." Marxist socialists have generally opposed private property, except as a tactical concession, because it has been viewed as a vehicle for the re-establishment of capitalism.

This narrow view of private property as a kind of monolithic engine of capitalism is so distorted and so far from the reality that it is not a useful construct in its undifferentiated form for understanding macroeconomic structure. In this brief discussion, we will differentiate various kinds of private property in order to understand how they might or might not fit in with a peace system.

Capitalist theory is based on the idea that small-scale property is the foundation of capitalist enterprise. That model belongs more to the stuff of capitalist textbooks and mythology than to the realm of history and fact. The capitalist system, as it has always been, is a system which makes the small scale dependent on the large scale. Very often it has been destructive of small-scale enterprise. When one includes the destruction of local production in cottage industries around the world (including the Third World) in the history of capitalism, we can see that the net result of the last 200 years has not been to promote small private property but rather to destroy or subjugate it. Destruction of commonly held community property is another facet of capitalist history. In England, for example, the beginnings of capitalism lie in the "Enclosure Movement," during which large landlords deprived peasants of tenant rights and rights to use common land. This gave the landlords more property, but made poor peasants propertyless and drove them into the towns.

The property structures of capitalism have changed to consolidate the hold of large institutional property over individual, small-scale and community property. The larger economic structures of capitalism—central governments with their monetary and military powers and multinational corporations and banks—are really not "private property" in the same class or sense as the family farmer, small shopkeeper, garage owner or operator of a home improvement business. In the latter cases, the category of "net income" is not so much profit as a return-to-labor. Very often, the amount of this return is not too different from that which a person of comparable skills and experience might earn if they held a job in a large corporation for a comparable amount and type of work.

There is, of course, a continuum of sizes in which small business goes from providing a return-to-labor to producing a profit based on other people's work. The same distinction can be observed in corporate compensation policies. The compensation of both white and blue collar workers is generally of the same magnitude as what they might make were they in a similar business for themselves. However, the compensation of chief executive officers and others at the top of the corporate ladder is often so enormous that it does not correspond to any conceivable reasonable measure of relative value. The most flagrant single case of this is perhaps that of Michael Milken, the "junk bond king," jailed for fraud, who made five hundred million dollars in a single year, which is more than the Gross National Product of many small Third World countries. That clearly belongs in the category of profit, and looking to the trail of destroyed jobs and bankrupt companies, even in the category of plunder via the stock and junk bond markets.

The clearest view of the distinction between property held private-ly in a manner that provides its holders with control over their own lives and that held for profit is obtained by contrasting the situation of a peasant with a large corporation. The peasant is a property owner, often derided as "petty bourgeois" in Marxist literature. However, the earn-ings of a typical peasant family can not be described as profit by any stretch of the imagination. They are often less than that of factory wokers on an annual basis, and often far lower on an hourly basis, given the huge number of hours a typical farm family must work. Further, poor peasants in the Third World are often forced to go to moneylenders to borrow for seeds and food to eat during the planting season. A large proportion of the output of their labor then becomes profit for moneylenders. A similar situation prevails for family farmers in capitalist countries, although at much higher levels of income, with banks, agribusiness and commodity speculators sometimes playing a role similar to Third World moneylenders.

In fact, poor peasants in the Third World are hardly better off than the landless workers. In years of normal weather, landless workers may earn more and eat better during the planting season. A principal reason why poor peasants and other family farmers hold on to land, despite the considerable economic sacrifice it often entails, is that it is their in-surance policy for survival. In years of poor weather and poor harvest, they can sell or mortgage their land and survive; landless workers are usually the first to starve.

It is therefore incorrect to view the property of the poor peasant or small scale property held in a manner of a farmer in the same light as that held for profit. When earnings from such holdings are comparable to income from holding a job, it is more appropriate to view such forms of property as a means for the control of one's labor and as insurance for hard times.

Private property which people hold for use is similar to land held by small farmers in many respects. The largest single example for this is privately owned homes. Domestic animals, utensils, furniture, automobiles and home appliances also belong in this category. These kinds of property are usually not held for profit by their owners. However, within the context of capitalism all forms of property have the potential to become instruments of injustice and exploitation. One graphic example was provided in Part I of this book, where the mere membership in a Tokyo golf club can enable purchase of a thousand years of labor in the Third World. The ownership of homes or a plot of land can and often does become an avenue for profit.

There are two other kinds of institutions that provide a certain amount of control over income and over work to individuals, and can be thought of as property in that sense. The first is the professional license. The second is a job where wages are set much higher than those of others doing comparable work. In the latter case, it is easy to see that merely living in a capitalist country becomes a kind of control over income because the same work commands a much higher wage in a capitalist country than in a Third world country. That is the origin of a good deal of the pressure to emigrate from the Third World or from formerly socialist countries into capitalist countries. In situations where powerful, monopolistic unions use their power to exclude workers, as, for example, by race or caste, even holding a union card can fall into such a category.

The professional license is granted by governments and gives exclusive rights to certain kinds of work, such as the practice of engineering or dentistry to groups of people possessing certain qualifications. Such licenses may or may not have an exploitative aspect, depending on the kinds of control that are exercised, the levels of income, the availability of alternatives and so on. The granting of licenses to operate certain kinds of businesses, such as bars, also fall into a similar economic category.

Usufruct

To derive a principle of property ownership, we must distinguish between the large controlling economic institutions which operate in the exclusive pursuit of profit or, in the case of governments, in support of such profit-making structures, and small-scale property which is held for use or which provides income mainly as a return-to-labor. The Marxist view of latter is not in accord with the facts of human reality. Human life is lived individually, in families and in the small structures of communities. The intimate decisions of everyday life are best made at that level, if only because the knowledge of what needs to be done is greatest at the level. The love and nurture that are needed in everyday life also cannot be dispensed by macroecnomic structures, but must necessarily be in the small structures of everyday life. Whether it is husbanding the land, bringing up and educating children in homes and schools, deciding where a sign for a deaf child should be put up on a street or what parts of a house or office need fixing, or any of the myriad decisions that people make every day, considerable control over property at the local level is essential. In that respect, capitalist theory is certainly closer to what we need than Marxist theory or practice under Soviet-style socialism.

However, such control must be distinguished from license to do whatever one wants with property. Even within the home, not to speak of the multinatonal corporation, the English maxim "every man's home is his castle" fails to recognize the rights of the women within it. Neither does it care for future generations nor recognize the fact that air, water, soil and the ozone layer, and nature generally, are not limited to the boundaries of property. Even in the most intimate realm of the family, we recognize that parenting cannot be a license for child abuse and we put social, cultural and legal restraints upon individual and family discretion and action. Similar principles must apply to control of property in a peace system.

Control of property at the individual, family and community levels must be exercised in a way that enables everyone else as well as future generations to exercise similar control. There is a natural and enduring tension between the local control and enabling everyone to exercise that control. In a war system, that tension is resolved through violence domination and exploitation. The result is power and riches for the few and poverty and powerlessness for the many. In a peace system, the tension between the local and the global must be resolved through equity, neighborliness, friendship and consideration for others.

We must borrow from ancient times, from tribal peoples and from farmers the concept of usufruct as the foundation of the structure of property ownership. Control of property must be used to serve our need to provide for ourselves, our children, our families, our communities. But usufruct also means that property is held in trust for future generations, so that it cannot be violated for short-term profit, gain or even income, as is the norm today. It is the existence of the future that gives meaning to the present. If our system of use of resources (that is, our property laws) is such that it puts the future in jeopardy, it makes the present less meaningful too.

Property ownership or control at the local level creates obligations both locally and globally. This means that there must be economic, social, political, judicial and cultural structures through which those obligations are carried out, and appropriate sanctions imposed if they are not. The greater the scale of property control, the greater must be the scale of obligations and regulation. The greater the scale of profit, the greater the need for redistributional instruments, of which taxation is the best known.

Such a scheme requires macroeconomic institutions considerably different form the ones we have today. It needs means by which multinational corporations can be controlled. It needs measures to control a speculation. It needs a way to eliminate the injustices that arise out of monetary imperialism as well as ways to control resources, technology and ways to capital by multinational corporations and banks. It also needs systematic criteria by which the environment can be protected and enhanced for future generations.

Local Self-reliance

Local self-reliance is a principle which aims to reduce the scale of the economic enterprises and make them amenable to community control to serve broader social goals.

The question of scale in economic enterprise is the subject of considerable literature. In the twentieth century, the most notable early exponent was, of course, Gandhi with his village economy. In the last quarter of a century, the best known exponent has been Schumacher in his well-known essay *Small is Beautiful.* Even more recently, we have Paul Ekins' *The Living Economy,* Kirkpatrick Sale's *Dwellers in the Land: The Bioregional Vision,* and Leopold Kohr, *The Breakdown of Nations.* The term local self-reliance was coined by David Morris, who founded the Institute for Local Self-Reliance in the early 1970s.[7]

Johan Galtung, a pioneer in peace studies, has described the prin-

---

7   On Gandhi, see Ram Manohar Lohia, *Marx, Gandhi and Socialism,* Hyderbad: Nava Hind Press, 1963. Other works mentioned include Paul Ekins, ed., *The Living Economy,* London: Routledge & Kegan Paul, 1986; Kirkpatrick Sale, *Dwellers in the Land: The Bioregional Vision,* San Francisco: Sierra Club Books, 1985; and Leopold Kohr, *The Breakdown of Nations,* New York: E.P. Dutton, 1978. Among David Morris' publications which explore this concept are *Be Your Own Power Company,* Emmaus, PA: Rodale Press, 1983; and *Self-Reliant Cities: Energy and the Transformation of Urban America,* San Francisco: Sierra Club Books, 1982.

ciple of local self reliance in this way:

> ... [T]he basic rule of self-reliance is this: produce what you need
> using your own resources, internalizing the challenges this involves,
> growing with the challenges, neither giving the most challenging
> tasks (positive externalities) to somebody else on whom you become
> dependent, nor exporting negative externalities to somebody else to
> whom you do damage and who may become dependent on you.

* * *

> For instance an obvious way of preventing pollution of rivers from
> riverside factories would be to force the management of the factory
> to drink downstream water. . . . Those who have made their beds
> should have an obligation to lie upon them.[8]

Self-reliant communities are the basic units of a peace system. The
difficulty is that "community" today does not exist in the sense of a non-
exploitative, non-violent, nurturing unit. As we look at violence in the
home or in the streets and between religious groups, races, and landlords
and landless workers in villages, it is evident that today communities
do not exist in the sense to which we aspire in a peace system. From
wife-beating and dowry murders to closure of factories by corporations
seeking only to move to areas with cheaper labor, to city governments
so helpless that they compete with others for these corporations to come
in even though that means the loss of jobs in other areas, we do not have
the communities upon which to build self-reliance.

One basic reality of the war system is that the local exploiting classes have more important connections with those outside the community
on whom they rely for their local power. Thus, for example, landlords
and moneylenders rely on the military power of the state to protect their
property. Dowry murders go on because the murderers go scot free and
there is no enforcement of anti-dowry laws. In the southern U.S., local
whites relied on police powers of southern states and the non-interven-
tion of the Federal government to keep African-Americans in bondage
long after the Civil War. A corollary is that when oppressed groups rise
up, they generally need and ask for support from outside the local community so that they may not be annihilated by the violence of the oppressors. That was as necessary for African-Americans in the

---

8 Johan Galtung, "Towards a New Economics: On the Theory and Practice
   of Self-Reliance," in Paul Ekins, ed., *The Living Economy, op. cit.,* p. 101.

Mississippi delta during the civil rights struggle (and continues to be to a large extent) as it is for women in Delhi or tribal people in the Amazon forest fighting dams sponsored by the World Bank.

Locally, community-oriented economic development will require planning. Further, that planning must be in the hands of a democratically accountable local government rather than in the control of or heavily influenced by large corporations. This does not necessarily mean local government ownership. Ownership can be diverse and determined by local traditions and preferences, which will, in general, include private property ownership. However, it does mean that local government should give overall coherence to economic and environmental goals and that communities have enough economic power, democratically exercised, relative to corporations and to larger governmental units, to achieve that coherence. As Gar Alperowitz and Jeff Faux have noted for the U.S.:

> The fundamental answer to the increasingly short-term horizons in the private sector is a coherent full-production plan which reduces long-term investment uncertainty.
>
> Without firm guidelines to hold on to, public officials are vulnerable to the demands of any strong constituency that demands something they have the legal power to give. Only the existence of a specific plan gives government officials a way to defend themselves against the conflicting pressures of contending interest and constituencies. The more explicit the plan, moreover, the more an official is restrained from exercising arbitrary power.... Only an explicit plan, finally, provides the citizen with clear criteria to judge and discipline the bureaucracy.[9]

Today, corporations can and do plan; indeed, they regard it as essential. But local governments rarely develop comprehensive and meaningful economic development plans.

For local planning and investment to succeed and to be responsive to local needs, three weakness of local government must be remedied, at least in the U.S., and probably in most other countries. These weaknesses are:

1.   The Federal government has largely exhausted the tax base, strictly limiting the ability of state and local governments to

---

9   Alperowitz and Faux, *Rebuilding America, op. cit.*, pp. 254-255.

raise tax revenues. Indeed, this is one reason that so many local and state governments in the U.S. find themselves in financial crises today.

2.   The use of vast amounts of tax resources for military spending which, as Seymour Melman has often pointed out, has become an "industrial policy" affecting every state in the U.S. and most communities. This means that jobs and property values become linked to continued high military spending.

3.   Large corporations can move at will in and out of communities, and in and out of the countries altogether. This leaves communities economically vulnerable to the power of corporations.

The process of creating communities free of the threat and fact of the daily violence of the war system requires that we also reform those larger institutions on which local communities must rely to ensure that a minimum standards of human decency, human rights and economic justice prevail in all communities. Democracy at the local level and the establishment of non-oppressive communities not only requires the creation of democratic structures locally, but needs the institution of a larger system of safeguards that extends all the way to the global level. In many ways, the task of building community locally and the task of achieving economic justice globally are two aspects of the same process of change that we must accomplish.

For instance, achieving local self-reliance requires that a minimum set of global rules be put into place which at least subjects multinational corporations to global and local accountability. Rather than force business to be strictly local, the rules for global business should correspond to the need for all the communities involved to exercise control to see that their interests are served.

One broad principle for deriving these global rules for business is that the *mobility of capital should not exceed the mobility of people*. This is a minimum condition needed to create a democratic context for the operation of the global economic system. It is needed to respond to the reality that mobility of capital, without a corresponding mobility of people, has created immense seas of poverty and marginalization and vast differences of wages quite unrelated to labor productivity, the textbooks of capitalism notwithstanding. Further, there needs to be economic and environmental standards for all goods entering into world trade.

The intent is not to close off borders, or to stop trade—quite the contrary. Trade and movement of goods are needed for a variety of reasons. For instance, it may be much more desirable for a community or country in a wet cold area with oil resources not to use those resources and import hydrogen derived from solar energy in the Sahara. Social and economic intercourse between peoples is also needed to help overcome the parochialism, which can turn quite easily into a denial of the humanity of others and provide rationalizations for exploitation, violence and prejudice. This is one of the hallmarks of global apartheid. Finally, the protection of the global environment requires global economic cooperation. Without steps to ameliorate poverty and the immense inequalities that exist today, there is unlikely to be agreement on the nature of the investments needed to substantially reduce the risk of global environmental catastrophe. Among other things, this urgently requires that certain technologies, such as those that vastly improve energy efficiency and technologies that allow for phase-out of the use of ozone-depleting chlorofluorocarbons, be widely used in the Third World.

Galtung has proposed a principle that can guide the direction in which restructuring of the trade system can take place so that it is not exploitative, but mutually supportive. He proposes that trade between countries "be carried out so that the net balance of costs and benefits, including externalities for the parties to the exchange, be as equal as possible. In practice this will point to intrasectoral rather than intersectoral trade."[10] Intrasectoral trade means trade in similar goods, such as machine tools for airplanes, while intersectoral trade means trade in different kinds of goods, such as oil for airplanes.

In order to make this principle operational, international minimum standards will need to be established for the conditions of production of any item entering into world trade. The rules for multinational corporations, discussed above, are one major example. Further, production within communities will need to be much more diverse than it is today so that they can meet their needs directly or through intrasectoral trade. These objectives are consonant with the reduction of capital mobility, the democratization of corporations and the weakening of the economic-military boundaries of the global apartheid system.

The concept of self-reliance is a fundamentally sound one because it recognizes the human need for community. That need is both a value

---

10 Galtung, *op. cit.*, p. 102.

and a fact of life. Community integrates the non-economic and economic aspects of life (language, the nurturing of children and, in general, assuring the continuity of society despite the certainty of death for every person as an individual). We assume this to be one of the fundamental elements in a peace system.

Chapter 11

RESTRUCTURING THE INTERNATIONAL SYSTEM

Security of International Trade

The most powerful capitalist countries have often justified immense arsenals under the guise of maintaining "freedom of the seas." Formally, "freedom of the seas" is supposed to mean security of international trade and freedom to trade. But freedom of the seas has long been a leading excuse for imperialist aggression, occupation of others' lands and exploitation of the powerless. An abandonment of this long-held militarist tenet, by which powerful countries have arrogated to themselves the authority to dictate what security of international trade shall mean and under what rules that international trade will be conducted, is essential to a peace system.

This requires us to address the real question of security of international trade apart from its imperialist aspects. Countries and communities may want to trade and they should be free to do so. Thus, we can define security of international trade as enabling countries and communities to trade without the threat of violence. It also encompasses not forcing those to trade who do not want to trade. For example, the South African apartheid government has long inflicted severe violence on the trade routes of the front-line states with the objective of making these countries physically dependent on the trade routes through South Africa, and thus subject to South African economic and military power. Such behavior should not be acceptable.

In the long-term, we need a United Nations armed force to guarantee security of international trade. This would take away the only rationalization remaining for huge naval forces on the part of any single country or group of countries, whether this be the U.S., Japan, Germany, the European Economic Community or some other combination of the powerful and the rich.

An international force under the auspices of the United Nations can be seen as a transition step to a world in which armed force is not required for the conduct of trade, and in which people are free to move and trade or not to move and not to trade.

A number of steps are necessary to create the process by which a U.N. force could become an effective instrument to serve the ends of economic justice. Some of these would have to be changes in the U.N. itself. For instance, veto-power for the five nuclear weapons states in the Security Council would have to be abolished. This too will require a long-term effort.

The need for abolition of veto powers by those states with nuclear weapons is pointed up by the way the United States, using its economic and military clout, pushed through a dozen resolutions in the Security Council in 1990 to give it the authority to wage war on Iraq, with the agreement of the other nuclear powers and of most other temporary members of the Security Council. At the same time, many other gross injustices continue. Why should the United Nations authorize the use of force in such a hurry to restore an undemocratic government in Kuwait, yet fail to protect trade routes in southern Africa from the trepidations of the South African apartheid regime or to dispatch troops to South Africa to assist in the liberation of the long oppressed peoples? Why does the Security Council do nothing to enforce the decision of the World Court that the U.S. violated international law by mining Nicaragua's harbors and collect the seventeen million dollar fine? Why was there no military action to enforce Security Council resolutions which declared South Africa's occupation of Namibia to be illegal?

The reasons lie, of course, in the economic power of the capitalist states, the collapse of the Soviet economy and the internal political disintegration in the Soviet Union. China's acquiescence with U.S policy relates more to its own international economic position and objectives rather than to any considerations of global equity or justice. This then is not so much the rule of law, but the selective application of rules of the rich and powerful, by the rich and powerful, for the rich and powerful.

Other changes relate to eliminating the aggressive posture of foreign military forces of powerful countries. This applies especially to the capitalist powers, since the Soviet Union has made some of the transition already, although much remains to be done. For example, the Soviet Union has renounced the first use of nuclear weapons and use against non-nuclear powers, although how the nuclear weapons situation will evolve in the context of the tensions between nationalities in the Soviet Union is a huge, important unresolved question.

For the United States, this will require some very fundamental restructuring of military policy. Since the Second World War, the United States has claimed the right to use nuclear weapons first in any conflict. It has made many veiled and not-so-veiled nuclear threats against non-nuclear powers. It has also arrogated to itself the authority to police the seas. The most immediate needed changes are a comprehensive nuclear test ban treaty and an abandonment of the policies of using nuclear threats and the prerogative of first use of nuclear weapons. It also means that nuclear weapons powers dismantle foreign bases and eliminate "tactical nuclear weapons" which are aimed at nuclear as well as non-nuclear countries as part of the global goal of eliminating nuclear, chemical and biological weapons as well as other weapons of mass destruction. Such changes are complementary to the democratization of U.N. institutions.

In the meantime, the emergence of a united capitalist Europe armed with nuclear weapons of France and Britain poses new problems for the prospects for economic justice and disarmament.

The adoption of a truly defensive policy by capitalist countries would open up the possibility of vast reductions of military budgets. It would enable a vast reduction in the quantity and variety of armaments that are made. This is not only domestically important for economic conversion but is also important internationally. A major source of the current massive arms trade lies with the Soviet Union and the U.S. In order to reduce the costs per weapon of the arms produced to fight each other, they have encouraged the production and sales of many of their weapons to other countries. A great deal of the international arms trade, which has been so destructive to people's well-being, has been driven by the logic of the immense variety of weapons that are being produced by the U.S., Soviet Union and other major arms manufacturers and by cost reduction per unit by these same manufacturers.

Today, moreover, a denial of armaments by the U.S. and the Soviet Union or any of the other powerful countries to the Third World states happens on the basis of inequalities which reflect larger realities on the distribution of political and economic power. Even though the denial of such weapons may be justifiable or desirable in many situations, this basic and fundamental inequality creates an appearance and even the fact of injustice because the United States and the Soviet Union retain the military ability to strike against the very countries to whom they would deny weaponry. (Such are the injustices of the war system!) This creates nationalistic reactions in the countries which have been denied weaponry. That in turn has made it politically easier for them to justify acquisition of more weaponry, or in the case of nuclear weapons, to develop the capability to make the weapons and delivery systems themselves.

Thus, the adoption of a defensive posture by the capitalist countries and the Soviet Union and a change in the structure of armaments production would create some of the conditions for a corresponding reduction in military expenditures in the Third World. It is essential to liberate resources being used for military build-ups to enable their use for the improvement of the conditions of life for the vast majority of the world's people who suffer in poverty today.

Such a defensive posture and reduction of armaments production and expenditures is also fundamentally compatible with the creation of the United Nations security force discussed above.

The process of democratizing the United Nations and its institutions cannot be complete without democratization in the Third World. As we have discussed, governmental repression and violence are more the norms rather than the exception, so that Third World governments generally do not represent the aspirations of the vast majority of their peoples, although they may wear the mantle of nationalism abroad. But this aspect too is linked to the deadly trade in armaments fostered by multinational corporations as well as by many governments. That in turn is linked to the heavy military expenditures of the powers that dominate the world today.

The International Monetary System

Within the present structure of capital mobility and the control of capital by large corporations (including banks) for the purpose of profit, it is unlikely that there can be any serious or equitable worldwide prospect of providing meaningful and productive work to all who need it in order to end poverty and marginalization.

As discussed in Part I, a central element of the international system of inequalities and exploitation since World War II has been the international monetary system. Indeed, the last few decades of the exploitation of the Third World may well be termed "monetary imperialism." This monetary system operates to keep wages low in the Third World, far below the relative productivity of workers in the Third World.

Economic theory has it that when labor is more productive, then wages can be higher and prices lower at the same time. This is often used to explain the relatively high wages and affluent standard of living in the capitalist countries.[1] However, if we compare the prices of most goods in capitalist and Third World countries at the present exchange rates, we find that the same dollar can purchase more in Mexico, Bangladesh or Brazil than it can in New York, Paris or Tokyo. This contradicts the prevailing theory which would have it that the prices should be lower where the economy is deemed to be more productive.

The issue is not so much that the amount of production per unit of time per worker in Mexico is higher overall than in the United States. Rather it is that *the Mexican currency is valued much lower than the relative productivity of Mexican workers collectively.* Of course, on the average the amount of investment and efficient equipment available to Mexican farmers and workers is far lower than in France, Japan or the U.S., and thus, on average, they produce fewer goods per unit of time when we compare specific areas of production. However, while the average amount produced per unit of time by workers in Mexico, Brazil or Bangladesh is lower than in France, the United States or Japan, the *difference in wages at present exchange rates is much bigger than the difference in productivity.* This explains why the purchasing power of

---

1   There are two quite distinct concepts of labor productivity. One is a physical concept which measures how much a set of workers produce of a particular product in a unit of time. The other is an economic concept in which different activities and products are grouped together to yield a composite measure expressed in monetary units per hour of labor. Comparisons of productivities in different countries in this second economic sense involves the use of exchange rates to make the units of economic measure comparable. Thus, if an exchange rate is set so that the currency of country A is undervalued with respect to the currency of country B, then the productivity of labor in country A will be correspondingly underestimated.

U.S. dollars, French francs or Japanese yen is much bigger in Mexico, Bangladesh or Brazil than it is in their countries of origin.

The world's monetary system does not set values of the currencies on the basis of relative productivity of workers. Rather it sets values of currencies on the basis of balance of payments considerations. This has had serious negative impacts both within the Third World countries and the capitalist countries. The miserable conditions, which are widespread within Third World countries, are partly tied to the fact that their domestic products are drastically undervalued in relation to what those countries can buy in the international marketplace. In these circumstances, Third World countries are at a structural disadvantage in their trade with the capitalist countries. The extent to which the goods and labor of Third World countries are undervalued can be gauged by an overall calculation of the amount of time that people in the capitalist countries work to import the immense amount of Third World resources and finished products they consume. All of the imports to the capitalist countries from the Third World, including oil, raw materials, agricultural products and manufactures are paid for with less than 5 per cent of the monetized labor-time worked in the capitalist countries. It is not surprising then that the Third World cannot purchase very much from the capitalist countries, and that it has chronic balance of payments deficits.

For the capitalist countries, low wages in the Third World have meant that it is cheaper and more advantageous to shift manufacturing to the Third World from the capitalist countries. As previously noted, this has depressed wages within the U.S. and elsewhere.

Similarly, the relative undervaluing of Third World natural resources based on the relative weakness of Third World currencies has encouraged a throw-away society in capitalist countries which over use the world's resources with grave environmental consequences. When manufacturing can be done with cheap labor and resources in the Third World, then it becomes more attractive to throw away goods than to repair them in the capitalist countries where labor is more expensive. This affects every stage of manufacturing from material selection in design to the overall reduction in the durability of goods.

To help reverse these tendencies, we need to change the way in which currency exchange rates are set. The present system is based on balance of payments considerations and on capital flows. Therefore, exchange rates are basically driven by capital mobility and corporate and banking interests. We need to put in its place a system in which currencies of countries are valued by the relative productivity of monetized labor. Such a system would equalize the purchasing powers of currencies and continuously adjust them for inflation. An international monetary system in which an international currency is created with constant purchasing power in all countries is one necessary element in a system in which trade between countries is carried out on an equitable basis.[2] It is important to note here that any monetary system can only address the question of the conditions of exchange of labor which is monetized. It inherently omits non-monetized labor as well as environmental destruction. These questions need to be addressed through the kinds of measures that we have discussed elsewhere in this book.

A monetary system based on relative productivities of monetized labor, as proposed by Makhijani and Browne, would have the following principal features:

- the determination of exchange rates of currencies according to the relative prices of "baskets" of comparable consumer goods;

- the issuance by a world central bank of a new international currency, a unit which would have fixed purchasing power in every country in terms of the "baskets" of consumer goods;

- the creation and maintenance in each country of stocks of commodities of a monetary value proportional to that of the country's foreign trade as a guarantee against balance of payment deficits.

This approach is essentially different from the present system, which is driven by balance of payments considerations and currency speculation. (The amount of trade in currencies exceeds within a few days the monetary value of the world's annual international trade.) The present system exacerbates rather than corrects economic disparities and environmental destruction.

The proposed system, which we call the "productivity-standard system," would do away with the trading of currencies. All transactions between one currency and another would flow through the central banks

---

2   For a detailed discussion of this proposal, see Arjun Makhijani and Robert S. Browne, "Restructuring the International Monetary System," *World Policy Journal*, Winter 1986. Most of the rest of the discussion in this section is based on this paper, which is reprinted in the Appendix to this book.

of countries and be conducted via the a world central bank. While this would appear at first sight to be more centralized than the present system, that is not the case.

Within countries, the present system is conducive to considerable centralized control in cases where the central bank of a country directly controls all foreign exchange transactions. It is also amenable to considerable decentralization, since in many countries private banks and corporations can carry out foreign exchange transactions under broad central bank charters.

The present system is highly centralized in some respects. The central banks of monetary powers, such as the U.S., Japan, Germany and Britain, coordinate their policies through the Bank of International Settlements in Basle, Switzerland. And even among these, the role of the U.S. Federal Reserve and Treasury are pre-eminent and usually decisive, although this may change with the emergence of a single European currency. Flows of foreign exchange are greatly influenced by central banks of these countries when they set interest rates.

The monetary imperialist powers also coordinate the policies through an informal institution known as the "G-7." (The abbreviation stands for "Group of 7," which consists of U.S., Japan, Germany, France, Britain, Italy and Canada.) This is the informal coordinating forum from which these countries make major economic decisions and also influence major policy decisions of the International Monetary Fund. In brief, a small minority of countries, and within them a small minority of officials and institutions, control the world's monetary system today—and through it, much else.

Under the productivity-standard system, monetary power would be much more decentralized in that all countries would be free to set their own internal monetary policies within a set of modestly constraining general rules. The degree of regulation of transactions within countries can be decided on by governments. There could be a central bank of all foreign exchange transactions. At the other extreme, central banks of countries could authorize private banks to carry out transactions directly via the world central bank. The main requirement of the international monetary system would be that central banks—and through them, all countries—remain responsible for keeping foreign accounts in balance within a narrow range. In political terms, this means that the governments of countries would be responsible for the overall consequences of the financial transactions carried out by people and institutions located within their jurisdictions.

The larger freedom that countries would have for carrying out internal policies can be illustrated by an example. For instance, over a certain period, Ghana may have need for policies which are more stimulative (in Keynesian terms) that those of France. This would tend to create an internal inflation in Ghana larger than that of France during that period. Suppose these rates are 15 percent and 5 percent per year respectively. This would not have severe external repercussions, even if it persisted for a prolonged period. It would merely mean that the value of France's currency would be depreciated with respect to the international currency at the rate of 5 percent per year and that of Ghana by 15 percent per year. This would automatically create a revaluation of French francs relative to Ghanaian cedis. If the situation were reversed later on, then an automatic revaluation of Ghanaian cedis would take place relative to French francs.

Flows of capital (whether as money or as financial instruments, such as bonds and stocks) across boundaries would not be restricted as a feature of the monetary system. That would be a matter of the policies of countries. But, as with other international transactions, all capital flows between countries would be directed via the world central bank.

From the point of view of the monetary system, the flows of capital would register as the mirror image of the trade in goods and services. The export of capital, that is, making a foreign loan, would look like an import of goods or services. Borrowing money abroad would register as an export of goods or services. It is clear that no monetary system, including the proposed productivity standard system or any other, can guarantee that countries will not get into excessive debt by borrowing in order to import goods and services for present consumption. That is a situation which can only be controlled by other means, internal and external.

Such a system would provide a stable, non-inflationary international currency with real commodity backing without requiring the management of the price of any commodity. Countries would be free to pursue internal monetary and fiscal policies according to their internal needs. Their currencies would be automatically revalued or devalued accordingly as the price of the "basket" of basic consumer goods went down or up in the local currency.

In principle, there is no reason why the main features of the monetary system discussed here for the global economy should be restricted to the international sphere. As information systems become more capable of connecting the local to the global, it may be possible to create sub-national regional currencies which can be used, via inter-regional banks, to carry out transactions between regions. Such an approach holds interesting possibilities. For instance, it may enable different regions to integrate environmental values into the overall economy more rapidly than is possible at the national level, while still allowing for inter-regional trade and exchange in a non-restrictive way.

The productivity-standard system would result in substantial revaluations of the currencies of Third World countries, the more so for the ones with lowest relative wages under the current system with respect to the currencies of capitalist countries, including the U.S. dollar. The direct result would be to increase relative wages in the Third World. This would:

- increase purchasing power in the Third World for importing industrial goods and foodstuffs;

- increase commodity prices, thus reducing the real burden of debt repayments for many Third World countries;

- reduce greatly the incentive for multinational corporations to invest in the Third World mainly to take advantage of the vast differences in wages for labor having similar productivity in physical terms;

- permit both the capitalist and Third World countries to more easily *lower* trade barriers, since much of the protectionist pressure comes from the existence of arbitrary wage differences across boundaries.

A restructuring of the monetary system would affect diverse portions of the global economy and diverse groups in varied ways. Raising relative wages in the Third World across the board by instituting an equitable system of setting exchange rates would increase the purchasing power of workers and farmers in the Third World so far as goods produced in the capitalist countries are concerned. Thus, it would spur exports from the capitalist countries to the Third World. China would experience similar effects. The consequences for Eastern Europe and the Soviet Union should, in principle, be similar, although the collapse of these economics and their chaotic reintegration into capitalism has created very special pricing problems.

The proposed system would tend to decrease capital flight both from the Third World to the capitalist countries and vice versa. Capital flight from the Third World is driven mainly by three factors where the operation of the monetary system is concerned. First, Third World currencies are much more restricted in their circulation than "hard currencies." Hence, the range of goods that can be purchased with Third World currencies is limited. Second, Third World currencies have poor international purchasing power due to the relative undervaluation of Third World labor. Finally, both internal policies, such as excessive printing of currencies, and external impositions, such as devaluations, cause instability and uncertainty leading to a search for safe havens for money. On the other hand, capital flight from the capitalist countries to the Third World is driven largely by the search for cheap, productive labor.[3] Since the productivity standard would revalue labor in the Third World, this incentive for capital flight would be greatly reduced.

The negative economic effects of the restructuring would be in the areas of reduced corporate profits for many multinational corporations and banks and increased prices for many resources. Unlike the increased price of oil in the 1970s and early 1980s, which was the result of a cartel arrangement setting the price much higher than the cost of production, the increases in resource prices due to the restructuring of the monetary system proposed here would come from increased relative wages in the Third World, thus increasing their costs in a structural way. It would also reduce the economic power of the capitalists in the Third World linked to the exploitation of cheap labor and resources for exports.

As with the U.N. Security Force, or the abolition of boundaries between countries, the establishment of an international monetary system in which countries and even communities can relate to each other on the basis of equality, so far as the monetary system is concerned, is a long-term goal. The achievement of an equitable international monetary system in which communities are not exploited by virtue of their past subjugation and present poverty is as necessary a means toward achieving a peace system as the abolishment of nuclear weapons and other weapons of mass destruction. It is something we must demand, and work for. But we must also work for intermediate- and short-term steps toward the long-term goal of restructuring the monetary system. Some of these short- and intermediate-term policies are:

---

3 Capital does not necessarily go the countries with the lowest wages. A number of factors, such as the availability of infrastructure (roads, reliable electricity, etc.), the locations of resources, the politics of the government and the rules for profit repatriation play decisive roles.

- Cancellation of that part of the Third World debt on which interest payments and fees have exceeded the principal.

- Public disclosure by banks in all countries of the identities of the holders of all foreign accounts in excess of $50,000. This must be a minimum condition in allowing banks to participate in international transactions. Similar conditions must be imposed on foreign holdings of stocks, commodity futures, bonds and other financial instruments. This will allow people to expose and catch corrupt transactions which have played a large role in problems as diverse as the maintenance of dictators in power, the Iran-contra affair, the Third World debt crisis and the failures of savings and loan banks in the U.S.

- A tax on all foreign exchange transactions to reduce currency speculation.

- Requirement for disclosure of the source of income and expected area of tax liability before foreign bank deposits (or purchases of financial instruments) exceeding $25,000 can be made.

The bank accounts in Switzerland, the Cayman Islands and other "havens" for the capital of the corporations, drug dealers, Mobutus and Marcoses, and the defrauders of the U.S. savings and loan banks are important vehicles of corruption in world politics and economics. These rules would restrain unnecessary, speculative trade in currencies as well as corrupt transfers of money by corporations and individuals all over the world.

Redistribution of wealth between the capitalist and Third World countries and within countries is in accord with the overall goals of limiting riches, reducing wasteful consumption of resources and abolishing poverty. Restructuring the monetary system is a basic part of a break with the war system since it would help make progress toward all these goals.

A restructuring of the international monetary system will not be enough to achieve the goals of distributive justice which are fundamental to creating a minimum economic standard of living for the majority of the world's people. Redistributive mechanisms must also be put into place within countries. Further, not all the international inequalities can be addressed by changing the monetary system. There are many other structural inequalities, such as the present maldistribution of land and inequitable structure of investments, that also need to be redressed.

In brief, changing the international monetary system will not in itself be sufficient to take care of the enormous inequalities which currently grip the world, but it is one necessary factor.

Chapter 12

RESTRUCTURING WITHIN COUNTRIES

Local struggles for justice related to class, gender, environmental sanity, race and so forth are in many ways the basis on which more global struggles can be conducted, because it is within the local, personal context that people come to discover the wider inequities of the system. For large numbers of people throughout the world even simple demands for jobs at minimally decent wages, a reliable supply of drinking water, affordable health care and good education seem to be out of reach.

These basic needs are unobtainable not because of some insufficiency of resources or a lack of productive capacity. There is quite enough in the world to feed everyone and to provide everyone with jobs, water, good health care and education. The problem is one of inequalities of power and control of resources. It is not a lack of political will on the part of political leaders that prevents simple things like water and vaccinations and vitamin A from reaching the children of the world. It is the forceful presence of political and military and economic power used to maintain the present order which is responsible.

The class structure in most countries, and especially in Third World countries, is highly differentiated. For the most part, the elites in the Third World who dominate most of these countries are intimately connected to the global war system and their privileges are closely dependent upon it. Moreover, they derive from external sources a good portion of the money and the weapons they use to repress the people. In return, they provide the kind of "healthy" environment for corporations which U.S. National Security Memorandum No. 68 sought to establish after World War II.

While there are many differences between the programs and policies which are needed in the Third World and in the capitalist countries, some common principles and policies should apply to all countries. Some of these are:

1. Guaranteed employment (including adequate job training).

2. Unemployment compensation for all who want jobs but cannot get them.

3. Minimum wages set high enough to enable one wage to support a small family above locally defined poverty levels.

4. Adequate day-care facilities.

5. Security of people in their homes, even if these be huts in villages or shanties in cities.[1]

6. Universal health insurance or other form of guaranteed health care.

7. Minimum rules of accountability and responsibility for all corporations operating within single countries.

8. Establishment of the economic rights of women, especially in relation to the immense amount of non-monetized work they do, for example, by allocation of family property rights, pen-

---

1   For instance, wholesale destruction of townships and settlements is not only a feature of South African apartheid; it is a routine feature of economic life for the poor in the Third World, especially in large cities. The class divisions in the Third World are so strong that such destruction often goes by the name "beautification." This destruction of people's homes is one of the most egregious aspects of the lack of economic democracy within countries. It must be stopped.

sions, social security and so on.

The experience of Kerala demonstrates how these goals can, in large measure, be achieved even in a low-income area.

Kerala, India

There have been many comparisons of China and India. The elimination of the worst aspects of poverty in China, despite a higher population and considerably more difficult resource situation in many respects, has been one of the great accomplishments of the Chinese Revolution. The contrast with India with its great extremes of poverty and wealth and much higher infant mortality (and the violence it implies) is painfully clear.

Yet, as we have discussed, China has found neither an economic nor a political model to undergird these economic gains. The wide swings in political and economic policy have, in part, been a consequence of that failure.

One area of India may provide an example to serve as a guide to the achievement of the goals of economic justice and political democracy. That is the state of Kerala in India. On the subcontinent's southwestern coast, it is the most densely populated state in India and was the objective of the first European traders and imperialists, known as the land of spices, coconut trees and lovely lagoons. Kerala's popular radical politics, rooted in simple demands for land, minimum wages, health and education, have combined with a history of struggles against age-old caste discrimination and more recent British imperialism to create a most remarkable achievement.

In Kerala, land reform, grassroots organization and electoral politics have produced considerable political freedom and economic progress. Kerala has a long tradition of militant struggle against exploitation. Its people gave the British imperialists a rough time for almost a century and a half. In 1957, the people of Kerala elected a government led by the Communist Party of India in multi-party elections, much to the displeasure of the Congress Party, which dominated the country politically.

Over a period of two decades, in and out of government, leftist forces organized multi-party electoral politics. They did this within the context of non-violent struggle, the substantial local political space created by a long tradition of militant struggles, and the considerable freedom of expression which has prevailed in most periods in India since political independence in 1947.

The situation today is that there has been significant redistribution of land (implemented by the government-led Communist Party of India [Marxist] in 1969), establishment of minimum wage laws, considerable progress in the reduction of caste prejudices and discrimination against women and even modest pensions for agricultural workers.

Because these popular struggles were led by grassroots organizations in the towns and villages of Kerala, the reforms persist and gains continue to be made, although the Communist Party of India (Marxist)-led governments have been in and out of power in the state several times since 1957.

The real improvements in the lives of the people are seen in the measures of human welfare that we used in Part I to compare various economic systems. Richard Franke and Barbara Chasin have made such a comparison, using data for 1979 to 1980 from Kerala, the whole of India, other low-GNP Third World countries and the United States.[2]

Table 6 below shows life expectancy and infant mortality for India, Kerala and the United States. It also shows per-person gross national product. Kerala has a lower per person income than the rest of India, not to mention the United States, but the indicators of human well-being are closer to those of the U.S., where the level of GNP is almost 100 times higher and the level of material consumption over an order-of-magnitude higher. In fact, overall conditions of life in Kerala in human terms are better than those prevailing in many U.S. inner cities. It is pertinent to note the utter failure of monetary statistics, especially in terms of present-day exchange rates, to capture the human reality of the comparison.

This is possibly the most hopeful subnational region in the world in terms of building a non-violent and just economic system. It shows that the evils of poverty and misery can be substantially reduced with radical reforms that are compatible with grassroots power, with private property and with a multi-party electoral system. Further, this has been accomplished without shifting burdens to any other part of the country or the world.

It is important to remember that it has been Communists and other leftists, with a practical dedication to both democratic values and to

---

2   Richard W. Franke and Barbara H. Chasin, *Kerala: Radical Reform as Development in an Indian State* (Food First Development Report No. 6), San Francisco, Institute for Food and Development Policy, 1989.

economic equity, who, despite many odds, have been at the forefront of this achievement. Kerala has the highest literacy and newspaper readership in India. By 1990, Kerala had achieved universal literacy and boasts a vigorous "peoples science movement," which has popularized science education and has spread to many other areas of the country.

Table 6
QUALITY OF LIFE INDICATORS OF KERALA
COMPARED TO SOME OTHER AREAS, 1979-80

Indicators	Kerala	All India	Low-GNP Countries	USA
GNP per Person, (US $)	182	290	200	17,480
Adult Literacy Rate (%)	78	43	?	96
Life Expectancy, Years	68	57	52	75
Infant Mortality per 1,000	27	86	106	10
Birth Rate per 1,000	22	32	43	16

Source: Franke and Chasin, *Kerala, op. cit.*, p. 11.

The difference in infant mortality between Kerala and the rest of India, and between Kerala and other poor areas of the world, is one measure of the structural violence that is occurring for lack of even a modicum of internal distributional justice in the rest of India and in most Third World countries. Kerala's relatively low infant mortality is due fundamentally to the fact that its health care resources are directed in a manner that substantially includes the poor with stress on preventive care. For want of similar health care, the death rate of infants in the rest of India is three times higher. This means additional deaths of about one-and-a-half million infants in India alone every year. No external aid or resources are needed to reduce infant mortality (and hence also the birth rate) in India. It is internal resource misallocation and the intense oppression of women which prevent this same achievement from being replicated all over India and most of the rest of the Third World. Franke and Chasin have described Kerala as "an experiment in radical reform as a modern development strategy."[3]

There are other signal features of Kerala's success. It is the place in India where there is the least caste, ethnic and religious strife. The situation of women is far better in Kerala than in most of the rest of India and, indeed, much of the Third World. The result of that can be seen in the far lower infant mortality rates, birth rates and in the gender ratio. In India as a whole, there are about 7 percent fewer females than males because of the systematic social and economic discrimination against women through the dowry system and many other factors. In Kerala, these are slightly more females than males, which is normal.

Their thorough-going commitment to redistribution of access to productive resources, minimum wages, meeting the essential needs of even the poorest in society and grassroots organization and democracy has enabled the people of Kerala to create this model of development. It deserves close attention and international study, particularly at a time when its lessons might be broadly applicable not only to the Third World, but also to Eastern Europe, the Soviet Union, China and other socialist countries seeking to marry multi-party systems with social justice and private property ownership. It may also hold some lessons for the capitalist countries where anti-communism is still rife.

These successes have been achieved in the face of considerable odds and difficulties. Kerala has a number of features which should be noted here. Coastal Kerala, where most of Kerala's people live, is one of the most densely populated areas in India and the world. The land reform which was carried out was not thoroughgoing because it faced a number of obstacles. The distribution of income and control of property, especially in industry, continues to be in the hands of the rich both from Kerala and from outside the state. Big industry and large-scale fishing have caused considerable environmental damage to the land and oceanic resources of Kerala. This has affected the poor adversely. As a result of these factors, there continue to be serious problems of poverty, high infant mortality relative to the capitalist countries unemployment, inadequate housing and a lack of other resources. These require additional financial resources—a difficult proposition in the face of very low income.

---

3 Franke and Chasin, *op. cit.*, p. 10.

Kerala's high unemployment persists despite the large number of people who have gone outside the state (to Bombay, for instance) and outside India (mainly to the Persian Gulf region). Its economic successes internally are now partly dependent on remittances from abroad, making it vulnerable to the kinds of disruption which occurred with the Iraqi occupation of Kuwait in August 1990 and the international sanctions that followed. There are, therefore, many factors which will strain Kerala's ability to sustain its economic gains over the long term without supporting changes in the larger national and global economic system of which it is a part.

Another jarring note and serious problem is the rhetoric of the various Communist parties in India which still harks back to the authoritarian texts about the "dictatorship of the proletariat." That phrase cannot even take into account the historical reality that in this century most revolutions and their accomplishments have been generated by poor peasants out of a desire for their own piece of land—and that this desire has been a positive force for economic justice. Further, the gains in Kerala occurred where those political forces committed to redistributive justice built popular organizations at the grassroots, defying other political parties not as committed to redistribution and even those bent on capitalist exploitation. These popular organizations have often been started and built by leftist parties and individuals. Today, those gains have become consolidated, independent to a large extent of the party which holds the seat of government, because a considerable amount of power resides with grassroots organizations in the towns and villages of Kerala. No party dare undo the land reform or stop enforcing minimum wage laws. As Franke and Chasin have noted:

> The shifting sands of Kerala's electoral politics are one aspect of the state's radical political history. With left governments in power, major laws have been passed to redistribute income and income-producing assets, such as land, to the dispossessed. But even when conservative governments have held control of the state assembly, Kerala's workers and peasants have won some reforms. This has come about because the left parties, unlike the electoral parties familiar to most people in the United States, are made up of highly organized, militant peasant associations and labor unions. The groups continue to agitate for change no matter who is holding formal power in the state.[4]

---

4   Franke and Chasin, *op. cit.*, p. 8.

The reality of the accomplishment of the people of Kerala and its grass-roots power and democracy in the context of a multi-party electoral system is a beacon for the future of local efforts for economic justice. It also points up the larger political space which has been available in India for radical change compared to many other Third World countries.

The United States

Internal restructuring is also needed in the U.S. and other capitalist countries. Over the 1980s, the poor in the U.S. have become poorer and the rich, richer. Tax write-offs for the rich and huge military budgets have been possible in part because of the ability of the U.S. to draw capital from abroad. But at least some of the growing difference between what the U.S. government earns and what it spends has been made up by cutting programs for the poor and by taxing working people more heavily. A litany of problems has already been discussed in Part I. The question is, then, what can be done about them?

Systems of economic allocation of resources need to be fundamentally restructured within the U.S. That requires action in a number of areas. For example, a drastic reduction of military spending in tune with a move to a defensive posture is in order. This may mean a reduction from the current spending level of about $300 billion per year to a level of roughly $50 billion per year. Similarly, we need changes in the tax structure so as to encourage rather than discourage job creation and environmental protection.[5]

Some reductions in military spending will have to be redirected to civilian spending to create productive jobs in a highly dispersed manner in communities all over the country. Seymour Melman of Columbia University has long discussed the subversion of the U.S. industrial structure by military spending and the necessity of improving productivity and investment in the civilian economy by reducing military spending. Many organizations, such as the Center for Economic Conversion, the Congressional Black Caucus, the Council on Economic Priorities and Jobs with Peace, have outlined alternative budgets and peace conversion policies. The problem of the conversion of military facilities to non-military uses is now urgently being taken up by many

---

5 Arjun Makhijani, "Reagonomics: Policies, Results, Alternatives." Unpublished draft paper, October 1986.

unions and state and local governments across the country.

One of the most important areas of increasing jobs would be through making available a vast increase in the quantity and quality of education available to people of all ages from primary school children on up. The number of school days, the standards of achievement in mathematics, science, writing and reading are unsatisfactory for a large proportion of school and even college students. In addition, the acquisition and enhancement of management and financial skills and awareness of resource conservation will have to be systematized. In this context, the following areas of job creation and investment appear to have the potential for creating large numbers of jobs in communities all over the country, while fostering the resource conservation and enhancement (of land and water resources) that will be needed:

- Production of high quality goods, such as furniture, clothes and houses, which perform their functions well and last for a long time.

- Maintenance programs for household appliances and cars—run like annual service contracts, but community sponsored.

- Devotion of more resources, which are free of toxic chemicals, to the local production of healthful food that preserves soil and limits water consumption.

- Extensive soil, water and other resource conservation programs to repair the damage already done.

- The clean-up of toxic wastes now present, including both radioactive and non-radioactive wastes.

- A drastic reduction in fossil fuel use and a shift to energy conservation and renewable energy sources.

- Large increases in the quality and quantity of resources devoted to education.

- The restructuring of industrial and agricultural production in order to move steadily toward the goal of eliminating seriously toxic products altogether.

The first two items—production of high-quality goods and community-based maintenance programs—need some elaboration. In the current economic structure, high resource consumption, planned obsolescence and, to some extent, low quality of goods in use is in large part a result of the large and increasing differences in the costs of maintenance and repair versus the costs of manufacturing. The latter tend to be lower, especially because manufacturing can now be shifted to low-wage areas in the Third World. But if the international monetary system is restructured as suggested above, higher wages in the Third World and attendant increases in raw materials prices will provide incentives both for production of higher quality goods and for maintenance of the existing stock of goods. In some areas, such as automobiles or heating equipment, it will be necessary to develop means to improve their efficiency and environmental performance and to allow for their more rapid replacement with more efficient and cleaner equipment.

Harbingers of Hope: Internationalism at the Grassroots

In the U.S., as in other capitalist countries, it is especially necessary to connect local action with international aims to prevent corporations or national governments from meeting local demands and simply transferring the problems elsewhere. In such a manner the war system pits people against one another. To prevent this, we must link grassroots groups and non-governmental organizations, generally (as well as local governments) across national borders and address common concerns through joint action.

In the United States, some of this movement has already begun, partly as a response to the Reagan era. The reality of Reaganomics was the strengthening of large corporations, the Pentagon, the nuclear weapons establishment and the rich, but its rhetoric was of decentralization. And indeed, there has been over the last decade a shaping of grassroots democracy in the U.S. in response to budget cuts for states and local governments, the aggressive assertion of federal authority over local government on environmental issues and a regression in civil rights. Public interest groups, city, state and county governments, local environmental activists, labor unions, local advocacy groups and peace activists have seized the initiative and passed and implemented laws at the local level, ranging from CFC recycling to assistance for sister cities in Nicaragua and South Africa.

Consider the Sanctuary Movement. Churches in the United States, in defiance of the Immigration and Naturalization Service, provided sanctuary to people fleeing from Central American wars financed and sponsored by the United States government. They did this on pain of prison and at considerable personal and financial expense. They did not ask whether the refugees were economic or political refugees, for in reality this distinction is a false construct designed to discriminate against those people fleeing from the military, political and economic horrors in countries with dictatorial capitalist-supported regimes like El Salvador. These acts of solidarity and compassion have created a basis for long-term cooperation between the peoples of the U.S. and Central America.

Or consider the Potters for Peace. In that movement, potters from the U.S. helped build Nicaraguan pottery cooperatives in the midst of the U.S.-sponsored war against the Sandinista government, which also was a war of economic and physical destruction waged on the people of Nicaragua themselves. Yet Potters for Peace and many other organizations not only helped resist the U.S.-sponsored war; they helped the people rebuild and continue to do so. Ben Linder, the engineer who was killed by the Contras as he helped with a hydroelectric dam, worked in that spirit of resistance and creation. Similarly, an international effort was undertaken to help the people of Nicaragua market their coffee in the U.S., despite the U.S.-imposed trade embargo which lasted until 1990.

There are many other examples of such struggles within the capitalist countries. One recent example involved the fight to reduce and then eliminate hazardous waste production. Many corporations confronted with citizen protest on toxic waste dumps in the capitalist countries have tried to export hazardous waste to the Third World and in some cases, succeeded. However, militant action by environmental groups and protests in the Third World against toxic waste from Europe being dumped—for example, in West Africa—were so strenuous and so powerful that further dumping of hazardous wastes in the Third World has become politically very difficult. In 1989, an international agreement was arrived at by which any toxic waste disposal in a country other than the country of origin would have to conform to certain minimum standards wherever it was disposed of, even if it were in a Third World country. While this still leaves the door open to some abuse, it is a beginning toward *a minimum global structure in which local struggles for environmental sanity and clean water can support similar struggles elsewhere, including in the Third World.*

Another example has been the work of the Quixote Center to send medicines and supplies to Nicaragua to compensate in some measure for the economic destruction that the U.S.-sponsored war caused in Nicaragua during the 1980s. In the same spirit is the effort of the Quakers in the United States to assist the people of Laos to rehabilitate their country. They provide them with the tools needed to plough their fields with less danger of being blown up by unexploded bombs and other remaining ordnance.

In recent years, there has been a rapid growth of the municipal foreign policy movement. In this movement, cities and communities across boundaries have become linked, and assist each other in problem-solving. For example, the struggle of people in the community of Lawaaikamp in South Africa to remain in their homes and not have them bulldozed by the apartheid regime has been supported by its sister city, St. Paul, Minnesota. After many years of struggle, a dwindling population of Lawaaikamp, from 5,000 to 1,200 under the apartheid regime's pressure, were able to fight back with support from the people of St. Paul. Under international pressure, the government of South Africa announced that it was going to allow the present inhabitants to remain in the area and also permit the previous inhabitants to apply for resettlement.[6]

At a United Nations conference of local governments in September 1990, local governments recently considered ways in which they can cooperate to foster sustainable development. Transnational environmental problems are both immediate and urgent and provide great room for combined efforts internationally. The struggles to eliminate ozone-depleting chlorofluorocarbons and other chemicals began in a few capitalist countries when scientists in the 1970s first hypothesized that chlorine emissions would damage the ozone layer. In the 1980s, as we were confronted with the enormity of the damage that human activities, primarily in the capitalist industrialized countries, have done to the Earth in terms of destroying the ozone layer, the dimensions of the international struggle also grew. For the first few years, it was primarily a struggle carried out in the capitalist countries to phase out these chemicals—that is, where the emissions were concentrated. At the same time, cooperation between the countries of the world, including the countries in the Third World, to eliminate or reduce the risk of severe

---

6   Richard Trubo, "Striking a Blow for Freedom," *Municipal Foreign Policy Bulletin,* Spring 1990, pp. 28-29.

ozone depletion has been in greater evidence, although much more remains to be done. That cooperation was greatly enhanced in the the June 1990 accords to phase out ozone-depleting chemicals, which included provisions for alleviation of the financial burdens that are being imposed on Third World countries due to pollution mainly caused by emissions from the capitalist countries.

An increasing appreciation of the global nature of environmental problems, not only by national bodies but by local organizations and by people in their everyday lives, is one of the most important elements in moving toward a system of economic justice and environmental sanity in the world. It is a harbinger of a global civic culture.

Chapter 13

MONEY, HUMAN NEEDS AND THE ENVIRONMENT

Monetized and Non-monetized Work

We should try to create a society in which it is never a tragedy to be pregnant.

—Annie Makhijani[1]

It is essential that the work of parenting, of maintaining homes, of looking after the sick in the family and the many other vital tasks which tend to be almost exclusively those of women today be immediately included in the accounting of productive labor. As has been suggested by Marilyn Waring and others, the keeping of international economic accounts must be changed to include all such work as productive labor, essential to the functioning of the economic system.

No program can adequately address the immense issues of work, jobs and meeting human needs unless a clear accounting and inclusion of all non-monetized work is made.

These accounts are needed for a number of reasons. For instance, they are needed to assess the utility of goods which are made today.

---

1   Annie Makhijani, personal conversation around 1986.

Monetary value does not take into account the non-monetized labor required to maintain goods in usable condition unless that maintenance is part of the monetized economy. Thus, although it may take much longer to wash and iron a shirt over its life than to make it, economic accounting and the design of the product does not systematically take that into account. Sometimes we see indirect effects. For example, when more women work in the monetized sector, then we see an increase in no-iron shirts.

Estimates of the amount of maintenance labor required to maintain the utility of a product as well as estimates of the lifetime of the product should also be required of manufacturers. The utility per unit of labor time to produce and maintain consumer goods can, in most cases, be calculated at least approximately—hours of wear over a shirt's lifetime, number of calculations a computer will perform before being junked and so on. In terms of productivity over the long haul, it may well be that techniques of construction used by master carpenters to build Japanese temples that have withstood earthquakes and the rigors of climate for centuries might be more productive than the glued plywood of today.

Of course, one need not monetize all aspects of social activity to recognize their social worth and "pay" for them. That would probably not be desirable in many cases. But policies can be put into place to take practical account of non-monetized work. For example, pensions and social security benefits should be instituted for parenting, for attending to the sick and for other non-monetized work. The provision of paid pregnancy leave and parenting leave could be made a social expenditure rather than a corporate expenditure. That is already the case, for instance, in France and some other countries.

While it may be impractical or even undesirable to directly monetize parenting, cooking and other work at home, there is no reason why it cannot be indirectly monetized. For instance, the work of parenting can be indirectly recognized as part of the money economy, without monetizing it by making the earnings of both parents legally common property. This is already the case in some countries, but in most of the Third World it could have a considerable liberating effect and provide women with some security with which to organize their struggle for economic and social equality.

Human Needs and the Environment

Our robbery of the environment of future generations is at least as grave as any injustice we are visiting upon our own generation. The term "sustainability" has been used to describe the attributes of the economic system which does not mortgage the future. Sharad Lele has defined sustainability as having the following attributes:[2]

- Dynamic equilibrium.

- Adaptability (or the capacity for evolutionary change to changing circumstances).

- Resilience (or the capacity to recover from shocks or sudden changes in conditions).

- Reliability.

How these attributes are to be measured or evaluated, what tensions there are among them and between them and the goals of productivity for meeting present needs and equity is a complex matter which has begun to be explored systematically only in recent years.

However, it does not require detailed theoretical development to note that the transformations which human activities are making in the environment from the local to the global are generally in a direction which is opposite to that of sustainability. Major examples are the build-up of greenhouse gases, the Antarctic ozone hole, severe air pollution, destruction of tropical forests, loss of topsoil as well as widespread contamination of land, groundwater, rivers and seas with toxic wastes. We need initiatives that will create the economic incentives to reverse the increasing threats to the Earth and also meet the need for meaningful and productive work oriented toward human needs.

A brief discussion of greenhouse gas emissions shows one way in which environmental and economic goals can be joined. The principal greenhouse gases are carbon dioxide, methane and chlorofluorocar-

---

2   Sharad Lele, "A Framework for Sustainability and Its Application in Visualizing a Peace Society." Draft paper commissioned by The Exporatory Project on the Conditions of Peace, 1989; available from the Institute for Energy and Environmental Research, Takoma Park, MD 20912.

bons. These gases primarily come from activities in the industrialized capitalist and (formerly) centralized socialist countries. The accumulations of carbon dioxide in particular have resulted from about a hundred years of use of fossil fuels in the capitalist countries, the Soviet Union and Eastern Europe. Considerable reduction in their use is possible using available technology. In addition, we also need to greatly improve the efficiency of fuelwood and other energy in the Third World and stop the burning of savannahs and forests. These activities in the capitalist and formerly socialist countries and in the Third World are contributing to the risk of catastrophic climatic changes. Yet, at the same time, we must provide larger amounts of useful energy to people in the Third World so that there is some hope of at least modest levels of material well-being for them.

While improvements in the conditions of living for the vast majority of people in the Third World do require an increase in the useful work that energy can perform, a great increase of energy use is not required. Poor people use energy very inefficiently *because they do not have the resources to invest in equipment that can provide efficient use.* As one dramatic example, I have calculated that the same amount of wood is used to produce charcoal for cooking for one person in Kenya can be used to generate electricity providing cooking fuel for fifteen people.[3] In this instance, there exists the scope for increasing efficiency by fifteen times, simply by first converting the wood to electricity in an efficient boiler, and then having people cook with electricity. The real problem, of course, is that the poor cannot afford electricity and electric stoves and so they use wood and charcoal to the great detriment of their own health, their children's health and the health of the planet. Often they are denied electricity because of skewed investment priorities in the Third World and as a part of a larger denial of land and housing rights to the urban poor.

Resources for drastically cutting back on fossil fuels can come from an increase in the relative price of fossil fuels. For instance, a tax on carbon emissions from fuels which escalates gradually has the potential of providing substantial resources over the next two decades both within the capitalist countries and internationally. The proceeds of such a tax can be used for projects which are designed to improve the ef-

---

3 For a detailed discussion of how energy effectiveness can be improved without substantially increasing energy use in the Third World and reducing it in other countries, see J. Goldemberg, et. al., *Energy for a Sustainable World,* New Delhi: Wiley East, 1988.

ficiency of energy use and increase renewable energy use all over the world. It can also be a major source of revenue for guaranteed employment schemes to meet human needs in all countries, and especially in the Third World. Other schemes, such as the use of tradable vouchers instead of taxes, may also be viable.

These projects can do more than meet global environmental needs. They have the potential to meet the needs of the poor for health care, water, decent jobs and such other basic human rights as shelter and education. The need for decently paid work as well as the amount of work that needs to be done is enormous. There is a great dearth of housing, clean water, production of healthy food and health care. At the same time, there are very large numbers of qualified or nearly qualified people, or people who can be trained to fill these needs. What is lacking is the means to mobilize and rechannel financial resources from their present environmentally destructive, militaristic patterns into sustainable, equitable, peaceful patterns.

Sufficient resources can be generated from such measures as a carbon tax to create large numbers of jobs, including jobs in the Third World. These jobs must be in the proper sectors to ensure that the financial resources are transferred to those areas within the Third World that need them most. Currently, in most Third World countries the interests of the rich generally prevail. The channeling of resources to the poor which are raised through international taxation will require vigilance and support and cooperation across borders among those struggling for economic justice.

Non-governmental organizations can play an important role in this. They are, in any case, coming to have a bigger role in world affairs. For instance, in environmental issues it has been non-governmental organizations which have taken the lead over both government and industry. Non-governmental organizations have struggled hard for stringent limits on emissions of ozone-depleting substances and faster phase-out schedules. Without their efforts, the situation regarding ozone-depleting substances would be even more unsatisfactory than it is today. Similarly, within Third World countries it is largely the non-governmental organizations, whether they be environmental groups, unions, peasants demanding land or women fighting the dowry system, which lead the struggle for economic and social justice and environmental sanity. The linking of these organizations across the boundaries of countries can help create the minimum political conditions to ensure that at least a substantial fraction of resources allocated for international environmental restructuring meet the needs of the poor, and especially women and children.

The transformation to a peace system requires steps at many different levels. Changes in the international economy and changes in the national economies are all tied to improving both living conditions and the environment. Including the value of the environment (covering also non-renewable resources) and the value of the non-monetized work of women and children is critical to a true redistribution of wealth among the people who now live in the world and between people of this generation and people of the next. It is also a key element in transforming social attitudes. Changes in the tax structure to account for environmental damage and in social security to pay for currently non-monetized work are steps toward a peace system.

Chapter 14

ECONOMIC CULTURE

A critical aspect of the war system is expressed in the greed it tends to engender in people. The ideology is one in which the well-being of neighbors, not to speak of neighboring countries or future generations, can be widely disregarded without shame. Limitless consumption and acquisition are often overriding goals in a war system.

Both the social system under the Egyptian Pharaohs and the feudal and imperial systems of Asia and Europe were progenitors of modern economic culture in many ways. They all depended upon the exploitation of land in rural areas and of large numbers of workers and slaves and women in villages and cities for the provision of luxuries. In ancient Greece, neither women nor slaves could be citizens. This enabled "consumerism" to flourish in times past among a small minority.

In all war systems, the existence of vast riches creates two kinds of poverty: absolute poverty, in which people die for want of food and medicine and water and shelter; and relative poverty, in which wants multiply, driven by the cultural example of the rich. These two are not always separate. The drives generated by relative poverty often take precedence over those of food, water and shelter—that is, in the competition for resources between vegetables and VCRs, the latter often win.

Over the last 200 years of consumerist culture, which formerly could be practiced only by the ruling classes, strictly defined as kings, feudal lords, capitalist merchants and slave-owners, has come within reach of large numbers of people. This possibility has derived from three sources:

1. The vast increases in machinery and energy consumption which immensely accelerated the human ability to produce and consume resources.

2. The huge areas that were suddenly brought into the compass of resource exploitation, including vast areas underground and undersea.

3. The practical expropriation of resources from the Third World so that their consumption could be concentrated within the capitalist countries.

These factors provide the possibility of a widespread culture of consumerism. Besides the example of the ruling classes, who have always defined "the good life" for the rest of the people, today's culture of consumerism is also driven by systematic corporate policies and the structure of the world economy. Rapid discarding of goods produces more profits than careful construction. Frequent changes of fashion are more profitable. Unneeded consumption by the rich produces profits while the needs of the poor, which are not backed up by money ("effective demand"), produce none. An immense morally and intellectually dishonest and corrupt system of promotion of goods underlies the culture of consumerism, where the act of purchase sometimes appears to be more the goal than the possession, let alone use, of the object that is purchased. We have discussed some examples in this book.

By these means, a culture of consumerism, driven by a permanent feeling of relative poverty despite increasing consumption, has become thoroughly consolidated in the capitalist countries, especially in the last half-century. This consumerist culture is not limited to the capitalist countries, however. It has seized the popular imagination of rich and poor alike, of capitalist and communist alike, throughout the world. The foundation in imagination of this culture is that it knows no limits of consumption. There is no notion of "enough."

Today, the problems of global environmental damage are often blamed on the large numbers of people in the world and increasing population. However, the fact that about one-third of the world's people are consuming considerably in excess of 90 percent of the monetized resources, when we include the rich of the Third World in the calculation, is causally connected to the reality that hundreds of millions of people in the world are living at the margin of existence in great poverty with hardly any access even to clean water, let alone productive resources such as land.

Those who consume large amounts of resources are frightened of the "population problem" and see the poor as a threat because the poor are demanding that they be allowed to consume to the material standard that the wealthy have established in the popular culture and imagination as desirable. It is not the present consumption of the poor which defines "overpopulation." It is primarily the consumption of the rich that threatens to exhaust the world's resources and cause irretrievable damage to the environment.

In a sense, the wealthy are right to be afraid. With the present level of technology and culture of limitless greed, the poor cannot become just like the wealthy without destroying the Earth. However, this is not a problem of population as such. With far fewer people, the same structure of greed would still result in despoliation of the Earth.

We see the spectacle today of people being dissatisfied with enormous homes. In Beverly Hills, a home of 6,000 square feet becomes too small and the rich move on to 10,000 square feet, and then to 50,000 square feet with a bowling alley. The requirements of energy resources to heat and to air condition these modern palaces are so great that no conceivable pattern of production along the present lines could satisfy even a considerably smaller population with such aspirations. We may say that there are two population problems, rather than only one. For the rich there are too many poor, and for the poor there are too many who are too rich.

The extent of consumption often seems to have little connection to the utility of the goods that are being consumed. The chairman of Coca Cola Corporation is pleased with the accomplishment of his company and others like it that people in the United States drink more soft drinks than water. However, in terms of human health, the quality of one's teeth and the condition of one's body, this is clearly a step backward from the time when one might have been able to drink a few glasses of clean water every day. Consumerism creates desires for "high-definition television" with bigger and bigger screens. But we do not seem to remember that we see programs with lower and lower quality.

Overall, we might consume as many resources today, in the typical "middle-class" family of the capitalist countries as Marie Antoinette may have done when she advised the poor to eat cake. The degree to which we have deprived future generations in terms of the despoliation of the environment and putting the entire atmosphere of the planet in peril is greater than was done by the feudal lords and kings of centuries past. (There were also far fewer of them.)

Cooperation within communities and between communities as the basis of trade and mutual benefit, and consideration for future generations, cannot be established securely unless we also establish the principle of enough as part of our economic culture. The ideology of limitless consumption goes hand-in-hand with the ideology of greed and limitless profit and limitless riches. That ideology has contributed to the production of grave inequalities, nuclear weapons, militarized borders and much other violence in order that the rich and the privileged may protect themselves from the poor. Yet it is not a system conducive to human happiness even for the rich and for their children.

At the same time, the system of greed and exploitation creates in the poor the idea that they must also be rich. So those few who escape poverty usually become established within that same system and adopt its values. It is these structural conditions which give the war system its resilience. And it is these structures of the war system which must be dismantled and replaced by the principles of a peace system. One of these is the principle of limits to material wants in our desires and in the economic structure of society.

In global apartheid, the hungers, desires, tears, joys, the very humanity of the dispossessed, do not register as parts of the economic system. The process by which we rid the world of economic depravity and excess is surely the same one by which we organize to end the suffering of the children who die of want and of their parents who must bury them. That will be the process by which the present economic system based on exploitation, violence and environmental destruction will be replaced by one in which human well-being, neighborliness, friendship and nurture of the Earth will flourish.

Appendix

RESTRUCTURING THE INTERNATIONAL MONETARY SYSTEM*

Arjun Makhijani and Robert S. Browne

Today, the characteristics of the third World's debt are such that they constitute a great threat to national sovereignties and our peoples' right of self-determination.[1]

—Aldo Ferrer, President,
Banco de la Provincia de Buenos Aires

---

* This paper is based on a study prepared by Arjun Makhijani for the International Labour Office of the United Nations, in which he explores the connections between human labor-time and productivity and the use of energy—of oil in particular. [2] Reprinted with permission from *World Policy Journal*, Winter 1985-86, pp. 59-80.

153

The experience of world development has demonstrated with increasing force that it is impossible to implement a genuine international development strategy without fundamental restructuring of the international monetary system . . . . This must be capable of achieving monetary stability . . . and it must be supportive of a process of global development, especially for the countries of the Third World, which contain the majority of the world's poor.[3]

—The Arusha Initiative

For more than a decade now, in U.N. speeches, in scholarly studies and in declarations like the Arusha Initiative, Third World leaders have sought to draw attention to the inadequacy of the international monetary system. The world's monetary arrangements, they have argued, are particularly ill-suited to the needs of their countries' economies and require fundamental restructuring. But in the West, which effectively controls the international monetary system, these calls for change have fallen on deaf ears or [have] been interpreted as political maneuvers by the "have-nots" as just another round in their campaign to redistribute the wealth of the "haves." Washington, in particular, has dismissed these demands as unworthy of serious consideration; the present administration still holds the same basic position.

Events of the past 10 years, however, should have dispelled any reasonable doubts about the Third World's contention that the current monetary system is itself a major obstacle to economic growth and development. The moderate economic successes that Third World countries managed to achieve during the 1960s and early 1970s were abruptly derailed in the early 1980s, in large part by narrowly conceived U.S. macroeconomic policies whose impact was transmitted abroad through the international monetary system. Washington's relentless effort to bring domestic inflation under control—an effort initiated by the Carter administration and vigorously pursued by the Reagan administration—wrought considerable economic havoc in Third World countries. The drastic tightening of U.S. monetary policy beginning in 1980 pushed real U.S. interest rates as high as 8 percent—the equivalent of 20 percent for some Third World countries, when based on terms of trade. The resulting recession slowed the growth of Third World exports and depressed the prices of Third World commodities. And high interest rates and an overvalued U.S. dollar encouraged capital flight from Third World countries and dramatically increased their debt-servicing burdens.

Yet it was not until these developments threatened Western

economies—through the debt crisis that erupted in 1982—that Western nations began to pay serious attention to the Third World's economic plight. Western officials, anxious about the recession induced by America's tight money policy, have recently begun to voice more and more anxiety about the global financial collapse that could be brought on if Third World borrowers massively defaulted on their debts. And as the overvalued dollar has begun to take its toll on U.S. industries and jobs, more and more U.S. policymakers—both Democratic and Republican—have begun to look more closely at the shortcomings of the international monetary system. Even though they have so far paid little heed to Third World arguments, they have nonetheless begun to recognize the need for some rethinking of the system.

This essay's goal is to contribute to that rethinking process—a process that we know will take considerable time. Human nature tends to resist new ways of looking at old relationships. Furthermore, any reform, including the proposals of our own that appear below, will necessarily cause some discomfort for those who derive excessive benefits from the existing arrangements. But we believe that, in the long run, the more rational approach to international monetary transactions that we propose will benefit everyone—those who now enjoy special privileges as well as those who are now unconscionably exploited.

The Bretton Woods Dollar-Gold Exchange System

The present international monetary arrangements derive from the system devised at the 1944 conference in Bretton Woods, New Hampshire. That system was based on the gold-exchange standard: the parities of currencies of all participating countries were to be fixed and adjusted in relation to the U.S. dollar, while the U.S. government promised to redeem paper dollars for gold at a fixed rate of $35 an ounce.

The basic idea was that the exchange rate of a country's currency—both its rate against the dollar and its rates against other currencies—would reflect the supply of and demand for that currency. These, in turn, were a function of the country's balance-of-payments equilibrium. The currency of a country with a surplus would be more in demand, that of a country with a deficit less so. Exchange rates were envisioned as helping to keep a country's balance of payments in approximate equilibrium.

Changes in economic relationships among countries might temporarily disturb the payments equilibrium. But it was expected that market forces and the requirements of maintaining credit would adjust the monetary flows as required to restore this equilibrium, thus allowing the exchange rate to remain fixed under normal circumstances. Should this mechanism fail and a deficit or surplus in the balance of payments become chronic, the system provided for a change in the exchange rate.

Such changes were discouraged, however. A country experiencing a serious disequilibrium was instead urged to bring its payments balance into line by making adjustments in its internal economic policies. To the extent that trade could flow freely—and a major impetus behind the establishment of the Bretton Woods system was the desire to facilitate trade and to discourage the beggar-thy-neighbor policies that had been so disruptive during the prewar period—countries could increase or decrease their trade balances by lowering or raising their internal price levels. (They could also manipulate the prices of particular products by subsidizing them, but this was frowned upon.) Another variable for countries to manipulate was the price of money—the interest rate—which allowed them some control over the volume and direction of non-trade-related capital flows. The IMF was created to monitor these operations and was empowered to make short-term loans to assist countries over periods of temporary monetary disequilibrium.

For the industrialized countries, the system worked reasonably well during the first two decades after World War II. It carried the world through the prolonged period of postwar reconstruction that was marked by the dollar shortage, a problem the United States handled by instituting the Marshall Plan and the succeeding foreign aid programs. By the late 1960s, however, a host of new realities had begun to undermine the system. At this point, the European and Japanese economies had fully recovered from the war, and the privileged position that had been granted to the dollar began to come under question. The dollar shortage had turned into a dollar glut, as Washington attempted to pay for the Vietnam War not by taxing U.S. citizens but by printing dollars and obliging its trade partners to hold them in ever-greater quantities. As America's inability to convert these dollars into gold became increasingly evident, dollar-holders grew more and more restive. In 1971, the United States ended gold convertibility, and two years later, after devaluing the dollar twice, severed the formal link between the dollar and gold. Soon after that, the system of fixed exchange rates was officially abandoned in favor of floating exchange rates.

Floating exchange rates, it was believed, would help restore equilibrium in countries' payments balances. But what has followed instead has been an increase in economic instability. International payments imbalances have been larger than ever. Currency speculation has become widespread. International financial transactions have skyrocketed, far surpassing the levels necessary to finance trade transactions. And a huge Eurodollar market—dollars held outside the United States and not subject to U.S. regulation—has sprung up. These developments—large payments imbalances, rapidly fluctuating exchange rates and massive unregulated capital flows—have complicated and distorted economic policymaking in the industrialized and developing countries alike.

Moreover, for most of the world, but especially for the Third World countries, the abandonment of the gold standard and the adoption of floating exchange rates have had the effect of making their economies even more vulnerable to U.S. economic policy. The U.S. dollar—the paper currency of a single country—continues to be the principal international reserve currency and the principal monetary instrument of international trade. The value of other countries' international monetary reserves and that of their products and commodities, as well as the flows of international capital, have therefore become critically dependent on the domestic monetary and fiscal policies of a single country. Because the value of the dollar is not backed by any commodity, the value of other countries' financial reserves, like that of the international monetary unit itself, is only a nominal value determined by the United States, which holds a monopoly on its issuance.

While these features of today's international monetary system pose problems for all countries, they pose special problems for Third World countries. This is made clear if we examine two areas of concern: Third World balance-of-payments problems and the inappropriateness of the IMF conditionalities intended to solve those problems, and the effect of the international monetary system on Third World terms of trade.

Balance-of-Payments Problems and IMF Adjustment

Under the current system, the International Monetary Fund is charged with overseeing countries' balance-of-payments situations and has thus taken the leading role in handling the Third World debt crisis. As a condition for extending new loans to debtor countries, the IMF requires them to adopt what are called adjustment policies. The IMF's standard prescription calls for currency devaluation, export expansion and a number of other belt-tightening austerity measures. This program has come under increasing attack in recent years as being harmful not only to the debtor country but also to the world economy. Such programs have failed to produce economic growth in Third World countries and have not made the Third World more able, or likely, to repay its debt. If anything, the opposite has occurred—the Third World's economic situation has deteriorated, in large part because the IMF program addresses only the symptoms and not the underlying structural causes of the current problem.

J. J. Polack, one of the architects of the IMF's theoretical approach, has argued that, in general, "balance of payments problems are associated with inflationary causes: and moderation in credit expansion is generally prescribed as a preventative or a curative for payments difficulties."[4] In this view, Third World economic crises almost always result from the same sequence of events: Governments spend far in excess of their revenues, causing budget deficits and inflation. These governments' failures to adjust exchange rates to reflect this internal inflation result in overvalued currencies. The economic situation is further damaged by insufficient government attention to supply-side factors, such as production, marketing, pricing and exchange rates.[5]

Underlying this analysis lie two main theoretical premises. First, the IMF assumes that a country's internal economic policies—monetary, trade and fiscal—are the primary factors determining both the country's economic well-being and the amount of capital flowing into and out of it. Second, the IMF holds that appropriate changes in a country's monetary, trade and fiscal policies and in the exchange rate of its currency will correct unhealthy and unstable internal conditions, as well as solve balance-of-payments problems.

One major shortcoming in these assumptions is immediately apparent: the IMF's analysis and prescriptions relate primarily to the internal economies of countries and fail to take into account the importance of international economic relationships. More specifically, the IMF gives no systematic central place to the effect of the U.S. dollar and of U.S. policy on the international economy and on the balance-of-payments positions of other countries.[6] Yet, as suggested earlier, the economic policies of the industrialized countries, particularly the United States, weigh at least as heavily in the balance-of-payments situation of the developing countries as the policies the latter may pursue.

Consider, for example, the Third World debt crisis, which has its origins in the West's reaction to the OPEC oil shocks. In the early 1970s, the United States and, to varying extents, the other OECD countries, responded to OPEC's increases in oil prices by heavily expanding the money supply. The resulting inflation, together with the administered pricing policies in many basic U.S. industries, sharply increased the prices of U.S. exports and thus the cost of many imports to Third World countries. Such an inflationary policy enabled the OECD countries, as a group, to keep their current accounts in balance, despite the large oil price rises.[7] At the same time, however, the industrial economies were also experiencing unemployment and frequent recession, which depressed the demand for Third World goods.

Thus the U.S. response to the OPEC moves created a two-way squeeze on the Third World: its exports to the United States slowed while its imports from the United States became more expensive. In effect, the United States largely insulated itself from the oil price hikes by passing the burden on to the Third World, whose current account deficits mounted. The Third World, in turn, tried to ease this burden by borrowing heavily rather than by deflating. These contrasting responses to the oil price hikes created a good deal of financial instability: the heavily indebted borrowers were increasingly unable to sell their wares to the depressed economies of their creditors. This instability was exacerbated at the beginning of the 1980s, when America's highly restrictive monetary policy produced the highest real interest rates and one of the worst worldwide recessions of this century, and its loose fiscal policy led to mammoth budget deficits that kept interest rates high after the recession had ended.

For the indebted Third World countries, these U.S. policy choices have been an utter calamity and have greatly increased their debt problems. To begin with, much of the Third World's debt was contracted at variable interest rates—up to 75 percent for some major borrowers, and 40 percent overall—which has made them extremely susceptible to the effects of the high interest rates that U.S. economic policy has dictated over the past six years. In 1984, it was estimated that a 1 percent rise in interest rates added about $3 billion per year to the interest charges on all Third World debt.[8] The high interest rates have also encouraged capital flight to the United States from other OECD countries and from Third World countries. These flows are high but not easily measurable, as is clear from the burgeoning Errors and Omissions figures in many countries' balance-of-payments accounts.

The overvalued dollar that has resulted from the high interest rates has had equally far-reaching effects. Although this strong dollar has encouraged a flood of imports into the United States, many of them from Third World countries, its negative impact has been severe. It has greatly increased the cost of U.S. products to those countries that need them. Because oil prices are denominated in dollars, it has raised the effective price of petroleum to the oil-importing nations—despite the decline in the posted price of oil. It has also raised the prices of and thereby cut the demand for those Third World exports whose prices are customarily quoted in U.S. dollars but sold to non-U.S. buyers. And it has raised the real cost of servicing Third World debt, most of which is dollar-denominated. As a result, Third World countries must now sell a larger volume of goods to service a given volume of debt.

Finally, and ironically, Washington's high-interest-rate/strong-dollar policy has quickly transformed the United States itself into a debtor nation—soon to be the largest in the world—and has saddled the country with a trade deficit so large that the calls for protectionism are becoming difficult to resist. Consequently, some of the major Third World debtor countries like Brazil and South Korea have become the object of U.S. trade retaliation. These protectionist pressures only darken the prospects for Third World economic growth and the successful repayment of Third World debt.

Thus a great deal of the economic damage [that] the Third World has suffered since 1980 has been the result of deliberate choices of U.S. policy, whose negative effect is often exacerbated by the IMF's actions. Trade has been depressed. A growing number of Third World countries face debt-servicing obligations in excess of 50 percent of their export earnings. And the combination of high debt-servicing obligations and declining capital inflows has transformed many Third World countries into net capital exporters.

This means that resources are being transferred from the world's poorest countries to its wealthiest ones—a highly perverse state of affairs.

The IMF regularly points out the negative impact U.S. policies have on the global economy. And normally the IMF has leverage over countries that are encountering payments deficits. But despite the fact that the United States is experiencing sustained balance-of-payments deficits, the IMF has no leverage over U.S. policy, since the dollar is the international reserve currency and since the United States exercises veto power over all major IMF decisions.[9] Thus even though many individuals, including a few Western officials,[10] have recognized the impact of U.S. policy on the international economy—and particularly on the debt crisis—the IMF has failed to take steps that could lessen this

impact. Instead, it has plowed ahead with its practice of placing virtually the entire burden of adjustment squarely upon the shoulders of the
Third World. It has continued to apply its standard prescriptions for
countries suffering balance-of-payments deficits—currency devaluation, export expansion and trade liberalization—even though these
measures are in many cases unrelated to the real causes of the payments
imbalances.

But the problem is not just that these policies do not address the international factors behind the debt crisis or that there is a lack of sym-
metry in the IMF adjustment process, but also that they are applied
indiscriminately. For one of the fundamental flaws in the IMF approach
is the assumption that the internal economic structures of different
countries are essentially similar, so that similar policies will have
similar effects both internally and on the balance of payments. These
measures may have had the desired effects when applied to the Western
industrialized nations during the postwar period. But now, when applied
in a world whose economy has grown more and more interdependent,
and to Third World countries that are still relatively unindustrialized,
these policies fail to produce the intended effect.

The IMF's trade-related prescriptions illustrate how
counterproductive the IMF's approach to adjustment can be. This approach calls for Third World debtor countries to expand theit exports
and limit their imports as a way of improving their balance-of-payments
position. But such an approach as applied by the IMF cannot only retard
the growth of domestic demand and undermine productive capacity, but
can also create deflationary pressures in the world economy. The latter
problem is especially acute when the IMF encourages large numbers of
countries simultaneously to expand exports and restrict imports: who
will buy in a world full of sellers? This deflationary approach to adjustment can lead to increased protectionism and a shrinkage of world trade,
which in turn only compounds the adjustment problem. In essence, this
is what we see occurring today.

Moreover, as part of its prescription for increasing exports, the IMF
typically requires a currency devaluation, which makes a country's exports cheaper and its imports more expensive. A currency devaluation
thus can expand the exports of countries that have a range of goods to
sell, and may do some good for countries that have reached a certain
level of industrialization (assuming, of course, that industrialized
countries' markets remain open). But it does little to expand exports for
many Third World countries, whose exports consist primarily of one or
two commodities, such as coffee, copper and rubber. If markets for these

products become poor, the countries do not have a range of other products to sell. And even if markets do remain strong, demand for these commodities, which are consumed primarily in OECD countries, remains highly inelastic. Moreover, because commodity producers, with the exception of OPEC, have never been able to organize themselves sufficiently to influence the prices at which their products are sold, these prices remain externally determined. Thus when currency devaluation is implemented, Third World countries will probably feel the internal inflation that usually results, but they are unlikely to experience any significant increase in their export earnings. The problem is that the IMF's pressure is being applied to the relatively passive Third World sellers, but not to the major actors—the industrialized country buyers.

Even if a devaluation does work to increase a developing country's exports, it creates other, more serious problems. For example, such a devaluation shifts the terms of trade more in favor of the industrialized countries, even though poor terms of trade are a major cause of the original balance-of-payments problem. Furthermore, the inflationary effects of the devaluation, combined with other typical IMF prescriptions, such as cutbacks in consumer subsidies and freezing of salaries and wages, generally lead to a reduction in real wages in the debtor country—where real wages are already quite low.

Relative Wages and Exchange Rates

This brings us to an equally serious flaw in the present international monetary system: its tendency to depress real wage levels in the Third World and to institutionalize poor terms of trade between industrialized and developing countries. It is generally recognized that Third World wages are much lower than those in the West. In the manufacturing sector in Third World countries, wages range [from] 3 to 30 percent of wages in the United States.[11] (These are 1975 statistics; at current exchange rates, the disparities are even greater.) But what is not generally recognized is that the low level of wages is intimately linked not to low productivity of labor-time, as classical economic theory would suggest, but to undervalued exchange rates and the workings of the international monetary system.

According to classical economic theory, wages are based on the productivity of labor; and because wages are a major determinant of the price of most traded goods, the relative prices of goods should reflect a country's relative labor productivity. But this is not the case in the Third World. Indeed, labor productivity in the Third World export sector is often higher than in the OECD countries. Richard Barnet has given some examples of this:

> The product that export platform countries in the Third World are selling is not merely cheap labor, but highly productive labor. In Singapore . . . McGraw-Hill produces in one year an encyclopedia that takes five years to produce in the U.S. . . . Mexican metal workers are 40 percent more productive than U.S. workers, electronics workers 10 to 15 percent more productive, and seamstresses produce 30 percent more sewing per hour than their U.S. counterparts.[12]

The same disparity shows up in the exchange rates of currencies: they do not reflect the average productivity of labor-time in monetary terms. For if this average productivity were lower in the Third World than in the OECD countries—as current exchange rates would indicate—the average prices of commodities would be higher in the Third World than in the West. The reality is quite the opposite. Apart from imported commodities, which are made costly by the current system of setting and changing exchange rates, average prices in the Third World are generally much lower than in the OECD countries, particularly the United States. For example, while 50 U.S. cents converted to rupees or taka would buy a good meal made from local foodstuffs in a small-town restaurant in India or Bangladesh, it barely sufiices for a small glass of orange juice in the United States. Similar price differences can be observed in many consumer commodities, such as clothing or public transportation.

Thus the average productivity of labor, measured in terms of prevailing prices at current exchange rates, is generally much higher in the Third World. At the prevailing exchange rates, many more comparable meals are produced per U.S. dollar in Bangladesh than in the United States.[13] The fact that exchange rates of currencies do not reflect local purchasing power has been the object of considerable inquiry. Many international institutions, such as the United Nations, the World Bank and OECD, have sponsored research on the subject. The *1983 World Bank Atlas*, referring to several of these studies by Irving Kravis and his associates, noted:

> The use of official exchange rates to convert national currency figures to the U.S. dollar does not, of course, measure accurately the relative purchasing power of currencies. The United Nations International

Comparison Project (ICP) has developed measures of real gross
domestic product (GDP) on an international comparable basis by
using purchasing power parities instead of exchange rates as conversion factors.[14]

Using purchasing power parities related to the gross domestic
products of various countries, these U.N. and World Bank studies calculated that the GDP of Third World countries was substantially higher,
often as much as threefold or more, than if calculated at official exchange rates. This means that if exchange rates were set according to
purchasing power parity, most Third World countries' currencies would
be worth substantially more than they are now.

All this implies that the currencies of Third World countries are *undervalued* both in relation to productivity in the export sector and in
relation to average productivity. We recognize, of course, that the assertion that the currencies of the Third World are undervalued runs quite
contrary to the common assumption that they are overvalued—a position presumed to be generally substantiated by the existence of currency black markets in the Third World. These black markets exist,
however, largely because of the inequitable structure of the international monetary system. Third World countries' perpetually poor terms of
trade, along with the heavy dependence of their economies on export
earnings, lead to restrictions—often severe—on the amounts of foreign
currencies available in the Third World. This fact, combined with the
great inequalities of income distribution within Third World countries
and the widespread insecurity among the rich of the Third World,
generally creates a large demand for foreign currencies, as [a] means
both to export money and to purchase foreign commodities and services. Currency black markets usually do not disappear with devaluation; in fact, devaluation and fears of devaluation can increase capital
flight. Furthermore, currency black markets exist not only because of
the monetary policies and political climates within individual countries,
but also because of the international monetary structure and specific
U.S. policies, such as the currently high interest rates.

If Third World currencies are undervalued, as our analysis suggests,
then the current system artificially lowers relative wages in the Third
World and builds poor terms of trade into the international economic
system.[15] This systematic undervaluation of Third World currencies is
one of the main reasons the Third World has so little command over
world resources. In the heyday of the Victorian era, Britain's economic
maxim was, "Selling dear, buying cheap."[16] As Tanzania's President

Julius Nyerere has noted, for the Third World this has meant, "We sell cheap and buy dear, whether we like it or not." The workings of the international monetary system help explain why Nyerer's formulation persistently holds true.

The current exchange-rate system, then, complements and exacerbates the theoretical deficiencies that characterize the IMF's demand-based, monetarist analysis of the source of the balance-of-payments problems. This system does not, and cannot, address the structural realities that differentiate the economic situation of the Third World from that of the United States and other OECD countries. It therefore cannot yield correct "prescriptions" for resolving the Third World's economic difficulties.

These two shortcomings, of course, are not the only flaws in the international monetary system—increasingly currency speculation, massive unregulated capital flows and widely fluctuating exchange rates create serious problems. But the two specific aspects we have discussed do suggest how the system operates against Third World development—and thus, sustained world economic growth—and why international monetary reform is critical.

Basics of a New Approach

In order to correct the present monetary system's theoretical flaws and practical inequities, it will be necessary to abandon balance-of-payments criteria—or increasingly, capital-flows criteria—as determinants of currency exchange rates. It will also be necessary to create a stable, truly international currency whose value cannot be changed by a single country or bloc of countries. Thus a new international monetary system that addresses the immediate problems of the debt crisis as well as more long-term, structural problems would need to introduce several major changes:

- Exchange rates of currencies should be determined according to the relative prices of basic consumer goods in each country. This would better reflect the productivity of monetized labor-time. It would also allow each country monetary independence in decisions on internal policy, without making outside parties vulnerable to the consequences of those decisions.

- A new international currency should be issued. A unit of this currency—which we would call the International Currency Unit—would have a fixed purchasing power in every country, as it would be valued in terms of a "basket" or composite of consumer goods. International trade would greatly benefit from the existence of such a noninflationary and stable international currency and unit of account.

- Each country would set aside certain stocks of commodities whose monetary value would be proportional to that of the country's foreign trade. These would serve as a guarantee against obligations arising from balance-of-payments deficits. The stocks would also provide real commodity backing for the international monetary system, without requiring commodity price control or management.

These technical features of our proposal are geared to two fundamental realities. First, most of the world, especially the industrialized countries and the Third World, have constituted one economic system for quite some time. Second, within that system there are structural differences between the OECD countries and the Third World countries that arise from the specific way in which the world economy has evolved. Our proposal recognizes the necessity both of stable, continuing trade and of structural change that would help create a more equitable system, one that promotes Third World development and, in so doing, world development. In fact, we would argue that the world economy's present instabilities have arisen precisely because of the system's structural inequities—particularly the unjustifiably vast differences in wages. These inequities must be redressed in order to ensure the economic stability that benefits all countries.

Exchange Rate Determination

A system of exchange rates based on the relative prices of consumer goods has a different underlying premise than the present system: instead of reflecting balance of payments or capital flows, currency values would reflect average productivity in each country relative to human needs. Instituting such a system would bring about substantial revaluations of the currencies of most Third World countries, and to a lesser extent of many OECD countries as well, with respect to the U.S. dollar. These revaluations would tend to be larger for the countries with the lowest wages, such as most sub-Saharan African countries and

South Asian countries, because it is these countries' currencies that are most undervalued when measured in terms of average productivity of labor-time.

Further changes in the real values of countries' currencies would occur over time according to changes in the productivity of labor-time as it concerned basic consumer goods. A country whose productivity increased in relation to that of other countries would experience a corresponding rise in the value of its currency.

This approach is essentially different from the balance-of-payments approach. In the latter, exchange rates are determined primarily by the prices and quantities of commodities that are imported. This might be satisfactory in a hypothetical world in which all countries had similar internal economic structures and wage levels—that is, in a world in which economic, social and political barriers to the movement of workers and capital did not exist. But as we have seen, in the real world the system is not at all satisfactory: it exacerbates rather than corrects existing economic disparities. Moreover, exchange rates are increasingly determined less by balance of payments in traded goods and more by the trading of currencies themselves. Because the trading of currencies encourages speculation and involves political and economic considerations that are unrelated to labor productivity, it only exacerbates the problems of the balance-of-payments system.

Our approach, in contrast, would do away with the trading of currencies (as will be discussed later) and recognizes and allows for the differences in countries' internal economic structures by creating a unit of value that relates to basic consumer goods—or basic human needs, to use a more common phrase. As we have seen, the prices of basic consumer goods, although affected by imports and exports, are determined mainly by the productivity of labor within that country. This is because the production of basic consumer goods—such as food, housing, medical care and transportation—tends to involve a high amount of domestic labor-time. Setting exchange rates on the basis of the relative prices of these goods—and hence of the average productivity of the country's labor—would have several effects. For one, it would remove one of the principal means by which colonial economic relationships have been institutionalized in the world economy. It would also help to alleviate one of the main causes of the debt crisis—poor terms of trade. And because it would bring about revaluation of Third World currencies, it would substantially raise wages in the Third World relative to wages in the OECD countries, although in many cases they would remain considerably lower in Third World countries.

We have chosen the term "basic consumer goods" only tentatively, since we are keenly aware that in most Third World countries the amount and type of items consumed are largely dictated by poverty. People eat rice and beans, often in insufficient quantities, not because they would not prefer chicken or cheese or do not need more food, but simply because they eat what they can afford. Cultural factors also influence what people consume. In India, for example, beef is much cheaper than chicken, partly for cultural reasons.

These differences would have to be taken into account in the selection of the appropriate "basket" or composite of consumer goods to use as the basis for the exchange rate. In making this selection, it would also be important not to institutionalize differences that arise mainly from the present poverty of most of the Third World's inhabitants. For this reason, we have not suggested using average prices in the entire composition of the GDP but would instead suggest a more specific "basket."

This basket might, for example, consist of one traditionally desirable, 1,000-calorie meal served in a restaurant. Exchange rates would be set so that one International Currency Unit would buy one such meal in all countries. The value of this composite would result from several factors, including the price of food ingredients, the productivity of the workers and the price of floor space. In practice, this composite might prove too narrow; other items such as housing and health care would probably need to be taken into account. But some such composite would provide a reliable basis for comparing average productivity in relation to basic consumer goods, and it would not institutionalize the patterns of consumption that arise from poverty. Using this kind of composite as the basis for determining exchange rates might well cause the currencies of some countries—such as Bangladesh and many sub-Saharan African countries—to be revalued by factors of five or more over their present values relative to the U.S. dollar.

In addition, the prices of traded commodities would change with changes in the exchange rates of currencies. The size of these changes would depend on the specific commodity, and, to a lesser extent, on the length and nature of the transition to the new monetary system. Since the principal effect of the revaluation would be to raise relative wage rates in the Third World, the U.S. dollar prices of Third World commodities would tend to rise insofar as Third World labor contributed to the overall price of the commodity. Thus the price of oil would be essentially unaffected; the price of cocoa would probably rise substantially; the price of copper would increase in lesser measure, since it reflects not only Third World wage's but also interest and depreciation on equipment imported from the OECD countries.

Overall, one could expect a substantial improvement in the Third World's terms of trade. Exactly how much each country's terms of trade would improve, and what effects the new monetary system would have on the prices of and demand for various commodities, would have to be worked out during the technical preparations for formal negotiations toward a new monetary order. But in general, the revaluation of Third World currencies would have a number a beneficial effects. Third World debt, in real terms, could be reduced without altering the dollar amount of it. The new system would promote more open trade on a mutually beneficial and equitable basis. Over the short and medium term, the Third World would be able to import more food and other essentials and, also, to increase the level of investments in agriculture and industry. And the cost of oil for Third World importers would be substantially reduced without severely decreasing oil exporters' revenues, since most of the oil is imported by the OECD countries.

The OECD countries themselves would also benefit from the changes we have proposed. The international monetary and trading system, which is essential to their economies, would be vastly stabilized. The new monetary system would structurally alleviate the debt crisis that now threatens to precipitate widespread financial collapse. It would also help relieve the increasing protectionist pressures that threaten to set off retaliatory trade wars. In the short and intermediate term, Third World markets for manufactures and farm goods from the OECD countries would expand. And it might also be possible for OECD countries to increase jobs in sectors that are now threatened with extinction because of the growing numbers of imports from high-productivity, low-wage Third World industries.

Inflation within individual countries would also become much less of a problem for the international economy. Under our proposed system, inflation or deflation in individual countries' currencies would lead to their automatic devaluation or revaluation with respect to the International Currency Unit. In this way the International Currency Unit would maintain constant purchasing power in all countries, thus protecting the value of the reserves held in International Currency Units. At the same time, this arrangement would allow individual countries to pursue the internal monetary policies of their own choosing, without outside interference or "conditionalities."

For example, if France were experiencing an annual inflation rate of 10 percent in the prices of basic consumer commodities, the French franc would be devalued by 10 percent relative to the International Currency Unit. An inflation rate of 5 percent in Ghana would cause the Ghanaian cedi to be devalued by 5 percent with respect to the International Currency Unit. Such adjustments would be carried out every time the price of the "basket" of basic consumer goods changed by a prescribed fraction of a percent. Thus holders of the International Currency Unit would have constant purchasing power, on the average, in both France and Ghana, irrespective of the inflation rate in either country: they would still be able to purchase the same amounts of goods as before in both Ghana and France, despite the inflation in each country and despite the differences between the two countries' inflation rates. In addition, with these inflation rates, the value of the cedi would automatically increase relative to the franc.

As a result of this automatic adjustment, countries would have much greater independence in pursuing internal policy than they do under the current system. Now, when the IMF is making a loan to a country whose policies it considers to be too expansionary or inflationary, it imposes "conditionalities" that usually involve severe and specific restrictions on that country's monetary, fiscal and even wage policies. In contrast, the system we propose would require no such conditionalities but would instead leave countries much freer to set their own internal monetary and fiscal policies. At the same time, our system would insulate the holders of International Currency Units from particular countries' inflationary or deflationary policies, because their holdings of International Currency Units would maintain constant purchasing power. Furthermore, as we shall discuss in more detail later, the system we propose, like the original Bretton Woods system, would not allow trading of currencies. Consequently, the instabilities that now result from runs on currencies and rapid fluctuations in exchange rates would be controlled—in essence, eliminated.

These are vast claims, to be sure. But we believe that our proposal addresses the principal structural causes of the instability and inequity in the present system. Our system would allow for a defusing of the debt crisis, would put into place a flexible and stable monetary instrument and would lay an inflation-free and equitable basis for trade relations between the Third World and the industrialized countries. At the same time, it would enhance internal monetary and fiscal independence, which are sharply limited under the present system. This feature would have the additional benefit of making it easier for those countries in the Council for Mutual Economic Assistance that are not now IMF members to join the restructured system, thus establishing the basis for a truly universal system.

World Central Bank and the Balance of Payments

Stability in trade will require not only an inflation-free currency, but also an appropriately structured international bank—which we would call the World Central Bank—and a method of settling balances of payments. During the Bretton Woods Conference in 1944, John Maynard Keynes actually presented a British proposal for an international bank—to be called an "International Clearing Union"—where all international transactions would be cleared, much as checks are cleared in domestic banks.

> The Central Banks of all member States (and also of non-members) would keep accounts with the International Clearing Union through which they would be entitled to settle their exchange balances with one another at their par value as defined in terms of the bancor [Keynes's name for the proposed new international currency]. Countries #ith a favourable balance of payments with the rest of the world would find themselves in possession of a credit account with the Clearing Union, and those having an unfavourable balance would have a debit account. Measures would be necessary . . . to prevent the piling up of credit and debit balances without limit, and the system would have failed in the long run if it did not possess sufficient capacity for self-equilibrium to secure this.[17]

The International Clearing Union was designed to prevent the United States from subjugating the international economy to its own domestic policy considerations. It is precisely this feature of Keynes's proposal that is needed today. Even if it had been created and empowered to function at the end of World War II, such a bank could not, for any practical purposes, have been independent of U.S. domestic policy, given America's overwhelming economic and military predominance then. In fact, one could say that it is only now, when American hegemony has declined and when the inadequacy of the U.S. dollar as the international reserve currency is becoming painfully obvious, that a truly international bank for a truly international currency could be established.

The international currency we have proposed, based on a basket of consumer goods, addresses the problem of the stability of the monetary unit, but leaves unanswered the question of how to deal with balance-of-payments problems. We suggest that this issue be resolved by the creation and maintenance in each country of stocks of commodities whose value, in International Currency Units, would correspond to a portion of that country's trade. These commodity stocks would serve as deposits with the World Central Bank, which would verify them from time to time. They would guarantee countries that held credit accounts with the World Central Bank that these accounts were backed up by real commodities in the countries with deficit accounts—commodities that could be sold, with the proceeds going to credit account holders, as necessary. Thus the international currency would, in effect, be underpinned by a variety of real commodities rather than simply by gold and paper dollars.

Using commodity stocks as balance-of-payments guarantees would also bolster confidence in the International Currency Unit: those who held it would be assured that they could realize a certain commodity value from their monetary holdings. This would eliminate one of the main reasons for currency speculation. Furthermore, this confidence in constant, realizable purchasing power could, in its turn, provide the stability that goes with a commodity-based system without the problems that go with trying to fix commodity prices. Instead, the quantities of commodity stocks would vary according to changes in commodity prices. The mix of commodities could also be allowed to vary, provided the total value in International Currency Units remained the same.

The monetary system we are proposing combines the advantages of a system based on commodities, which provide real value to an international currency, with those of a fixed exchange-rate system, which under special circumstances can provide for stability. But in contrast to the gold or gold-exchange standards, which require management of the price of gold, our system does not require that the price of any commodity be managed. Nor does it depend on any technical and economic conditions of production for the commodities that give the currency its backing. Indeed, if particular commodities were to become less economically attractive—because of changes in technology, for example—the composition of the stocks would tend to change automatically to accommodate such economic realities.

Furthermore, our proposed system would possess the attractive features of the fixed exchange-rate system—predictability and resistance to inflation—without its rigidities. The values of the currencies of countries would change, but they would do so in response to the policies and economic conditions that prevail inside those countries. Imbalances and strains between internal conditions and external exchange rates would not be allowed to build up into crises, as they frequently do under the fixed parity system.

The proposal has a number of other advantages. Since it does not require the management of commodity prices, the range of commodities in the reserve stocks could be very wide. Indeed, the wider this range the better, since that would decrease the extent to which the selling of commodities to cover payments deficits would depress the price of any particular commodity. Further, a wide range of commodities would permit most countries to build and maintain commodity stocks largely or even wholly from domestic production.

Finally, our proposed system would be able to largely avoid the deflation-creating conditionalities and adjustment measures that plague countries experiencing deficits under the current system. In most cases, the only condition a country would have to satisfy would be the maintenance of commodity stocks at a certain level related to the total value of their trade. For countries that consistently ran large deficits, however, there would have to be additional rules. Countries who were members of this system might, for example, be required to trade with the deficit country on a cash-only basis until its situation was corrected. Countries that consistently ran surpluses might be required to deposit them, or corresponding quantities of commodities, in special accounts in the World Central Bank.

Thus our system of dealing with balance-of-payments deficits would not require countries to adopt recessionary measures across the board; in particular, depressive wage policies could be avoided. Similarly, requiring that consistent surpluses be deposited in the World Central Bank would enable countries to handle those surpluses without taking sudden measures to drastically depress their exports or increase their imports, actions that would disrupt their internal economic structures. Such an approach might also help prevent the erection of trade barriers against countries with large balance-of-payments surpluses.

We should note that international monetary transactions would be carried out by countries' central banks, which would maintain accounts for that purpose with the World Central Bank. This would mean that international currency transfers outside the jurisdiction of the central banks, which have become common practice for multinational banks and corporations over the past two decades, would have to stop. Channeling currency transactions through the central banks would restore some regulation and order to international capital flows. As under a fixed parity system, there would be no trading in currencies. Given the scale and speed of current capital transfers and the large volume of world trade, making the transition to such a system would require that a number of technical problems be worked out. The benefits of increased international monetary stability would, however, be enormous.

A Mutually Beneficial System

The international monetary system we are proposing can be established only through the cooperative efforts of most Third World and OECD countries. Although it might seem that the Third World would derive most of the advantages to be had from this system—decreased debt-servicing costs, freedom to pursue internal growth and employment policies, the ability to increase imports of farm commodities and industrial goods, improved terms of trade—there would be substantial benefits to the OECD countries as well. A structural defusing of the debt crisis would eliminate the threat of collapse and chaos that now hangs over the international monetary and trade system. A reduction in the exploitation of ill-paid Third World labor would halt or at least slow the loss of many industrial jobs in the West and help reduce the current pressures for protectionism. And there would be a growth in Third World markets for Western farm exports as well as such manufactures as machine tools, electronics and agricultural implements.

The principal cost to OECD countries would be increases in the prices of those Third World commodities that are now relatively cheap because of underpaid Third World labor. The profits of the transnational corporations that depend heavily on such labor would tend to decline. In many Third World countries, jobs in the export sector might be affected by declining foreign demand, which would require that these economies be restructured toward internal demand. These types of issues would have to be worked out during the transition from the present to the new monetary system. But such detailed work can have meaning only if there is a general acceptance of the need for restructuring the present system—a process that will require agreement on convening a new Bretton Woods-type conference on international money and finance.

This kind of conference has been advocated by countries, such as France and New Zealand, as well as by the nonaligned nations. The Reagan administration continues to resist such calls—which is not surprising, since the policies that brought the debt crisis to a head are the same ones that produced the Reagan-era economic growth. But as the present system's inadequacy to all parties concerned becomes more severe and more apparent, we believe that the forces of resistance will yield to sound judgment. That is, at least, our hope.

Notes

1   Aldo Ferrer, "Debt, Sovereignty and Democracy in Latin America." Presentation at the New York Society for International Affairs, New York, May 10, 1984, p. 19.

2   "The Arusha Initiative," in *Development Dialogue,* Dag Hammarskjöld Foundation, Uppsala, Sweden, No. 2, 1980, pp. 17-18.

3   Arjun Makhijani, *Oil Prices and the Crises of Debt and Unemployment.* Final Draft Report to the International Labour Office of the U.N., Geneva, April 1983.

4   J. J. Polack, "Monetary Analysis of Income Formation and Payments Problems," in *Monetary Approach to the Balance of Payments* (Washington, DC: International Monetary Fund, 1977), p. 15.

5   Robert S. Browne, "Conditionality: A New Form of Colonialism?" *Africa Report,* September/October 1984, p. 15.

6   The IMF also fails to take into account the interposition of some other industrialized currencies between the U.S. dollar and some Third World currencies—for example, the many African countries that are in the French franc zone. When the French franc declines with respect to the U.S. dollar, so does the currency of the Central African Republic, regardless of what internal economic policies it follows.

7   Makhijani (note 3), Chapter 1.

8   *The Debt Crisis and the World Economy.* Report by the Commonwealth Group of Experts, London, 1984, p. 18.

9   The problems created by the dollar's privileged position in the international monetary system have long been recognized. John Maynard Keynes, one of the principal architects of the Bretton Woods system, was vigorously opposed to the use of the dollar (or any other national currency) as the basic international monetary unit. He warned that the dollar's role as the domestic U.S. currency would conflict considerably with its role as a stable instrument of international trade. His fear has been fully justified.

10   For example, Beryl Sprinkel, undersecretary of the U.S. Treasury until

January 1985 and now chairman of the Council of Economic Advisers, acknowledged while testifying before Congress that "the debt crisis is, to a large extent, an indirect result of our success in curing inflation and revitalizing the American economy." (Congressional testimony of March 19, 1984, reported in the *Washington Post,* March 30, 1984.) Although Sprinkel made this statement while trying to explain to Congress the benefits of the tight monetary policy, his assessment of the U.S. role in the debt crisis essentially coincides with that of Aldo Ferrer (note 1).

11 Computerized data on international wages from the U.S. Bureau of Labor Statistics, cited in Makhijani (note 3), Chapter 4.

12 Richard J. Barnet, *The Lean Years* (New York: Simon & Schuster, 1980), p. 247.

13 Makhijani (note 3), Chapter 3.

14 *1983 World Bank Atlas: Gross National Product, Population, and Growth Rates* (Washington, DC: World Bank, 1983), p. 27.

15 Makhijani (note 3), Chapter 4.

16 James Morris, *Pax Britannica: The Climax of an Empire* (New York: Harcourt, Brace & Jovanovich, 1968), p. 108.

17 "International Clearing Union: Text of a Paper Containing Proposals by British Experts for an International Clearing Union," originally published by the British Information Services in *Proceedings and Documents of the United Nations Monetary and Financial Conference, Bretton Woods, New Hampshire, July 1-22, 1944,* 2 vols. (Washington, DC: U.S. Government Printing Office, 1948), Vol. II, p. 52.